The Spirit of Jesus in Scripture and Prayer

The Spirit of Jesus in Scripture and Prayer

James W. Kinn

A SHEED & WARD BOOK

ROWMAN & LITTLEFIELD PUBLISHERS, INC.
Lanham • Boulder • New York • Toronto • Oxford

A SHEED & WARD BOOK
ROWMAN & LITTLEFIELD PUBLISHERS, INC.

Published in the United States of America
by Rowman & Littlefield Publishers, Inc.
A wholly owned subsidiary of The Rowman & Littlefield Publishing Group, Inc.
4501 Forbes Boulevard, Suite 200, Lanham, Maryland 20706
www.rowmanlittlefield.com

PO Box 317
Oxford
OX2 9RU, UK

Copyright © 2004 by Sheed & Ward/Rowman & Littlefield Publishers, Inc.

All rights reserved. No part of this publication may be reproduced, stored in a retrieval system, or transmitted in any form or by any means, electronic, mechanical, photocopying, recording, or otherwise, without the prior permission of the publisher.

British Library Cataloguing in Publication Information Available

Library of Congress Cataloging-in-Publication Data
Kinn, James W., 1931–
The Spirit of Jesus in Scripture and prayer / James W. Kinn.
 p. cm.
Includes bibliographical references and index.
ISBN 0–7425–3189–9 (alk. paper) — ISBN 0–7425–3190–2 (pbk. : alk. paper)
 1. Holy Spirit. 2. Catholic Church—Doctrines. 3. Holy Spirit—Biblical teaching. 4. Bible. N.T. —Theology. I. Title.
BT121' .3—dc22
2003026776

Printed in the United States of America

∞™ The paper used in this publication meets the minimum requirements of American National Standard for Information Sciences—Permanence of Paper for Printed Library Materials, ANSI/NISO Z39.48-1992.

Contents

Acknowledgments		vii
General Introduction		xi

First Part: The Spirit of Jesus in Scripture

Introduction	The Old Testament	3
Chapter 1	Paul	5
Chapter 2	Luke	29
Chapter 3	John	43
Chapter 4	Other New Testament Writers	65
Chapter 5	Descriptions of New Testament Pneumatologies	71
Chapter 6	Comparisons between the Work of the Spirit of Jesus in Paul, Luke, and John	91

Second Part: The Spirit of Jesus in Prayer

Chapter 7	Luke	117
Chapter 8	Paul	123

Chapter 9	John	127
Chapter 10	The Spirit of Jesus and the Stages of Prayer	135
Chapter 11	Intimacy with God	155
Chapter 12	The Spirit of Jesus as the Agent of the Sacraments	165

Third Part: Comparison between the Spirit of Jesus in the Early Church and Today

Chapter 13	Every Church Is Divine and Human	173
Chapter 14	Experienced Presence versus Presence by Faith	181
Chapter 15	How Is It "Better for You That I Go"?	185
Chapter 16	Problems Regarding the Spirit of Jesus in the Modern Church	191
Chapter 17	The Spirit of Jesus and Christology	199
Chapter 18	A Simple Pneumatology Based on Luke, Paul, and John	207

Select Bibliography	213
Index	219
About the Author	233

Acknowledgments

Appreciation

I am deeply grateful to three friends who reviewed this whole book and greatly improved its content and style: Joseph O'Brien for his encouragement and theological suggestions; John Lodge for his insight criticisms and theoloical expertise; Mary Lou Larkin, BVM, for her valued comments and careful critique of my style.

Greatful acknowledgment is made to the following publishers and authors for permission to reprint sections from copyrighted material:

All Scripture texts are taken from the *New American Bible*, Donald Senioe, general ed. Copyright © 1986 by the Confraternity of Christian Doctrine, Washington, DC.

Alba House, for the *Christian Lives by the Spirit* by Ignace De la Potterie and Stanislaus Lyonnet. Copyright © 1971 by Alba House, Staten Island, NY.

America Press, for *The Documents of Vatican II*, edited by Walter Abbott, S.J. Copyright © 1966 by Anerica Press, New York, NY.

Crossroad Publishing Co., for *The Content of Faith* by Karl Rahner. Copyright © for the English translation, 1993 granted by Copyright Clearance Center, Inc., Danvers, MA.

Doubleday Publishing Co., publishers of *The Anchor Bible*, for *The Gospel and Epistles of John (vols. 29, 29A and 30)* by Raymond Brown. Copyright © by Doubleday Publishing Co., New York, NY for vol. 29, 1966; for vol. 29A, 1970; for vol. 30, 1982.

Doubleday Publishing Co., publishers of *The Anchor Bible*, for *The Gospel of Luke (vols. 28 and 28A)* by Joseph Fitzmyer. Copyright © by Doubleday Publishing Co., New York, NY for vol. 28, 1970; for vol. 28A, 1985.

William B. Eerdmans Publishing Co., for *I Believe in the Holy Spirit* by Michael Green. Copyright © 1975 by Michael Green.

Harper and Rowe Publishers, Inc., for *Catholicism* by Richard McBrien. Copyright © 1981 by Richard McBrien.

Herder and Herder, for *Theological Investigations*, vol. 7 by Karl Rahner. Copyright © 1971 by Herder and Herder, New York, NY.

Herder and Herder, for *The Gospel According to John, 3 vol.* by Rudolph Schnackenburg. Copyright © 1992 by Kent, Burns, and Oates, London.

ICS Publications (Institute of Carmelite Studies), for *The Collected Works of St. Teresa of Avila, 3 Vols.*, translated by Kieran Kavanaugh and Otilio Rodriguez. Copyright © 1980 by Washington Province of Discalced Carmelites ICS Publications, Washington, DC.

ICS Publications (Institute of Carmelite Studies), for *The Collected Works of St. John of the Cross*, translated by Kieran Kavanaugh and Otilio Rodriguez. Copyright © 1991 by Washington Province of Discalced Carmelites ICS Publications, Washington, DC.

Liturgical Press, for *Preaching the New Lectionary* by Reginald Fuller. Copyright © 1974 by the Order of St. Benedict, Inc., Collegeville, MN.

Pauline Books and Media, for *The Spirit, Giver of Life and Love* by Pope John Paul II. Copyright © 1996 by Daughters of St. Paul, Boston, MA.

Paulist Press, for *Biblical Exegrsis and Church Doctrine* by Raymond Brown. Copyright © 1985 by Raymond Brown, S.S.

Paulist Press, for *According to Paul* by Joseph Fitzmyer. Copyright © 1993 by the Corporation of the Roman Catholic Clergymen, MD.

Pocket Books (a division of Simon and Schuster), for *The Private Prayers of John Paul II* by Pope John Paul II. Copyright ©2001 (English translation) by Libreria Editrice Rogate. Published in English under agreement with Compulsion Sub, LLC.

Seabury Press, for *I Believe in the Holy Spirit 3 vols.* by Yves Congar. Copyright ©1983 by Seabury Press, New York, NY.

Sheed & Ward, for *Christ, the Sacrament of the Encounter with God* by E. Schillebeeckx. Copyright © 1963 by Sheed & Ward Ltd., Chicago, IL.

Westminster Press, for *Jesus snd the Spirit* by J. D. G. Dunn. Copyright © 1975 by SCM Press, London, England.

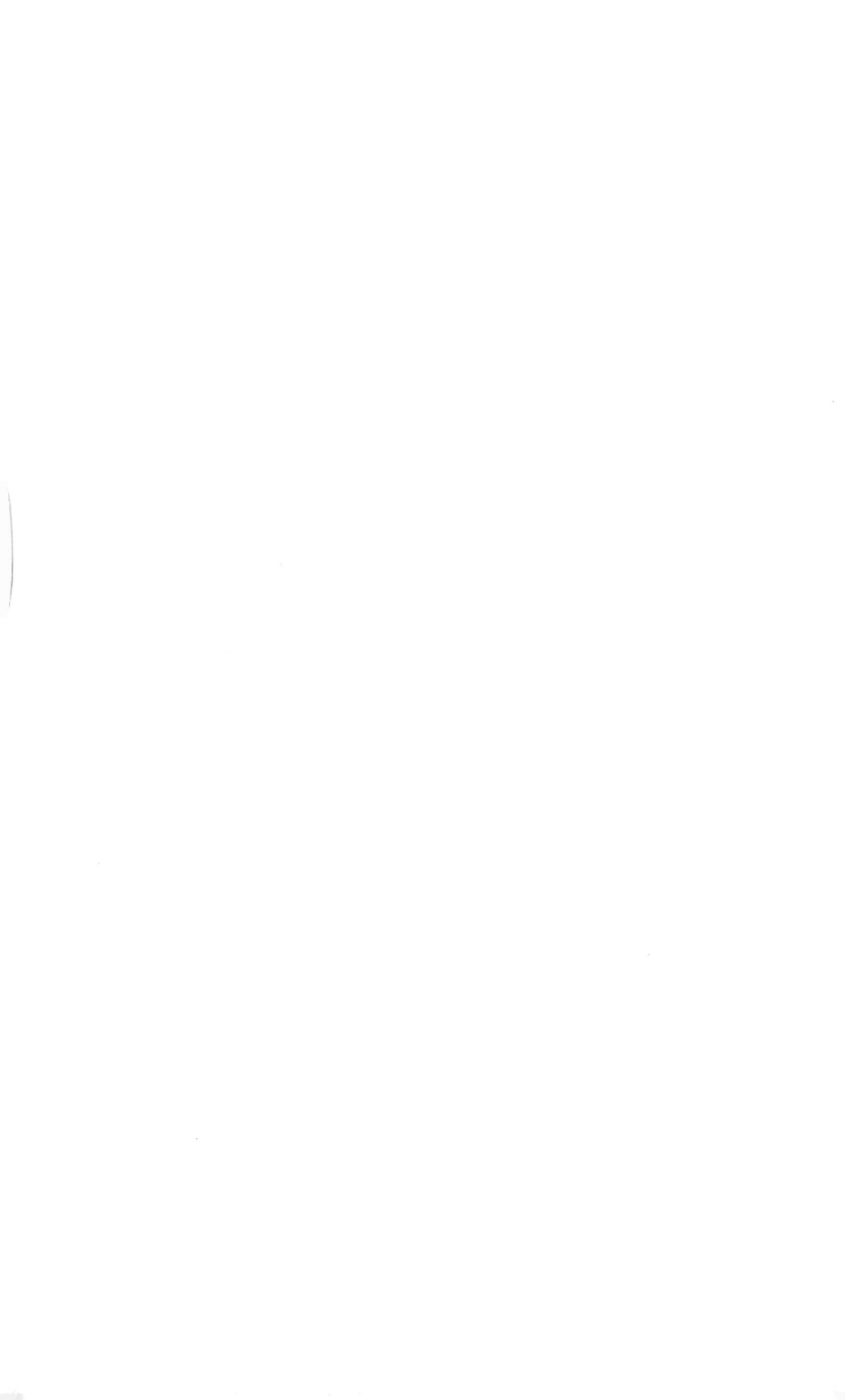

General Introduction

A. Neglect of the Holy Spirit in the Past

The Holy Spirit has frequently been called "the unknown God."[1] Western theology has largely neglected the study of the Spirit of God: "Perhaps the most neglected area of theology in the West is that of the Holy Spirit."[2] Several popes have urged a renewed devotion to and study of the Holy Spirit. Pope Leo XIII, in his encyclical on the Holy Spirit, deplores that the "Christians have only a very poor knowledge of the Holy Spirit. They often use his name . . . but their faith is encompassed with great darkness."[3] In 1973, Pope Paul VI asked the question: "What is the greatest need of the church today?" His own succinct response was, "The Holy Spirit."[4] Then, Pope John Paul II, in his encyclical on the Holy Spirit, urged: "the ecclesiology of the [Second Vatican] Council must be succeeded by a new study of and devotion to the Holy Spirit, precisely as the indispensable complement of the teaching of the Council."[5]

Many things throughout history have contributed to the neglect of the Holy Spirit. Scripture itself gives us many impersonal similes for the Holy Spirit such as wind, air, fire, water, seal, gift, dove, anointing, power. These similes refer mostly to the functions of the Holy Spirit using inanimate symbols. So they tend to make the Spirit impersonal and elusive, rather than a knowable, real person. Even the great councils of the early church did not help to make the Holy Spirit either vital or personal. While they carefully defined the mystery of our God as one and three and laboriously defined the two natures in Jesus Christ, they had great difficulty trying to describe the nature of the Holy Spirit. Sadly, the East and West ultimately split apart over the procession of the Spirit; the East insisted that the Spirit proceeds from the Father alone, while the West affirmed the Spirit comes forth from the Father **and** the Son (*filioque*). This disastrous rift exists to this day between the Catholic and the Orthodox Churches.

The second shattering division in the church came with the Reformation in the sixteenth century. In this case, a major part of the dispute concerned how the Holy Spirit functioned in the church and in individual Christians. The critical question of the Reformation was this: Could the Holy Spirit speak through the Scriptures in such a way that Christians could challenge the teachings of the church hierarchy? The Protestant groups insisted that the Spirit speaks in Scripture independent from the hierarchy, while Catholics believed the hierarchy was the proper interpreter of Scripture and faith. We can even note a further division among Protestants: Calvin and Luther insisted that the Spirit speaks through the Scriptures in the church, while charismatics and some Pentecostals taught that the teaching of the Spirit could be determined by each one individually.

Even modern theology has obscured the place of the Spirit in the church. The Holy Spirit does not play an outstanding part in our theological discussions and consciousness. In 1983 Ray Brown observed: "There is an almost total absence of *comprehensive* books on the Spirit in the New Testament" (emphasis in the original).[6] In the last several years, there have been notable efforts to improve our appreciation of the influence of the Holy Spirit in our Christian life.[7] Hopefully this book will add to this necessary dialogue and encourage us to relate more personally to the Spirit of Jesus.

B. New Place of the Holy Spirit Today

Let me suggest some of the elements that may awaken a new appreciation of the Holy Spirit in our contemporary theology and personal spirituality. First, modern Scripture scholars show that the gift of the Spirit is at the heart of the three major New Testament theologians' soteriology. For Paul, Luke, and John, the primacy of the Holy Spirit is unequivocal. When they deal with objective salvation, they focus on Jesus Christ as the author and cause of our salvation; when they speak of subjective, internal salvation, they teach that the Holy Spirit is the principle of all grace and is God dwelling in us. Second, when modern theology focuses on the Trinity, it no longer emphasizes the **internal life** of the Trinity. Such lengthy explanations about the way that the Son and the Holy Spirit internally proceed from the Father took up much of the traditional treatise on God. Rather, now there is more emphasis on the **external works** of the Trinity, that is, on how the three persons relate to us; scholars even describe the relationships among the three persons of the Trinity by focusing on how they individually relate to us in terms of the whole economy of salvation. They make it clear that we need to consider all three persons to form any adequate sense of God's plan of salvation. Thus, the history of our salvation necessarily describes the mystery of God as our creator and Father, of Christ as the one who revealed everything about God and accomplished our objective salvation, and of the Holy Spirit as our individual possession of God's grace dwelling within us. Or more simply, our spiritual life has its origin in the Father, its effective center in the Son, and its individual presence in the Spirit. Here is one example of modern theology's description of the trinitarian work of salvation:

> [I]t is the Father who remains the ultimate source of the saving activity of both Christ and the Holy Spirit, for "it was God [viz., the Father] who reconciled us to himself in Christ." (2 Cor. 5:18) But [God the Father] brought about [our] redemption in the human nature of the second person, the Son of God. . . . [Christ's passion, death, and resurrection] sanctifies mankind, reconciles, establishes peace, redeems . . . and unites men in communion with God. . . . The Holy Spirit . . . now realizes and perfects in us that which was completed in Christ. . . . The Spirit makes actual in us that which Christ achieved for us once and for all.[8]

Third, modern spiritual theology does not struggle to find purely **separate** operations of the Spirit (which can hardly be attributed to the Father or the Son), but rather merely follows the lead of Scripture in **appropriating** certain functions to one or another divine person. As we shall see extensively in this study, especially in John's Gospel, many operations of Christ and the Father are similar, and many functions of Christ while on earth are quite similar to those of the Holy Spirit after his ascension. Nevertheless, we can very securely follow the manner of speaking of Sacred Scripture as it appropriates this or that work of salvation to one of the divine persons. It is important to follow this lead of Scripture and to appropriate these actions to the Holy Spirit, because through the years our theology has led us into a neglect of the proper role of the Spirit.

Our hope in this study is simply this: to restore the Holy Spirit to the proper place that Scripture gives the Spirit in the whole plan of our salvation.

Fourth, despite all the impersonal symbols used in Scripture, we can relate to the Holy Spirit in a most personal and intimate way by focusing primarily on him as the SPIRIT OF JESUS. We hope to show that the Holy Spirit is so closely joined to Christ that the Spirit becomes our personal contact with Christ and the one who continues the work of Jesus in us. Such a focus means that for each of us, however personal our relationship to Jesus himself is in our life, our relationship to the Holy Spirit will be similarly personal and intimate.

Finally, let me describe how my own experience has led to a new appreciation of the Spirit in theology and spiritual life. Our seminary training was quite similar to that of other seminaries of the fifties and sixties. Our theology courses properly began with *De Deo Uno et Trino* (the study of God, one and triune). The main emphasis in that course was to teach how God could be both one and three, and how to understand the relationships within the Trinity and how their external actions were common to all three persons. Then we spent most of theology on Jesus Christ and how he revealed God to us and redeemed us. To a high degree these courses were concerned with the objective salvation accomplished by Jesus our Savior. Vatican II inspired theologians with a new interest in the Spirit, especially by its two fundamental documents: *Lumen Gentium* (On the Church) and *Dei Verbum* (On Revelation). In section D, below, we will develop some of that teaching. Then with the explosion of Scripture study of the last thirty years, the work of the Spirit became more clearly focused, enriching my spiritual life in two new directions: first, my growing interest in Scripture study, especially through the *Jerome Biblical Commentary* and the whole Anchor Bible series of the New Testament; second, because of a renewed interest in all the writings of St. John of the Cross, whose mystical writings place such emphasis on the work of the Spirit as the agent of contemplative prayer. This book is the result of all those influences. May this Spirit of Jesus inspire us with a new appreciation of the Spirit's personal presence and grace.

C. The Trinity, Salvation, and Revelation

1. Salvation

In the New Testament it is clear again and again that our salvation can only be understood in a trinitarian form. That is, we cannot properly express what God has done for us in redeeming us unless we include the work of all three persons of the Trinity. As we attempt to describe this trinitarian salvation, we need to be careful to follow the lead of Scripture. Karl Rahner offers this overriding norm for us: "We must take Scripture and the expressions it uses in *as exact a sense* as we possibly can" (emphasis added).[9] Rahner himself offers this description of our economy of salvation:

> The history of . . . salvation brings us up against the ineffable mystery of the incomprehensible, unoriginated God who is called Father. . . . This one and incomprehensible God is unsurpassably close to human beings historically in Jesus Christ who is . . . the final and unsurpassable self-promise of this one God in history. And this one and the same God imparts himself to us in the innermost center of human existence as Holy Spirit for salvation and for the consummation which is God himself.[10]

Paul expresses this trinitarian creed of salvation in different ways; see, for example, Romans 8:1–9 and Galatians 4:4–6. Perhaps his clearest expression is in Romans 5:1–5:

> [S]ince we have been justified by faith, we have peace with God through our Lord Jesus Christ, through whom we have gained access by faith to this grace in which we stand, and we boast in hope of the glory of God . . . and hope does not disappoint, because the love of God has been poured out into our hearts through the holy Spirit that has been given to us.

Other examples can be found in the- nonauthentic Pauline corpus, as in Titus 3:4–7 and 2 Thessalonians 2:13. Ephesians 2:18–22 expresses God's plan of salvation this way:

> [F]or through [Christ] we both have access in the one Spirit to the Father. So then you are . . . members of the household of God . . . with Christ Jesus himself as the capstone. . . . In him you also are being built together into a dwelling place of God in the Spirit.

In a word, we cannot adequately describe God's work of salvation, unless we include the action of all three persons of the Trinity. Or, as theologians put it: salvation is necessarily trinitarian. For though salvation is God's activity from beginning to end, it was set in motion by sending his Son, our Lord Jesus Christ; Christ accomplished this salvation by his death and resurrection. And the effectual realization of that salvation is singularly the work of the Spirit, whom we first receive in baptism.

To be sure, Paul, Luke, and John did not have a fully developed theology of the Trinity; that clarity came only centuries later. They could not use the language of a later time and had a less explicit trinitarian faith. Here is how Gordon Fee describes Paul's knowledge: One may grant that Paul's trinitarian assumptions and descriptions, which form the bases of the later formulas, never move toward calling the Spirit "God" and never wrestle with the philosophical and theological implications of those assumptions and descriptions. But neither is there evidence that he lacked clarity as to the distinctions between, and the specific roles of, the three divine "persons" who accomplished so great salvation for us all.[11]

2. Revelation
Revelation and the plan of God are also described by Paul in trinitarian terms.

He reminds the Corinthians:

> I resolved to know nothing while I was with you except Jesus Christ and him crucified . . . and my message and my proclamation were not with persuasive words of wisdom. . . . Rather we speak God's wisdom, mysterious, hidden, which God predestined before the ages . . . this God has revealed to us through the Spirit. (1 Cor. 2:2–10)

We see that Paul insists that his whole message consists of God's wisdom proclaimed in Jesus and revealed to us through the Spirit. Then, in the Acts of the Apostles, Peter's first speech, at Pentecost, testifies about the "set plan of God" proclaimed to all: "God raised this Jesus; of this we are all witnesses. Exalted at the right hand of God, he received the promise of the holy Spirit from the Father and poured it forth, as you see and hear." (Acts 2:32–33) Thus Peter describes the "set plan of God" revealed in Jesus' death and resurrection and known by all who received the Spirit at Pentecost.

Let us finish with the famous trinitarian blessing of Paul, which beautifully summarizes revelation: "The grace of our Lord Jesus Christ and the love of God and the fellowship of the holy Spirit be with all of you." (2 Cor. 13:13) This is Paul's most deliberate triadic formula. All three genitives here are subjective genitives, meaning that God is the subject of each phrase. That is, Jesus bestows the grace, God is the one who loves, and the Spirit is the source of the gift of fellowship shared by believers. The order here is quite notable: Son, Father, Spirit:

> The order . . . is striking, and again reflects the order of Christian experience. It is in Jesus Christ and his gracious life and death that we encounter the love of God, and this encounter leads to our incorporation into the redeemed community in which we participate in the common life of the Spirit.[12]

Our entire Christian revelation and knowledge of God is trinitarian. That is, for us Christians, the knowledge of God is mediated in history by the historical event of Jesus; God is revealed to us historically by the person of Jesus and by his life and teaching. That same knowledge of God is actualized and comes to fruition in us individually by the work of the Spirit; we come to know God present in us and in our world by means of the Holy Spirit. In summary, then, salvation can only be defined adequately in trinitarian forms. For though salvation is God's activity from beginning to end, it was set in motion by his sending his Son, our Lord Jesus Christ. Christ accomplished this salvation by his death and resurrection. The effectual realization of that salvation is singularly the work of the Spirit, whom we first receive in baptism.

D. Scripture as Our Primary Source

This entire work is based primarily on Scripture.[13] Whatever is said about the Holy Spirit in our Christian life in general and in our prayer comes first from what Scripture teaches. It is critical then to explain here just what the church teaches about the inspiration of Sacred Scripture. Vatican II's *Dogmatic Constitution on Divine Revelation* (*Dei Verbum*) recapitulates the church's traditional teaching on inspiration. The third chapter of *Dei Verbum* begins:

> Those divinely revealed realities . . . presented in Sacred Scripture have been committed to writing under the inspiration of the Holy Spirit . . . [so that] the books of both the Old Testament and New Testament in their entirety, with all their parts, are sacred and canonical because, having been written under the inspiration of the Holy Spirit, they have God as their author and have been handed on as such to the church itself.[14]

The constitution goes on to quote 2 Timothy 3:16–17: "All scripture is inspired by God" as well as 2 Peter 1:19–21: "no prophecy of scripture . . . ever came through human will; but rather human beings moved by the holy Spirit spoke under the influence of God." Both of these quotes really refer to the Old Testament Scriptures, but Vatican II uses them to show that when it affirms the inspiration of the Holy Spirit for **all** of Scripture, it is in keeping with the traditional teaching mentioned in Scripture itself. Notice how inspiration is the work of the Holy Spirit:

[S]ince everything asserted by the inspired authors . . . must be held to be asserted by the Holy Spirit, it follows that the books of Scripture must be acknowledged as teaching firmly, faithfully and without error that truth which God wanted put into the sacred writings for the sake of our salvation.[15]

The point of Vatican II here is not only that Scripture is inspired and therefore worthy of our complete faith, but also that this inspiration is uniquely the work of the Holy Spirit. That is to say, all the teaching of Sacred Scripture is rightly **appropriated** to the Spirit, because all the sacred writers are inspired by the Spirit of God. Thus, the Spirit alone is the teacher and revealer of all that is contained in Scripture. But Vatican II goes further than this; it asserts that the work of the Spirit includes helping us to a constantly growing understanding of the Word of God throughout the history of the church:

This tradition, which comes from the apostles, develops in the church with the help of the Holy Spirit. For there is a growth in the understanding of the realities and words which have been handed down. This happens through the contemplation and study made by believers, who treasure these things in their hearts, through the intimate understanding of spiritual things, and through the preaching of those who have received . . . the gift of faith.[16]

This means that our understanding of sacred Scripture constantly grows and deepens throughout history and moves toward the fullness of divine truth with the help of the Holy Spirit.

Notes

1. Walter Kasper, *The God of Jesus Christ* (New York: Crossroad, 1986), 198.
2. George Montague, S.M., foreword to *The Spirit, Giver of Life and Love*, by John Paul II (Boston: Pauline Books and Media, 1966), 12.
3. *Divinum Illud Munus*, 1897.
4. Paul VI, "The Holy Spirit," *L'Osservatore Romano*, June 7, 1973.
5. John Paul II, *Dominum et Vivificantem*, *L'Osservatore Romano*, June 9, 1986; also published in Washington, D.C., by the U.S. Catholic Conference, 1986.

6. Raymond Brown, "Diverse Views of the Spirit in the New Testament," *Worship* 57 (May 1983): 227.

7. See Kasper, *The God of Jesus Christ*, 363, 85; also see Raymond Brown, *Biblical Exegesis and Church Doctrine* (New York: Paulist Press, 1985), 101.

8. Edward Schillebeeckx, *Christ, the Sacrament of the Encounter with God* (New York: Sheed & Ward, 1963), 20–25.

9. Karl Rahner, "Some Implications of the Scholastic Sense of Uncreated Grace," *Theological Investigations*, vol. 1 (London, 1963), 346.

10. Karl Rahner, *The Content of Faith* (New York: Crossroad, 1993), 375.

11. Gordon Fee, "Paul and the Trinity: The Experience of Christ and the Spirit for Paul's Understanding of God," in *Trinity: An Interdisciplinary Symposium on the Trinty*, ed. Stephen T. Davis, Daniel Kendall, and Gerald O'Collins (New York: Oxford University Press, 1999), 70.

12. Reginald Fuller, *Preaching the New Lectionary* (Collegeville, MN: Liturgical Press, 1974), 205.

13. The translation we will use throughout this work is from *The New American Bible*, Donald Senior, gen. ed. (New York: Oxford University Press, 1990).

14. Walter Abbott, S.J., ed., *The Documents of Vatican II* (New York: Guild Press, 1966), 118.

15. Abbott, *Documents of Vatican II*, 119.

16. Ibid., 116.

FIRST PART

THE SPIRIT OF JESUS IN SCRIPTURE

Introduction:
The Old Testament

The Hebrew word *ruah* serves to signify both "wind" and "spirit." It has many meanings in the Old Testament, but it most often refers to a sensible manifestation of the divine presence and power. The spirit is not a personal being in the Old Testament; it is rather a principle of life and vital activity that comes from Yahweh alone; it is communicated to living beings as their principle of life. When God takes away his spirit, living beings die; when he sends it forth, they are created and God renews the face of the earth (Ps. 104:29–30; Isa. 57:16; Ezek. 37:5–14). The spirit is especially active in the leaders of Israel as a divine power that moves a person above his known capacity, to effectively deliver Israel from her enemies. Thus, the spirit became a distinctive mark of the early leaders of Israel, as we see often in the book of Judges: Gideon (6:34), Jephthah (11:29), and Samson (14:6, 19); the spirit of God gave each judge the power to lead God's people to victory. Apparently, however, the gift of God's spirit was a passing phenomenon to help them in emergencies. In the era of the kings, the spirit was a permanent power conferred on them, as indicated by their anointing with oil; two early examples are: Saul (1 Sam. 11:6; but then God rejected him because of his disobedience: 15:23 and 16:14); and David (1 Sam. 16:13).

The operations of the spirit in prophecy are somewhat ambiguous. The spirit is the inspiring agent of the early prophets: Moses (Num. 11:17), Balaam (Num. 24:2), Elijah and Elisha (2 Kings 2:9–15); and again in the later prophets, especially Ezekiel (Ezek. 2:2, 11:5). But surprisingly the spirit is not evident in the classical period of prophecy, for example, in Isaiah, Jeremiah, Amos, and Hosea.

The spirit of Yahweh is expected to break out in a new fullness in the messianic era: the messianic king will be known by the operations of the spirit (Isa. 11:1); the "servant of Yahweh" will receive God's spirit (Isa. 42:1); the prophet announcing salvation will possess the spirit (Isa. 61:1; cf. Luke 4:18–19). And finally, the whole people of Israel will experience the spirit poured out on them (Isa. 32:15, 44:3; Ezek. 39:29; Joel 3:28) to give them a new heart (Ezek. 36:26).

In summary, in the Old Testament the spirit is conceived as a divine dynamic entity by which Yahweh accomplishes his ends. It saves, inspires, vivifies, and energizes; but it remains impersonal. All of these lines of development of the spirit in the Old Testament will be brought together in the New Testament by the revelation of the Holy Spirit as a divine person dwelling in individual Christians.

CHAPTER ONE

Paul

A. Introduction

*P*aul's teaching about the Holy Spirit is multifaceted. Relying only on the authentic works of Paul (Romans, 1 and 2 Corinthians, Galatians, Philippians, 1 Thessalonians, and Philemon), we will find in his writings the foundation for so many core teachings regarding the Spirit of Jesus: without the Spirit of God we are not Christians at all (Rom. 8:9); the Spirit is the bearer of divine revelation (1 Cor. 2:10), and the power behind the Gospel (1 Thess. 1:5); the Spirit is the power that leads to salvation (Rom. 1:16); the Spirit of Jesus is operative in baptism (1 Cor. 12:13); because of the Spirit, we are adopted sons/daughters of God, so that we can address God as "*Abba*, Father" (Rom. 8:14–16); we Christians are called "temples of God" because of the Spirit of God dwelling within us (1 Cor. 3:16); by this Spirit of Jesus we belong individually to the body of Christ (1 Cor. 12:12–13); this Spirit is the pledge of eternal life, the proof of our hope (2 Cor. 5:5), and God's gift of love in our hearts (Rom. 5:5).

Notice also how many and how diverse are the activities of the Spirit that Paul describes: the Spirit teaches (1 Cor. 2:13); cries out from within our heart (Gal. 4:6); intercedes for us with God (Rom. 8:26); leads us in the ways of God (Gal. 5:16–18); bears witness with us (Rom. 8:16); gives life to those who believe (2 Cor. 3:6); produces spiritual gifts in us (1 Cor. 12:11). Now Paul could only make the Spirit the subject of all these verbs if he understood the Spirit in very personal terms. For Paul, then, the Spirit is very clearly a person. Indeed Paul describes the Spirit as the Spirit of Christ, the presence of the risen Christ in him (Rom. 8:9; Gal. 4:6), and also the Spirit of God, the presence of God in him (1 Cor. 3:16–17; 1 Cor. 2:11–12).

Perhaps we can summarize Paul's teaching about the Spirit by saying that the Spirit is the presence of God within us, the subjective revelation of God, the agent of God's outgoing activity in us, the source of new life in Christ, the multifaceted gift of God's love.

B. We Are Children of God

"As proof that you are children, God sent the Spirit of his Son into our hearts, crying out, '*Abba*, Father.'" (Gal. 4:6; see also Rom. 8:16) Because we possess "the Spirit of his Son" in our hearts, we become individually a son or daughter of God, so that we can address God familiarly as "Father."

Paul means that the Spirit animates and activates us Christians, making us children of God. Our status is initiated through faith and baptism (see Gal. 3:26–27) but is activated and realized through the indwelling Spirit. This is our permanent status as a member of the family of God, and the foundation for that status is the permanent indwelling of the Spirit of God's Son. In fact, the gift of the Spirit constitutes our sonship/daughterhood: "Those who are led by the Spirit of God are children of God." (Rom. 8:14) When Paul talks about being "led by God's Spirit," it is his way of expressing the active influence of the Spirit in Christian life. He means that the Spirit animates and activates Christians, making them children of God.

Paul's term, both in Galatians and Romans, is not *huios* (son) but *huiosthesia* (adoptive sonship). *Huiosthesia* is not found in the Old Testament, probably because adoption was not a normal institution among the Jews; it is a borrowed word from the Greco-Roman world, expressing the legal assumption of a person into the status of sonship (or daughterhood) in a natural family; because of faith and baptism, Christians have been taken up into the family of God, have come under the paternal care of God, and have a legitimate status in that family.

Notice how Paul stresses the active dynamism of the Spirit: "The Spirit itself bears witness with our spirit: we are children of God!" (Rom. 8:16; cf. Gal. 4:6) That is, the Spirit not only constitutes the sonship itself but also makes us aware of our adoptive sonship; in fact, the Spirit concurs with us as we acknowledge in prayer that we have this special relation to God our Father.

The preceding quotes are from Galatians and Romans and date from about the year 55; they are the earliest attestation of such a manner of Christian prayer. It seems to be an echo of the prayer of Jesus himself in the garden of Gethsemane: "*Abba*, Father, all things are possible to you. Take this cup away from me, but not what I will but what you will." (Mark 14:36) In Matthew (11:25–27) and Luke (10:21–22), Jesus also used the simpler form of address, "Father," in his prayer; and Luke identifies Jesus' prayer as Spirit-inspired: "[Jesus] rejoiced in the Holy Spirit and said." (Luke 10:21) Now Paul encourages us to use the same Spirit-inspired words in our prayer.[1] To address God as "Father" is unheard of in the Old Testament. A few passages describe corporate Israel as the son of God (Exod. 4:22; Hosea 11:1; Wisdom 18:13), but the individual Israelite does not address God as "Father." Joachim Jeremias is probably the primary scholar on the topic of Jesus' calling God "Father."[2] After studying all of pre-Christian Palestinian literature, he found no evidence of God being addressed as *Abba* by an individual Jew in prayer. His conclusion is: "For Jesus to venture to take this step was something new and unheard of."[3] Joseph Fitzmyer, after carefully critiquing Jeremias, basically agrees with him:

> There is no evidence in the literature of pre-Christian or first-century Palestinian Judaism that "*abba*" was used in any sense as a personal address for God by an individual Jew—and for Jesus to address God as "*abba*" or "Father" is therefore something new."[4]

This means that this form of address was unique to Jesus: "'my Father' on the lips of Jesus expresses a unique relationship with God."[5]

And because it is unique to Jesus and not found anywhere else in early Christian literature, *abba* stands a good chance of being *ipsissima vox Jesu* (the very words of Jesus himself).[6]

Paul understood that Jesus expressed this unique relationship to God as "*Abba*, Father" and "my Father," and he taught that all Christians could rightly use that same form of address to God. Paul concluded that we Christians could also boldly address God so familiarly because we each possess the Holy Spirit, "the Spirit of his Son." The connection that Paul draws between Jesus' unique relationship to God as Father and our consciousness as sons/daughters of God because we possess the Spirit of his Son is original with Paul, and he bases that relationship realistically on "the Spirit of his Son" within us.

Without Paul's writings, we would still have a sense of God as "Father," for the Gospels use the designation "Father" 170 times! But would we boldly address him in prayer as "Our Father"? Notice how the use of this title in Scripture progresses chronologically: there are only 4 instances in Mark, but 15 in Luke, 42 in Matthew, and 109 in John. Jeremias sees this temporal progression as very significant: there is "a growing tendency to introduce the title 'Father' for God into the sayings of Jesus."[7] He ascribes this tendency to Christian apostles and preachers in the early communities who spoke in the name of Jesus and with his words. That tendency came to its logical conclusion in the Johannine Gospel. All of these quotes belong to stage 2 of the gospel tradition—the time of the Gospel writers. But so great a number of instances of the term "Father" being attributed to Jesus himself seems to be rooted in an attitude of Jesus himself in his historical ministry; that is, they must be rooted in stage 1 of the gospel tradition—in the actual words of the historical Jesus himself.

What could this teaching of Paul imply about faith in God? For some people, the image of God as judge and lawgiver so dominates their view of God that they find it hard to relate to God in any satisfying way. They can only deal with this omnipotent and righteous God by ignoring or dismissing such an almighty judge. What a difference it would make for them if they began to think of God as their forgiving and loving Father who wants nothing but good for them. This Pauline view of God would soften their image of God and fill them with confidence.

Others have a more immediate quarrel with God. Their notion of God's providence is such that all things are willed by God—both good and evil. So when terrible accidents happen to them or tragedies affect innocent people, they ask, "Why does God allow the innocent to suffer and die?" They have heard this Old Testament description of God as the cause of all that happens and do not realize that this is a protological way of thinking about God's providence. (By protological we mean a primitive Old Testament concept that is corrected by the New Testament.) In fact, Jesus himself corrected this way of thinking in the Gospels (e.g., in John 9:2–3; twice in Luke 12:2–5). Modern theology rejects the notion that evil comes directly from God as a punishment for sin; it insists that God's providence does not ordinarily interfere with nature or with human freedom, so that all the suffering and agony of so many people in our world have nothing to do with God but everything to do with the laws of nature, the imperfections of human beings, and the evil in human hearts. Paul's teaching, that we are children of God who possess the Spirit of his Son, would cast a whole new light on their view of God. They could begin to cry out "*Abba*, Father," as beloved children who belong to the family of God and possess the Spirit of his Son permanently in their hearts. All the evils of the world would still exist for them, but none of those could separate them from God's love:

> If God is for us, who can be against us? He who did not spare his own Son but handed him over for us all, how will he not also give us everything else along with him? Who will bring a charge against God's chosen ones? It is God who acquits us. (Rom. 8:31–33)

Finally, notice the context here, where Paul leads up to this encouraging image of God by describing the Spirit as the source of our hope (Rom. 8:23–24); because we have the Spirit as our pledge of eternal life, we know that none of the evils of this world can separate us from our eternal destiny with our Father.

C. The Indwelling Spirit

Paul's second teaching about the Spirit springs partially from his understanding of three Old Testament prophecies. Let us see how he interprets the indwelling of the Spirit among God's people and in individuals, and compare that teaching to prophecies found in Jeremiah and Ezekiel.

The first passage is the famous one from the prophet Jeremiah, who prophesies about a "new covenant" that the Lord will make with his people:

> The days are coming, says the Lord, when I will make a new covenant with the house of Israel. . . . It will not be like the covenant I made with their fathers the day I took them by the hand to lead them forth to the land of Egypt. . . . But this is the covenant which I will make with the house of Israel after those days, says the Lord. I will place my law within them, and write it upon their hearts; I will be their God and they will be my people. (Jer. 31:31–33)

Paul affirms that he is a minister of this new covenant in the Spirit: "[we are] ministers of a new covenant, not of letter but of spirit; for the letter brings death, but the Spirit gives life." (2 Cor. 3:6) And he quotes Christ when instituting the Eucharist: "this cup is the new covenant in my blood." (1 Cor. 11:25) So Paul sees the new covenant fulfilled in Jesus and animated by the Spirit.

But the most complete reference to Jeremiah is found in the Letter to the Hebrews; there the author (not Paul) quotes the whole passage from Jeremiah and remarks: "[Jesus] is mediator of a better covenant, enacted on better promises. . . . When he speaks of a 'new' covenant, he declares the first one obsolete." (Heb. 8:6, 13)

The second passage is from the prophet Ezekiel: "I will give you a new heart and place a new spirit within you, taking from your bodies your stony hearts and giving you natural hearts. I will put my spirit within you and make you live by my statutes." (Ezek. 36:26–27) Paul sees the Holy Spirit as the fulfillment of this "new spirit":

> [Y]ou are not in the flesh; on the contrary, you are in the spirit, if only the Spirit of God dwells in you. Whoever does not have the

Spirit of Christ, does not belong to him. . . . But if Christ is in you, although the body is dead because of sin, the spirit is alive because of righteousness. (Rom. 8:9–10)

Thus, Paul not only says that we possess the "new spirit" so that we can "live by his statutes" but also that we actually have the "Spirit of God," which makes us "alive because of righteousness."

The third quote is also from Ezekiel:

I will make . . . an everlasting covenant with them, and I will multiply them and put my sanctuary among them forever. My dwelling shall be with them; I will be their God and they shall be my people. Thus the nations shall know that it is I, the Lord, who make Israel holy, when my sanctuary shall be set up among them forever. (Ezek. 37:26–28)

In 1 Corinthians, Paul takes up this metaphor of the "temple of God" and relates it to the whole community; they form the temple of God because of the Spirit of God dwelling within them: "you are the temple of God, and . . . the Spirit of God dwells in you. . . . If anyone destroys God's temple, God will destroy that person; for the temple of God, which you are, is holy." (1 Cor. 3:16–17) Then in 2 Corinthians, Paul connects this image of the temple of God with the above quote from Ezekiel (Ezek. 37:27); he affirms that in keeping with Old Testament antecedents, God now lives with his people as in a temple: "We are the temple of the living God; as God said: 'I will live with them and move among them, and I will be their God and they shall be my people . . . I will be a father to you, and you shall be sons and daughters to me.'" (2 Cor. 6:16–18)

Notice here that the whole people of God is spoken of as a temple of God. Ephesians will use similar Pauline language in speaking of the church as growing into the temple of the Lord: "Through [Christ] the whole structure is held together and grows into a temple sacred to the Lord; in him you [Ephesians] are also being built together into a dwelling place of God in the Spirit." (Eph. 2:21–22)

These three Old Testament texts, then, speak of God's future covenant and new form of dwelling with his people by means of his spirit. Paul does not quote these passages from the Old Testament but seems to imply that they are fulfilled by the coming of the Spirit: he associates the Spirit with the new covenant; he affirms that the new presence of God with his people consists of the Spirit of God within individuals and the church; he affirms that the new temple of God is now formed by the Spirit of God.

In chapter 6 of 1 Corinthians, Paul applies this same image of the temple to individual Christians: "Do you not know that your body is a temple of the holy Spirit within you, whom you have from God, and that you are not your own? For you have been purchased at a price. Therefore glorify God in your body." (1 Cor. 6:19)

All of chapter 6 forms Paul's powerful argument against sexual misconduct; he urges Christians individually to live a holy, embodied existence, for their bodies are like a temple because the Spirit of God dwells in them. In fact, they do not own their bodies absolutely, since "you have been purchased with a price." His reasoning here is based on a parallel to commercial sales: once the purchase price is paid for any material, it belongs to the buyer; so once Christ paid the price for them (1 Cor. 3:23), their bodies belong to him and to God: "therefore, glorify God with your bodies."

D. The Body of Christ

Paul describes the church as the body of Christ and the Holy Spirit as the principle of its unity: "As . . . all the parts of the body, though many, are one body, so also Christ. For in one Spirit we were all baptized into one body." (1 Cor. 12:12–13) He reminds the Corinthians that they are incorporated into the body of Christ by means of baptism, which is Spirit-inspired. For Paul, this "body of Christ" is more than a metaphor; it expresses the intimate relation of the church to Christ and its profound union with him and in the Spirit. Most likely Paul is the originator of this wonderful description of the church; it represents his mature thinking about the church.[8] When he speaks of the body of Christ, he means the local church of Corinth. Later Ephesians and Colossians will relate this to the universal church: "[God] gave [Christ] as head over all things to the church, which is his body." (Eph. 1:22–23) What Paul means is that those who are united to the body of Christ and permeated with the Spirit through faith and Baptism are really members of Christ's body and form an inseparable life with him. Paul views "this relation between Christ and the church as close as can be conceived; the church has become 'in Christ Jesus' a unity which has no parallel in the natural realm, for in it all natural differences lose their validity."[9] So, this indwelling of the Spirit and incorporation into the body of Christ is one basis for our intimacy with Christ, for we are each members of his body.

Paul makes use of this image to describe the diversity and unity in the church: "Now the body is not a single part, but many. . . . God has placed the parts, each one of them, in the body as he intended. If they were all one part, where would the body be?" (1 Cor. 12:14–20) Just because they all form one body of Christ, Paul makes one strong point after the other: all the members are mutually dependent (12:21, 25), all the members must be honored (12:22–24), all share in the health or suffering of the body (12, 26).

Now this image of the body of Christ does not only relate to the church as a whole but also applies necessarily to individuals, for it is they who are the members. Paul makes this a little clearer in two places. First, when he makes his powerful argument against sexual immorality, he is speaking to individuals: "Do you not know that your bodies are members of Christ? Shall I then take Christ's members and make them the members of a prostitute? Of course not!" (1 Cor. 6:15) Also in Romans, when he urges, "offer your bodies as a living sacrifice," he explains that they can do this by exercising whatever gifts they are given, because "we are one body in Christ and individually parts of one another." (Rom. 12:1, 5) In both of these passages, his arguments are directed to individuals, not only to the body as a whole.

In summary, Paul teaches that all the members of Christ are bound together in the one body of Christ. The cause of that union is the same Spirit dwelling in all the members. This profound unity makes all the members interdependent, so that what is done to one member of the body affects the whole body. Each individual member must live as a worthy member of this body of Christ; each one, no matter what his function, is to be honored because he belongs to Christ's body through the power of his Spirit.

E. The Revealer of Truth

Paul's primary passage about the Spirit as the revealer of truth is found in I Corinthians:

> [W]e speak God's wisdom, mysterious, hidden, which God predetermined before the ages for our glory . . . as is written: "What eye has not seen, and ear has not heard . . . what God has prepared for those who love him," this God has revealed to us through the Spirit. For the Spirit scrutinizes everything, even the depths of God . . . [for] no one knows what pertains to God except the Spirit of God. But we have received . . . the Spirit that is from God, so that we may understand the things freely given us by God. And we speak about them not with words taught by human wisdom, but with words taught by the Spirit. . . . But we have the mind of Christ. (1 Cor. 2:7–13, 16)

This passage is Paul's first sustained reflection on the Spirit in 1 Corinthians; in it he focuses on the Spirit as the source of divine revelation. Paul is clear and insistent here. First, he boldly asserts that God revealed his truths to the Corinthians through the Spirit. In the context, he is speaking of the redemptive work of Christ and Paul's own proclamation to the Corinthians (2:2–4). By "the depths of God" he means God's eternal plan of redemption; this gospel message becomes known in all its depth and details only through revelation given "through the Spirit." His point is that the Spirit alone is capable of revealing the mystery of God, since only the Spirit has intimate knowledge of God. Then Paul denies that his own mode of expression and persuasive words are sufficient; rather his teaching is inspired by the Spirit ("with words taught by the Spirit"). And Paul also means that native intelligence alone is not enough for a person to believe God's message of salvation. In both teaching and believing, the Spirit is the bridge between humanity and God; only the Spirit knows the mind of God and can reveal it to us; only one who has received the Spirit of God can understand and believe his revelation.

Paul concludes this passage with the startling declaration: "we have the mind of Christ." Paul knows that the sublime truths he proclaims are not comprehensible by the unaided human mind. The mystery, wisdom, and power of God—the mind of the Lord—are matters for the Spirit of God. The Corinthian community can only come to possess these truths with the revelation made known to them by the Spirit and with the grace of faith.

If God is to remain God in our knowledge of him, we cannot tailor God to our own image, our own definition. If God desires to reveal himself to us, he must also give us the subjective power to know God. And that subjective possibility of revelation is the Spirit of Truth. To understand the definitive revelation of God that comes to us in Jesus Christ, we need the Spirit of God himself.

F. The Spirit of Freedom

Paul teaches that Christians are free—free from sin, death, and law. In fact, Paul connects the Spirit of Jesus and our freedom from law and sin in a unique way. When Paul talks about **law**, he generally (about ninety-seven times) means the Mosaic law (the Ten Commandments and other regulations from Moses in the book of Exodus). He is particularly insistent with the Galatians that they received the Spirit and are justified not by the Mosaic law but by faith in Christ: "O stupid Galatians! . . . I want to learn only this from you: did you receive the Spirit from works of the law, or from faith in what you heard? . . . Does [God] then, who supplies the Spirit to you . . . do so from the works of the law or from faith in what you heard?" (Gal. 3:1–5)

Paul tells the Galatians they are foolish if they believe that the observance of the Mosaic law is salvific; rather, Christ "ransomed them from the curse of the law" (Gal. 3:13) so that they could "receive the promise of the Spirit through faith." (Gal. 3:14) What Paul rejects principally here are the 613 prescriptions of the Mosaic law. But Paul also seems to mean that Christians are not under the regime of law of any kind, if by that is meant a universal demand on the Christian from without; thus he affirms: "if you are guided by the Spirit, you are not under the law" (Gal. 5:18; see also Rom. 6:14: "you are not under the law but under grace"). Such passages lead some exegetes to affirm that the concept of law in Paul "applies to any norm imposed on the human conscience from without."[10]

In Romans, Paul asserts that Christians are also free from **sin**; he begins chapter 8 with this famous assertion: "there is no condemnation for those who are in Christ Jesus. For the law of the Spirit [or spirit] of life in Christ Jesus has freed you from the law of sin and death." (vv. 1–2) For the next eleven verses Paul describes the conflict between the flesh and the spirit within us; the flesh leads to sin and death, the spirit leads to life. He tells the Romans: "you are not in the flesh; on the contrary, you are in the spirit, if only the Spirit of God dwells in you. Whoever does not have the Spirit of Christ does not belong to him." (Rom. 8:9) In Paul's conception, anyone who is bound by sin is not free, and anyone penetrated by the Holy Spirit becomes free; the Spirit liberates one from the tyranny exercised by sin and ending in death. The Spirit of Christ is now the dynamic principle of the new life in Christ; this life-giving Spirit of God dwells in justified Christians so that they can overcome the desire of the flesh: "live by the Spirit and you will certainly not gratify the desire of the flesh. . . . If we live by the Spirit, let us also follow the Spirit." (Gal. 5:16, 25) The sum of Paul's teaching is that we Christians are not only attached to Christ in some merely external identification with the cause of Christ but actually possess the Spirit of Christ that frees us from sin and empowers us to live for God.

G. Downpayment, First Fruits

Paul's Greek term, *arrabon*, means "down payment" or "pledge." Commercially, it is used in the sense of earnest money of the total amount due; it establishes a contract and guarantees its fulfillment.

In the New Testament, *arrabon* is unique to Paul; he refers it to the Spirit, as the guarantee of our future inheritance. For example: "the one . . . who anointed us is God; he has also put his seal upon us and given the Spirit in our hearts as a first installment." (2 Cor. 1:21–22; see also 2 Cor. 5:5) He means that the gift of the Spirit in us is God's down payment of our inheritance, the guarantee or pledge of the glory that is assured us. "He put his seal upon us" refers to the anointing or sealing connected with Baptism. In Romans, Paul uses a similar word, *aparche*: "we ourselves, who have the first fruits of the Spirit . . . groan within ourselves as we await . . . the redemption of our bodies." (Rom. 8:23) Here Paul uses "first fruits" in the sense of a guarantee of what is to come; that is, the Spirit that has been received is the guarantee or pledge of the glory assured for Christians. Both down payment and first fruits include a sense of eschatological expectation—awaiting the glory of eternal life; that is, the Spirit is our assurance of the coming salvation and our hope for the fullness of eternal life.

Such terms are another example of Paul's teaching of the "already" and the "not yet" of our Christian life now. He means that we are already in the process of being saved, for the Spirit is our beginning of salvation; but we are not yet in possession of the full harvest of our future inheritance.

H. Gifts of the Spirit

Paul's lengthy treatment of the extraordinary charisms, or gifts, is found in chapters 12 through 14 in 1 Corinthians. In chapter 12, he describes nine gifts given by the Holy Spirit to individual Christians:

> Now in regard to the spiritual gifts . . . I do not want you to be unaware. . . . Therefore I tell you that nobody speaking by the Spirit of God says, "Jesus be accursed."
> And no one can say, "Jesus is Lord," except by the holy Spirit.
> There are different kinds of spiritual gifts but the same Spirit.
> To each individual the manifestation of the Spirit is given for some benefit.

To one is given through the Spirit the expression of wisdom;
to another the expression of knowledge according to the same Spirit;
to another faith by the same Spirit;
to another gifts of healing by the one Spirit;
to another mighty deeds;
to another prophecy;
to another discernment of spirits;
to another varieties of tongues;
to another interpretation of tongues.
But one and the same Spirit produces all of these, distributing them individually to each person as he wishes. (12:1, 3–4, 7–11)

Notice first that the Holy Spirit is the very ground of Christian confession and charisms; that is, the variety of abilities that mark the members of the church are all the results of the Spirit's gifts. Apparently, Paul presents all of them as supernatural gifts for the benefit of the church community. He is aware that the Corinthians experienced some of these manifestations of the Spirit in their worship. He does not dispute the general authenticity of these gifts but cautions them not to let these extraordinary gifts disrupt the unity of the church and its worship. Let us try to understand each gift from Paul's own descriptions here in 1 Corinthians and in his other letters.

Wisdom
A prime example can be found in chapter 2: "we speak God's wisdom, mysterious, hidden. . . . This God has revealed to us through the Spirit." (1 Cor. 2:7–10) Twice in this lengthy passage (vv. 6–16) Paul reminds them that he is speaking "words taught by the Spirit." (vv. 10, 13)

Knowledge
Paul speaks about the gifts of knowledge and prophecy in chapter 13: "if I have the gift of prophecy and comprehend all mysteries and all knowledge." (v. 2) And the author of Ephesians speaks directly about the Spirit's gift of knowledge: "you also have heard the word of truth, the gospel of your salvation, and . . . were sealed with the

promised Holy Spirit" and continues with this prayer: "may [God] give you a S/spirit of wisdom and revelation resulting in knowledge of him." (Eph. 1:13–17; only some versions capitalize Spirit)

Faith
Paul seems to refer to a particular gift of supernatural faith that can "move mountains" (1 Cor. 13:2); that is, an unusual openness and confidence that enables the power of God to operate through oneself.

Healing
Both Paul and Peter exhibit this gift of healing in Acts. Also Paul reminds his Roman converts: "I dare to speak of . . . what Christ has accomplished through me by the power of signs and wonders, by the power of the Spirit of God." (Rom. 15:18–19)

Mighty Deeds
Paul defends his teaching to the Corinthians by asserting that it is not based on human wisdom but on the power of God: "my message and my proclamation were not with persuasive words of wisdom, but with a demonstration of s/Spirit and power, so that your faith might rest not on human wisdom but on the power of God." (1 Cor. 2:4–5)

Prophecy
The primary gift that Luke describes on the day of Pentecost is the gift of prophecy; Peter builds his whole sermon on the prophecy of Joel (3:1–5) and its fulfillment on the day of Pentecost. Paul considers prophecy as one of the great gifts of the Spirit: "strive eagerly for the spiritual gifts, above all that you may prophesy. . . . One who prophesies is greater than one who speaks in tongues." (1 Cor. 14, 1–5) Both in Acts 2 and in 1 Cor. 14, prophecy is prominent as a gift of the Spirit.

Discernment of Spirits
Paul probably refers here to discerning or judging prophecies, as in 1 Corinthians 14:29: "Two or three prophets should speak, and the

others discern." Again in 1 Thessalonians 5:20–21 Paul calls for a testing or discerning of prophetic speech: "Do not quench the spirit. Do not despise prophetic utterances. Test everything; retain what is good."

Speaking in Tongues
This is clearly the most controversial gift in the Corinthian church; it seems to be also the most prevalent. Paul takes great pains to caution believers regarding this manifestation of the Spirit.

He describes this gift of the Spirit in chapter 14: a. it is utterance inspired by the Spirit: "one who speaks in a tongue does not speak to human beings but to God . . . he utters mysteries in the S/spirit" (v. 2; the NRSV capitalizes Spirit here; cf. also 12:7); b. the one speaking in tongues is not out of control, for he is cautioned by Paul to speak "in turn" (v. 27); c. it is unintelligible both to the speaker (v. 14) and to others (v. 16: "he does not know what you are saying"); d. it is speech basically directed toward God. (v. 2)

Interpretation of Tongues
Paul probably refers to the ability to articulate or explain for the benefit of the community what the speaker in tongues has said. This is a companion gift to that of speaking in tongues, because the gift of tongues is basically unintelligible. Paul actually admonishes those who speak in tongues to be silent in church if there is no interpreter present: "if there is no interpreter, the person should keep silent in the church." (v. 28)

All of chapter 14 consists of Paul's lengthy response to a practical question in the church of Corinth: How should they deal with the many charisms that are occurring during their worship? Paul accepts these charisms as works of the Spirit; they are signs that the Spirit is guiding God's church. But he also knows that such experiences can be very emotional, engaging, even overwhelming. People can be very easily carried away by these extraordinary experiences; they can get emotionally caught up in them; some of them might be driven by their own pride rather then the Spirit; they can cause confusion in the midst of worship by all speaking out at once.

So Paul needs to give some guidelines regarding gifts of the Holy Spirit. We can find at least three guidelines in these chapters. Paul's first guideline comes at the very beginning of chapter 12: "nobody speaking by the s/Spirit of God says, 'Jesus be accursed.' And no one can say, 'Jesus is Lord,' except by the Holy Spirit." (v. 3) That is, the confession of Jesus Christ as Lord is a simple criterion for discernment of spirits, for "Jesus is Lord" is one of the earliest creedal statements of the church. So if the spirit influencing the individual utters anything that is contrary to this, it is not the work of the Holy Spirit; on the other hand, anyone who professes Jesus as Lord is empowered by the Holy Spirit.

A very apropos example of this is found in Matthew's Gospel: "When they hand you over, do not worry about . . . what you are to say . . . it will not be you who speak but the Spirit of your Father speaking through you." (Matt. 10:19–20) Again, anyone who believes in Jesus will be empowered by the Spirit to witness to Jesus. On the other hand, Paul, before his conversion, tried to force the opposite testimony; that is, he tried to make Christians utter a curse against Jesus (or God): "I punished [many followers of Jesus] in an attempt to force them to blaspheme." (Acts 26:11)

Paul's second guideline is: "let all things take place for building up [the church]." (1 Cor. 14:26) This is his constant norm in chapter 14, mentioned four more times: vv. 4, 5, 12, 17. That is, the true Spirit of prophecy will be a source for "building up [the church]" and not for personal satisfaction. Also, notice how Paul develops his forceful argument for unity in the body of Christ (12:12–30); again and again he draws the parallel between all the parts of our human body working together and all the members of Christ's body working together; he means that the body of Christ can only thrive if all work for the common good and serve the other members.

Paul's third guideline is only vaguely indicated in chapter 14: "you can all prophesy one by one, so that all may learn and all be encouraged. Indeed the spirits of prophets are under the prophets' control, since [God] is not the God of disorder but of peace." (14:31–33) Paul's point is that a number of people prophesying at the same time leads to confusion, not enlightenment. So the gift of prophecy should be exercised "one by one." (v. 31) The implication is that prophets have voluntary control over the prophetic spirit and should prophesy in an orderly fashion, so that they will effectively teach and encourage those who hear the prophecy. The true Spirit of God is the Spirit of peace, not confusion; so if someone is causing confusion and cacophony by the manner of his prophesying, his prophetic message is not from the Holy Spirit. In a word, Paul's test for the discernment of spirits is that the spirit must lead to peace, not confusion.

A similar test for discernment of spirits is found in the the First Letter of John:

> Do not trust every spirit but test the spirits to see whether they belong to God, because many false prophets have gone out into the world. This is how you can know the Spirit of God: every spirit that acknowledges Jesus Christ come in the flesh belongs to God, and every spirit that does not acknowledge Jesus does not belong to God. (1 John 4:1–3)

Here, 1 John recommends testing the spirits by a test similar to the Old Testament way of testing prophets. Thus, Deuteronomy teaches that if a prophet urges people to "follow other gods and to serve them . . . [then] pay no attention to the words of that prophet." (Deut. 13:2–4) So the Old Testament test of a prophet is what he teaches about God. Similarly, the New Testament test is what he teaches about Jesus. For John the test refers to "Jesus come in the flesh" (which those who left the Johannine community denied); for Paul the test refers to "not the God of disorder but of peace;" so, in either case the test involves a doctrine about God or Christ. Admittedly, the tests of Paul and of John are only vaguely similar.

In summary, we conclude that Paul has three guidelines to distinguish the true Spirit of prophecy: "Jesus is Lord" is a true prophecy, and anything contrary to that is not; the Spirit leads to "building up [the church]," not to personal satisfaction; and the true spirit of prophecy reflects "not the God of disorder but of peace."

I. The Fruits of the Spirit

"The fruit of the Spirit is love, joy, peace, patience, kindness, generosity, faithfulness, gentleness, self-control. . . . If we live in the Spirit, let us also follow the Spirit." (Gal. 5:22–25) This entire chapter 5 in Galatians is Paul's exhortation to Christian living. In the first twelve verses his main point is that Christians are not bound by the Mosaic law: "For freedom Christ set us free." (v. 1) In the rest of the chapter he presents the human struggle between the flesh and the spirit. Paul probably draws from the widespread philosophic and religious tradition of compiling catalogs of vices and virtues. In presenting his own two lists, Paul seems to describe the actions of two warring forces: the Flesh and the Spirit; he seems to personify these forces and present them as dominating their human subjects: "For the flesh has desires against the Spirit, and the Spirit against the flesh." (v. 17) First he presents a list of "the works of the flesh." (vv. 19–21) Though the Flesh is dominant in its subjects, human beings are still responsible for their actions: "I warn you . . . that those who do such things will not inherit the kingdom of God." (v. 21) Then he presents a list of "the fruit of the Spirit," as noted above.

Here, too, the Spirit is dominant, in the sense that the antidote to the Flesh is the Spirit, whom God has already sent into believers' hearts: "If we live by the Spirit, let us also follow the Spirit." (v. 25) The Spirit produces these fruits in believers: "live by the Spirit and you will certainly not gratify the desire of the flesh." (v. 16)

These fruits are in no way an exhaustive list; they are Paul's way of encouraging the Galatians to "live in the Spirit"; they describe what people will look like if they are following the lead of the Spirit; they are pointers to what a Christian looks like who is transformed into Christ's image: "those who belong to Christ have crucified their flesh with its passions and desires." (v. 24) What Paul intends by these fruits of the Spirit might be paraphrased like this: The effects of living by the Spirit are faithfulness, generosity, and self-control; the fruits of following in the way of the Spirit are love, joy, peace, patience, kindness, and gentleness.

Some of these fruits of life in the Spirit are found prominently in Paul's letters. Here are some of his own descriptions.

1. Love

In the Pauline perspective, love holds the pride of place. Here, just before our quote above, "Live by the Spirit," Paul tells the Galatians to "serve one another through love. For the whole law is fulfilled in one statement, namely, 'You shall love your neighbor as yourself.'" (Gal. 5:13–14) Paul's argument is forceful: the whole Mosaic law is fulfilled in one statement: "love your neighbor" (v. 14); but the Spirit has now replaced the Old Testament law, for "If you are guided by the Spirit, you are not under the law" (v. 18); therefore, "live by the Spirit" (v. 16) and "serve one another through love" (v. 13). That is why Paul mentions love as the first "fruit of the Spirit" (v. 22).

2. Joy
Paul's prayer for his converts at Rome connects joy, peace, hope, and the power of the Holy Spirit: "May the God of hope fill you with all joy and peace in believing, so that you may abound in hope by the power of the holy Spirit." (Rom. 15:13) He prays that God may be the source of joy and peace for all believers; he adds "by the power of the holy Spirit" to stress the active role of the Spirit in Christian life. Finally, Paul roots Christian hope in the gift of the Spirit, as he did earlier (Rom. 8:23).

Again in Romans 14:17, Paul describes Christian life in the kingdom of God on earth as one of joy, peace, and righteousness in the Spirit: "the kingdom of God . . . is a matter of . . . righteousness, peace and joy in the holy Spirit." That is, the essence of the kingdom consists in the freedom of the Christian to react to the promptings of the Holy Spirit. These three qualities—each of which is connected to the Spirit—mark the life of a Christian and are conducive to mutual upbuilding.

3. Peace
Perhaps the most direct passage connecting the Spirit and peace is from Ephesians: "Striving to preserve the unity of the spirit through the bond of peace: one body and one Spirit, as you were also called to the one hope of your call." (Eph. 4:3–4) This quote, though probably not authentically Pauline, speaks of the "unity of the spirit through the bond of peace" as a quality that is already given by the Spirit and needs only to be maintained.

4. Hope
Hope is not one of the fruits mentioned in Galatians but is often connected by Paul with the Holy Spirit: "If the Spirit of the one

who raised Jesus from the dead dwells in you, [God] . . . , will give life to your mortal bodies also through his Spirit that dwells in you." (Rom. 8:11) That is, the Spirit is the driving force and new vitality for Christian life and will assure our hope of resurrection.

Similarly in 2 Corinthians, Paul affirms: "God . . . has put his seal upon us and given the Spirit in our hearts as a first installment." (2 Cor. 1:22) That is, we have received the seal of the Holy Spirit in baptism, and this Spirit is the first installment and pledge of our eternal life.

But, to my mind, the primary quote of Paul regarding hope and the Spirit is the famous sentence in Romans: "hope does not disappoint, because the love of God has been poured out into our hearts through the holy Spirit that has been given to us." (Rom. 5:5) Paul's direct intention here is to bolster our hope in the midst of trials. "The love of God" is a subjective genitive; that is, it refers to God's love for us. Paul's point is that our hope is well founded because the Spirit dwells in us as the evidence of God's love for us. The Spirit is the divine presence in a justified Christian; God put his Spirit in believers' hearts as a guarantee of our future salvation, the "first installment." (2 Cor. 1:22)

J. The Spirit of Grace and Salvation

Paul uses the word *charis*, grace, in three different senses. The first sense of the word "grace" is as his common greeting: for example, "The grace of our Lord Jesus Christ be with you all." (I Thess. 1:1) This greeting can be found in every letter of the Pauline corpus. By it, Paul reminds his followers of the favor of God that they enjoy.

The second sense of the word "grace" is very prominent in Paul's writings and relates to the justification of God. Thus, Paul often speaks about grace, especially when he argues that we are saved not by the works of the Mosaic law but by the grace of God (Rom. 3:24, 5:15–21, 11:6; Gal. 2:21). For example, consider his famous text from Romans:

> [S]ince we have been justified by faith, we have peace with God through our Lord Jesus Christ, through whom we have gained access

to this grace in which we stand, and we boast in hope of the glory of God . . . and hope does not disappoint, because the love of God has been poured out into our hearts through the holy Spirit that has been given to us. (Rom. 5:1–5)

Paul first boasts that "we have been justified by faith," so that through Christ we stand in grace, and we have hope for eternal life because the Holy Spirit pours "the love of God into our hearts." What Paul means here by grace is our justification wrought by Christ, which has made our basic peace with God. Paul speaks of grace as the gift of God that justifies us.

But Paul also uses the word "grace" in the sense of a gift that is given to Christians: for example, "We want you to know, brothers and sisters, of the grace of God that has been given to the churches of Macedonia" (2 Cor. 8:1; also 9:14 and Rom. 12:6), and even more often as a gift given to himself: for example, "According to the grace of God given to me . . . I laid a foundation." (1 Cor. 3:10; also Gal. 1:15–16, 2:9; 1 Cor. 15:10)

Now this last sense of grace is a living reality, a gift of God that comes to us through the Spirit; it accompanies us or is in us. And this sense of *charis*, grace, is what led to the medieval idea of "sanctifying grace." To identify Paul's teaching here with our modern notion of sanctifying grace would be anachronistic, for Paul did not think of grace in such metaphysical or structured terms. But this is one scriptural basis for our theology of sanctifying grace. There is also a second scriptural basis that relates to the work of the Holy Spirit; that is all of Paul's teaching about the Spirit as the energizing force of God and the source of our new life in Christ.

Notes

1. Joseph Fitzmyer, S.J., *Romans*, Anchor Bible, vol. 33 (New York: Doubleday, 1993), 498–501. I am indebted to Fitzmyer for his excellent treatment here.

2. See Joseph Fitzmyer, *According to Paul* (New York: Paulist Press, 1992), 132–33; fn. 1 has a bibliography regarding Jeremias on this subject.

3. Joachim Jeremias, *The Prayers of Jesus*, Studies in Biblical Theology, 2/6 (London: SCM, 1967), 62; found also in Fitzmyer, *According to Paul*, 60.
4. Fitzmyer, *According to Paul*, 55.
5. Jeremias, *Prayers of Jesus*, 53–54; found also in Fitzmyer, *According to Paul*, 60.
6. Fitzmyer, *According to Paul*, 59–61.
7. Jeremias, *Prayers of Jesus*, 30 (emphasis in original); found also in Fitzmyer, *According to Paul*, 58.
8. Rudolph Schnackenburg, *The Church in the New Testament* (New York: Herder and Herder, 1965), 167.
9. Ibid., 170–71.
10. S. Lyonnet, "St. Paul: Liberty and Law," *The Bridge* 4 (1961): 237. Also: Luis Bermejo, S.J., *The Spirit of Life* (Chicago: Loyola University Press, 1989), 295.

CHAPTER TWO

Luke

∞

A. Gospel

A few points will help our perspective regarding the work of the Spirit in Luke's Gospel. First, Luke more than the other synoptics (Matthew and Mark) makes the Spirit an important feature of his Gospel. Mark mentions the Holy Spirit only six times; Matthew does so twelve times; Luke, seventeen times. Second, in most instances Luke depicts the Spirit as it appears in the Old Testament. That is, the S/spirit denotes the principle of life and vital activity relating to God, or the manifestation of the divine presence and power. As such, the Spirit is not clearly a personal distinct being. Third, as in the Old Testament, the Spirit appears sometimes as a passing phenomenon, when empowering leaders or prophets, and sometimes as a permanent power conferred on kings or messianic figures.

Still, Luke expands those previous notions both in his Gospel and in Acts. For example, Luke develops his own tripartite division of salvation history:[1] the period of **Israel**; the period of **Jesus**; the period of **the church**. And in each period, he carefully presents the power of the Holy Spirit as a driving force. In his Gospel Luke carefully presents the Spirit as the active force in the birth of Jesus as well as the beginning of his public life; then in Acts, he draws remarkable parallels between the birth of Jesus and the birth of the church—especially in terms of the charismatic power of the Spirit.

1. The Spirit's Influence on Jesus

At Jesus' birth, all the prominent figures are described as "filled with the holy Spirit": Mary is told, "The holy Spirit will come upon you" (1:35); "Elizabeth [is] filled with the holy Spirit" (1:41), as was her husband Zechariah (1:67); and Simeon prophesies what "had been revealed to him by the holy Spirit." (2:25)

The beginning of Jesus' public life is dominated by the Holy Spirit. The inaugural event for that is his baptism: "the holy Spirit descended upon him in bodily form. . . . And a voice came from heaven, 'You are my beloved Son; with you I am well pleased.'" (3:22) The descent of the Spirit here is the immediate preparation for Jesus' ministry, which begins in the next verse. Implied here is that the Spirit is now a permanent power dwelling with Jesus, the Son and servant (as was prophesied about the messianic king in Isa. 11:1 and 42:1; twice in the next chapter Luke adds to this continual influence of the Spirit: "Jesus returned to Galilee in the power of the Spirit." (4:14; also 4:1)

Luke continues to show the influence of the Spirit at important stages of Jesus' career: when the seventy-two return from their mission (10:21), and in his teaching on prayer (11:13) and about persecution (12:10, 12).Then Luke does not mention the Spirit again until the end of his Gospel (24:49).

2. Jesus' Final Commission in Terms of the Spirit

Each synoptic Gospel concludes with Jesus' final commission to the apostles; each evangelist relates an appearance of the risen Christ in which he commissions the disciples to carry out their future mission in his name; the commissions are quite similar, but each one is crafted to suit the major theme of that particular Gospel.

In Mark's Gospel, the commission reads: "Go into the whole universe and preach the gospel to every creature" (Mark 16:15–16; this is part of the appendix to his Gospel), for "**preaching the gospel**" is the dominant theme of Mark's Gospel. In Matthew's Gospel, the commission reads: "Go . . . make disciples of all the nations . . .

teaching them to observe all that I have commanded you" (Matt. 28:19–20); for Matthew carefully groups Jesus' teaching into five great discourses and mentions **discipleship** (*mathetes*) seventy-three times.

In contrast, Luke's formulation of the charge is: "repentance for the forgiveness of sin will be preached to all the nations. . . . You are witnesses of this! . . . I am sending upon you what my Father has promised." (24:48–49) The first item here is "**repentance**," which Luke mentions twenty-five times (as a noun or verb) in his Gospel and in Acts; the second item is "**witness**," for the theme of witnessing to God's salvation through forgiveness of sin is what the apostles will give witness to.

At the very beginning of Acts, Jesus explains his commission further: "you will receive power when the holy Spirit comes upon you, and you will be my witnesses in Jerusalem . . . and to the ends of the earth." (Acts 1:8) That is, Christ's commission is invested with *dynamis*, the power of the Holy Spirit for them to give witness to Jesus. Luke refers to this witnessing by the apostles often in Acts and sometimes connects their witness with the Holy Spirit (e.g., 2:4; 5:32). In his Gospel, then, Luke presents Jesus, our Savior, as permanently empowered by the Spirit; while in Acts, he will present the church as frequently strengthened and guided by the Spirit to witness effectively to Jesus throughout the region.

B. Acts of the Apostles

In Acts, the Holy Spirit is mentioned fifty-seven times. Because of that constant reference to the Spirit, some would like to call Luke's second book the Acts of the Spirit instead of the Acts of the Apostles.[2] Luke sets up this dynamic work of the Spirit in Acts at the end of his Gospel; he relates the promise of Jesus to his apostles, as we just saw above (Luke 24:49). Then in the beginning of Acts, Jesus explains: "wait for the promise of the Father about which you have heard me speak; for . . . in a few days you will be baptized with the holy Spirit." (Acts 1:4–5) Thus Jesus teaches that the Spirit is the promise or gift to be given to the apostles; and immediately afterward, Jesus summarizes the work of the Spirit as the power given the community to reach "to the ends of the earth": "you will receive power when the Holy Spirit comes upon you, and you will be my witnesses in Jerusalem, throughout Judea and Samaria, and to the ends of the earth" (1:8); Luke uses this verse as a programmatic verse in Acts, because it sets the scope of the spread of the word of God—from Jerusalem to the ends of the known earth. In other words, Luke presents the Spirit as the dynamic principle of the apostles' role as witnesses in the third phase of salvation history, that of the church.

1. An Overview of the Work of the Spirit in Acts

Now, consider how effectively Luke describes the primary work of the Spirit in Acts. First, the Holy Spirit empowers the apostles to preach and witness (Acts 1:5, 8; 2:4, 33) and inspires the early believers to speak in tongues and prophesy (2:4; 10:46; 19:6); then the Spirit comes upon the new believers in Jerusalem (2:38, 41; 4:31) and then upon the Samaritans by the laying on of the apostles' hands (8:15–17); this same Spirit marks out the first new assistants ("deacons") as those "filled with the Spirit" (6:30) and also directs individual missionaries (8:29–39; 10:19–20; 11:12; 20:22), and then, through Peter, inspires the first Gentile converts (10:44–46; 12:15); the Spirit also selects Barnabas and Paul (13:2, 40) and inspires the decisions of the great Council of Jerusalem (15:28); finally, the Spirit continues to aid the "presbyters" in tending the flock (20:28).

I believe that this constant inspiration and guidance of the Holy Spirit is the distinguishing feature of Lukan ecclesiology: that is, the continuous presence of the Holy Spirit in terms of giving impulse and guidance to the apostles, encouraging them to speak openly and confidently, choosing additional missionaries, and helping them decide crucial issues. It is worth noting, however, that for Luke the Holy Spirit is not clearly attached to any particular ministry, but rather inspires individual people to give witness to Christ. The Spirit also helps the church at decisive moments to decide which direction to take. In other words, the work of the Holy Spirit in Acts is to direct the growth of the church outward, to inspire the mission of the church, and to guide individuals in carrying out the witness to Jesus.

2. Pentecost

This dramatic event is Luke's portrayal of the fulfillment of Jesus' promise of the Spirit to the apostles. Just as the Spirit initiated the public life of Jesus, the Spirit now initiates the witness of the apostles and the early church to Jesus. Just as the Spirit was the constant power guiding Jesus, so now the Spirit is the source of life and growth of the early church. This gift of the Spirit is the fulfillment of the prophecy of Joel: "I will pour out a portion of my spirit upon all flesh, your sons and daughters shall prophesy" (Joel 3:1–2), meaning that the gift of the Spirit will transcend all bounds, and the Christian message shall come to all languages and cultures. This gift of the Spirit at Pentecost is the fulfillment of the promise of a new covenant: "We ourselves are proclaiming this good news to you that what God promised our ancestors he has brought to fulfillment for us." (Acts 13:32–33) And finally, the Pentecost event is the birthday of the church as an enthusiastic community, bound together by their common experience of the Spirit (Acts 2:38–47).

The meaning of Pentecost can be viewed in another way. Pentecost describes the inauguration of the church in terms of understanding and of power; that is, we see a profound difference between the community of Jesus' disciples before his death and resurrection and the primitive church after Pentecost. First, there is a dynamic difference in their understanding. During Jesus' lifetime, the disciples of Jesus completely fail to understand his person and his mission—"How slow of heart to believe all that the prophets spoke. Was it not necessary that the Messiah should suffer these things and enter into his glory?" (Luke 24:25–26; see also Luke 9:45; 18:34; 21:13–15)—whereas after the coming of the Holy Spirit, the early church shows a remarkable understanding of Jesus' suffering and death, his Messiahship, the meaning of Scripture, and the entire plan of God's salvation. See, for example, Peter's first sermon (Acts 2:14–36), his second sermon (Acts 3:12–26), his third speech (Acts 10:34–43), and Paul's sermon (Acts 13:16–41).

The church we see in Acts exhibits a new and creative insight into the meaning of Scripture and God's plan of salvation. And Luke indicates that the source of the church's inspired wisdom is the Spirit; for example, Luke first describes Stephen as "a man filled with faith and the holy Spirit" (6:5), then he notes the source of his wisdom: "they could not withstand the wisdom and Spirit with which he spoke." (6:10) Second, there is a remarkable difference in power. In Luke's Gospel, Jesus promises to give his followers the "power of utterance and wisdom which no opponent will be able to resist." (21:15) When he sent out the twelve, and then the seventy-two, they were effective in terms of healing but apparently not in terms of converts (9:1–6, 10:1–16). But in Acts, Luke attests to Peter's inspiration by the Holy Spirit ("Then, Peter, filled with the holy Spirit, answered them" ([Acts 4:8]), and has the Sanhedrin remark on his courage and power (4:13–17); similarly, Luke notes that some of the Christian community "were . . . filled with the holy Spirit and continued to speak the word of God with boldness." (4:31) The result of such boldness and power was that large numbers came to believe in Jesus. These two differences, then, show that something unique and powerful happened within the disciples because of Pentecost. That difference was the gift of the Spirit, imparting divine wisdom and power for them to give witness to Jesus.

3. Pentecost as the Foundation for Witness throughout Acts

Pentecost can also be seen from the unique perspective of Luke; his theme from the end of his Gospel as well as throughout Acts is that the disciples are to give witness to Jesus. That is, his final commission in the Gospel is: "You are witnesses of these things. And behold I am sending the promise of my father upon you" (Luke 24:48–49); then in Acts he repeats, "you will receive power when the holy Spirit comes upon you, and you will be my witnesses . . . to the ends of the earth." (Acts 1:8) Also, throughout Acts Luke consistently refers to the principal work of the early church as that of prophecy and witness and often indicates the Holy Spirit as the inspiration and power of that witness. Consider these ten examples:

> 2:17 (quoting Joel 3:1–2): "It will come to pass in the last days," God says, "that I will pour out a portion of my spirit upon all flesh. Your sons and your daughters shall prophesy, your young men shall see visions, your old men shall dream dreams."

Note: though Joel was not thinking of the Holy Spirit, Luke certainly intends that. And in fact he uses this quote as a programmatic text, preparing us to expect the Spirit as a general source of prophecies, visions, and dreams as we continue to read Acts.

4:31: As they prayed, the place where they were gathered shook, and they were all filled with the holy Spirit and continued to speak the word of God with boldness.
Note: here they all experience the Spirit and become bold.

7:55–56: [Stephen], filled with the holy Spirit, looked up intently to heaven and saw the glory of God and Jesus standing at the right hand of God.
Note: the Spirit effects this vision of the glory of God.

8:28–29: [The court official] was reading the prophet Isaiah. The Spirit said to Philip, "Go and join up with that chariot."
Note: the Spirit gives an instruction in the form of a locution.

10:19–20: As Peter was pondering the vision, the Spirit said [to him], "There are three men here looking for you. So get up . . . and accompany them without hesitation."
Note: here the Spirit directs Peter by means of a locution.

11:27–28: [S]ome prophets came down from Jerusalem to Antioch, and one of them, named Agabus, stood up and predicted by the Spirit that there would be a severe famine all over the world, and it happened under Claudius.
Note: here Agabus prophesies by the Spirit.

13:2–4: While they were worshiping the Lord . . . the holy Spirit said, "Set apart for me Barnabas and Saul for the work to which I have called them." Then . . . they laid hands on them and sent them off.
Note: Here the Spirit inspires and speaks to them in prayer.

16:6–7: [Paul and Timothy] had been prevented by the holy Spirit from preaching the message in the province of Asia. . . . [Then] they tried to go into Bithynia, but the Spirit of Jesus did not allow them.

Note: the Spirit here gives guidance in the form of some kind of dream or verbal guidance.

20:22–23: "[N]ow, compelled by the Spirit, I am going to Jerusalem. . . . in one city after another the holy Spirit has been warning me that imprisonment and hardships await me."
Note: Paul is warned by a verbal warning or vision.

21:10–11: [A] prophet named Agabus came down from Judea. . . . he took Paul's belt, bound his own hands and feet with it, and said, "Thus says the holy Spirit, 'This is the way the Jews will bind [Paul] . . . and hand him over to the Gentiles.'"
Note: here again Agabus prophesies, as he did in chapter 11, above.

4. Pentecost Transforms the Following of Jesus into a Missionary Movement

The first step in the church becoming a missionary movement is attributed to the Spirit with which the apostles were baptized and empowered to speak. On Pentecost itself, Peter urges three thousand listeners to be baptized and receive the Holy Spirit: "Repent and be baptized, every one of you, in the name of Jesus Christ . . . and you will receive the gift of the holy Spirit." (2:38) Soon after this, Peter reported that the Christian community could not be stopped by order of the Sanhedrin (4:18–30), but would continue their missionary preaching; his witness was strengthened by the Spirit: "the place where they gathered shook, and they were all filled with the holy Spirit and continued to speak the word of God with boldness." (4:31) Indeed, the Spirit became the active guide in their missionary activity, personally directing Philip (8:29, 39), Peter (11:15), and Paul (13:2, 4). Also, in the most critical decision of the missionary church, the Holy Spirit intervenes in the acceptance of the Gentiles into the church (10:44–47; 19:5–6) and in the Council of Jerusalem (15:8–9, 28). Later, the Spirit continues to orchestrate the missionary journeys of Paul (13:4; 16:6–8; 20:22–23). In a word, for Luke, the principal mover of the mission to the Gentiles was the Holy Spirit, and the driving force for the whole missionary direction of the early church was the Holy Spirit. Finally, when we realize that

Luke affirms the important influence of the Holy Spirit from the very conception of Jesus, to his public life, and throughout the whole Acts of the Apostles, we see how Luke is unique among our three great Scripture writers. For he alone emphasizes that the Spirit's driving force is a continuum between the ministry of Jesus and that of the apostles. In John, on the other hand, the Paraclete/Spirit takes over the work of Jesus only after he has returned to the Father.

5. Pentecost and the Gifts of the Holy Spirit

The seven traditional gifts of the Holy Spirit are found together only in Isaiah 11:2–3: "The spirit of the Lord shall rest upon him [the messianic king]: a spirit of wisdom and of understanding, a spirit of counsel and of strength, a spirit of knowledge and of fear of the Lord, and his delight shall be the fear of the Lord."

The spirit here, as in the entire Old Testament, is not a personal being, not the Holy Spirit. But the church has always referred to these as the seven gifts of the Holy Spirit and related them closely to the gift of the Spirit in Confirmation. Theologians describe them well, from Thomas Aquinas through modern theologians.[3] But there is no specific **scriptural** explanation of these gifts. I believe that a very fine development for some of these gifts of the Spirit is found in Acts and follows easily from what we just considered.

Wisdom

The Spirit is the source of Stephen's wisdom: "they could not withstand the wisdom and the Spirit with which he spoke." (Acts 6:10) That is, Stephen preached with a new wisdom about Jesus and God's plan of salvation. Similarly, Peter (10:42–43) finally knew the meaning of Jesus' death and resurrection once he "poured out his Spirit" on him and on all.

Understanding

At Pentecost, Peter shows a remarkable understanding of the Messiahship of Jesus and the fulfillment of all God's promises to his people Israel (Acts 3:12–21); also Paul, having been sent to Antioch by the Spirit, explains the whole history of God's promise and fulfillment (13:2; 13:16–39).

Courage

Luke's whole theme for Acts is found in his quoting Christ: "you will receive power when the holy Spirit comes upon you, and you will be my witnesses . . . to the ends of the earth" (Acts 1:8); then he continually shows how the apostles exhibit that power; one example is that of Peter's inspiration by the Holy Spirit and his obvious boldness (4:8; 4:13–17).

Counsel

Luke often refers to the guidance of the Holy Spirit, particularly in directing Peter and Paul; for example: "the holy Spirit said, 'Set apart for me Barnabas and Saul for the work to which I have called them'" (13:2; also 10:19–20 and 20:22–23).

6. What Is the *Ordo Salutis* in Acts?

That is, what is the proper order for the following elements of conversion: faith, Baptism, and the gift of the Spirit? Generally speaking, all three are found together in Acts; that is, the conversion-initiation pattern includes faith, Baptism, and the gift of the Spirit. Peter's first sermon offers the paradigm: "they asked Peter . . . 'What are we to do?' Peter said to them, 'Repent and be baptized, every one of you . . . and you will receive the gift of the holy Spirit.'" (2:37–38) Luke carefully follows this pattern and joins Baptism and the gift of the Spirit in 1:5; 2:38; 10:44–48; and 11:15–17. Within the same episode, the gift of the Spirit might follow Baptism (2:38; 19:5–6) or precede Baptism (9:17–18; 10:44–48), but they are both given together. Thus, Luke presents the human complex of hearing the gospel, faith, conversion, Baptism, and the gift of the Spirit not in a single, unchanging sequence; but Baptism and the gift of the Holy Spirit are essential and united. His approach seems to be very much in keeping with our human experience of justification, which does not follow a rigid sequence but varies slightly in different people and circumstances.

There is one passage that needs special consideration:

> [W]hen the apostles in Jerusalem heard that Samaria had accepted the word of God, they sent them Peter and John, who went down

and prayed for them, that they might receive the holy Spirit, for it had not fallen upon any of them; they had only been baptized in the name of the Lord Jesus. Then they laid hands on them and they received the holy Spirit. (8:14–17)

Here Peter and John are sent out deliberately for this purpose: "they laid hands on them and they received the holy Spirit." In Acts, Luke presents the apostles as the primary ministers of the Holy Spirit; that is, the Spirit operates only when there is communion with the apostles. But Luke continues to emphasize faith, Baptism, and the gift of the Spirit as the essential components of justification.

7. Baptism, the Gift of the Spirit, and the Church

Baptism and the gift of the Holy Spirit imply more than individual faith; they mark the beginning of a community of Christians. By insisting on Baptism, the early preachers established an important mark of a public society. Those who were baptized were known publicly as followers of Jesus and formed a visible community (*koinonia*). Luke constantly presents Baptism and the receiving of the Spirit as the acceptance into a community; he is careful to note how many were "added . . . to the communal life" (2:41–42), and "everyday the Lord added to their number." (2:47; see also 5:14; 6:7; 9:31) For Luke, the apostolic preaching had as its goal not simply an individual experience of conversion but the formation of a church community, the people of God; thus, he carefully noted many aspects of their communal life (2:42–47; 4:32–35) and described one model community: "The community of believers was of one heart and mind." (4:32)

The essential connection of faith, Baptism, the gift of the Spirit, and the church community is clarified by Peter at the conclusion of his first sermon on the day of Pentecost. The listeners asked Peter, "What are we to do?" Peter's answer was: "Repent and be baptized . . . and you will receive the gift of the holy Spirit" (2:38), but his answer also involved a communal response: "for the promise is made to you and to your children and to all those far off" (2:39); and the people immediately joined into a community: "They devoted themselves . . . to the communal life, to the breaking of the bread and to the prayers." (2:42)

The final part of Peter's response was: "you will receive the gift of the holy Spirit." (2:38) This implies that the Spirit is the final step in the process of conversion; that is, the Spirit is the final agent in this work of salvation and the continuation of Christ's ministry and work of redemption.

8. Luke's Symbolism for the Spirit of Jesus

Dove

At Jesus' baptism, Luke remarks: "the holy Spirit descended upon him in bodily form like a dove." (Luke 3:22) The precise symbolism of the dove is difficult to determine; scripture scholars have had much discussion over it.[4] To my thinking, the best origin for the dove symbolism in the Old Testament is in the Noah narrative. Noah sends out the dove, which returns with an oak leaf in its bill (Gen. 8:8–11). Thus Noah knew that the flood was over. In the next chapter, God makes a covenant with Noah (Gen. 9:8–11). So the dove is apparently a symbol of a new beginning, followed quickly with a divine covenant. In Luke's Gospel, when Jesus was baptized by John, "the holy Spirit descended in bodily form like a dove." (Lk. 3:22) This baptism marked a new beginning for Jesus, the start of his public life, leading to a "new covenant." (Luke 22:20)

In both cases we recognize water, dove, and new beginning—though there are also major differences. In Luke's tripartite division of salvation history, the dove marks a new beginning and covenant in the time of the Old Testament; the dove as the Spirit above Jesus marks the beginning of the time of Christ; then the Spirit appears at Pentecost as burning tongues of fire to mark the beginning of the era of the church. One quote from Gregory of Nyssa is quite apropos here: "Allow time for the dove [the Holy Spirit] to fly to you [in baptism], that dove which Jesus for the first time brought down in figure from heaven. That dove is guileless, meek and fertile. When she finds a man cleansed . . . she dwells with him and sets his soul on fire."[5]

Fire

Luke first connects the Holy Spirit and fire when he quotes John the Baptizer: "[The Messiah] will baptize you with the holy Spirit and fire." (Luke 3:16) Then in Acts, Luke describes the fulfillment of

John's prophecy at Pentecost. But Luke has a second reference to fire and baptism, quoting Jesus: "I have come to set the earth on fire, and how I wish it were already blazing! There is a baptism with which I must be baptized, and how great is my anguish until it is accomplished." (Luke 12:49–50) There is much that is unclear in this figurative language of Jesus. But in v. 49 Jesus may think of "fire" as a means of purification (similar to the fire of purification in Lev. 13:52 and Num. 31:23); but more clearly he intended this "fire" to have some relationship to 3:16 above. And the "baptism" in v. 50 likely refers to the ordeal of fire facing Jesus at the end of his life, as his "baptism of fire."

However, when Luke describes Pentecost in the Acts of the Apostles, he leaves no doubt about the symbolism of fire and the Holy Spirit: "There appeared to them tongues like flames of fire that parted and rested on each one of them. They were all filled with the holy Spirit and began to speak in other tongues, as the Spirit gave them to utter." (Acts 2:3–4) Fire is a symbol of the presence of God in the Old Testament (as with Moses and the flaming bush, Exod. 3:2). Here it is an external sign of the coming of the Spirit and the fulfillment of Jesus' promise (Luke 24:49). And the fire was in the form of tongues because the Spirit enabled the apostles to speak in various tongues, and because their mission would cross all language barriers. Throughout Acts, Luke continually refers to the Holy Spirit as the dynamic force of the mission of the apostles, as we saw above.

Notes

1. This three-stage salvation history idea was first worked out by Hans Conzelmann, *The Theology of St. Luke* (New York: Harper, 1961). Joseph Fitzmyer basically agrees with Conzelmann in *The Gospel of Luke*, (Anchor Bible, vol. 29), 181–87.

2. Raymond Brown, *The Churches the Apostles Left Behind* (New York: Paulist Press. 1984), 65.

3. Thomas Aquinas, *Summa Theologica*, II–II, 8, 9, 19, 45, 52, 121, 139. Also Adolphe Tanquerey, *The Spiritual Life* (Tournai, Belgium: Declee, 1930), 609–34.

4. Fitzmyer, *Gospel of Luke*, 483–84.

5. Gregory of Nyssa

CHAPTER THREE

John

A. Baptism in the Holy Spirit

In the first thirteen chapters of John's Gospel, the references to the Holy Spirit are few in number. The first instance is at Jesus' baptism by John the Baptizer:

> John testified . . . "I saw the Spirit come down like a dove from the sky, and remain upon [Jesus]. . . . the one who sent me to baptize with water told me, 'On whomever you see the Spirit come down and remain, he is the one who will baptize with the holy Spirit.'" (1:32–33)

Consider two points here, by way of introduction. All four Gospels describe the baptism of Jesus by John (although in John's Gospel his baptism is only implied); that event was most significant to all of them in terms of the beginning of Jesus' public life and his being filled with the Holy Spirit. Second, all four Gospels distinguish John's baptism as one of repentance and cleansing with water and Jesus' baptism with the Holy Spirit. They all clearly state the difference, and then in Acts (19:1–6), Luke continues to show this distinction.

Here Jesus himself first indicates the essential place of the Spirit in the whole work of salvation. He explains to Nicodemus, "Amen, amen, I say to you, no one can enter the kingdom of God without being born of water and Spirit" (John 3:5). The principal idea of this verse is the gift of the Spirit. Nicodemus himself could understand some of this teaching of Jesus in terms of Old Testament ideas about spirit and the life of God in us. But there is another level to this discourse (as there frequently is in John's Gospel), which could be understood by the Johannine church. For them, "being born of water and Spirit" would be seen as a reference to Baptism. In fact this passage in John is one of the few scriptural verses defined by the church. The Council of Trent applied this passage to Baptism: the water regenerates the soul by virtue of the Holy Spirit.[1] This connection between water, baptism, and the Spirit is made even clearer in chapter 4, in which John presents Jesus' discourse with the Samaritan woman at Jacob's well. Jesus slowly leads her from talk about water to talk about living water. He then explains, "the water that I will give him will become within him a fountain of water leaping up to eternal life." (4:14) This living water most likely refers to the Spirit communicated by Jesus, as Jesus himself explains in 7:37–38:

> "Let anyone who thirsts come to me and drink. Whoever believes in me, as scripture says: 'Rivers of living water will flow from within him.'" He said this in reference to the Spirit that those who came to believe in him were to receive. There was, of course, no Spirit yet, because Jesus had not yet been glorified.

Exegetes dispute many elements of this quote. However, they do agree that it relates to the Holy Spirit, as John explains: "he said this in reference to the Spirit"; so the Spirit is the living water whom Jesus gives to anyone who believes in him. However, as we will see again and again in John's Gospel, the abundant outpouring of the Spirit would only happen after Jesus' death and resurrection. Once Jesus has returned to the Father, the Paraclete/Spirit would continue the presence of Jesus in the world.

B. Spirit of Truth

In the five Paraclete sayings (which will be carefully considered below), Jesus describes the Paraclete as the "Spirit of truth" (14:17;

15:26; 16:13), and most of the functions of the Spirit relate to teaching, testifying, and guiding to all truth. Surprisingly, Jesus never directly describes the Paraclete as the Spirit of love. Why is that so? Why does John so emphasize truth with respect to the Spirit that he seems to ignore love? In order to understand John's thinking, we need to begin with his unique characterization of Jesus.

In the prologue of his Gospel, John constantly describes Jesus as the **Word** of God: "In the beginning was the Word"; and he repeats that same noun three times, concluding majestically, "And the Word became flesh." (1:1–14) Scholars agree that this prologue was composed independently of the rest of the Gospel. This seems particularly convincing, since John does not continue to emphasize the Word in the rest of his Gospel. But he does quote Jesus' referring to himself as **Truth** (8:26, 32; 14:6) and **Light** (3:19–21; 8:12; 9:5; 12:46) and as one who speaks the words of God (3:34; 7:16; 12:48–49; 14:10; 17:7–8). Also, the constant theme of John's Gospel is that faith in Jesus is the means to eternal life: "this is the will of my Father, that everyone who sees the Son and believes in him may have eternal life." (6:40; see also: 3:16, 18; 5:24; 11:25–26; 17:3; 20:31)

All this might be summarized by saying that in John, Jesus is the whole truth about God, he is the unique light come into our world, and his words express the whole revelation about God and salvation. We might even say that in John's Gospel, the revelation of God is a person, Jesus Christ. Or even: to believe in Jesus Christ leads to salvation. Such a stark and arresting statement needs to be understood in Johannine terms. John's Letters struggle mightily to correct false notions within the Johannine community; they explain that abiding in the truth includes keeping the commandments and following in the way of Jesus, which we will consider later. Here we focus merely on the dominant teaching in John's Gospel: Jesus is the whole truth about God and salvation.

If the Holy Spirit is to take the place of Jesus after he returns to the Father, then it is most appropriate for Jesus in John's Gospel to characterize the Paraclete as the Spirit of truth. If the Spirit is to be our new Advocate, then he must reflect the primary quality of Jesus (the first Advocate), who is the Word of God, the whole truth about God.

If we understand John's consistent paradigm of Jesus being the unique light of the world and faith in him being the single requirement for our salvation, then we are not surprised by the constant reference to the Paraclete as the "Spirit of truth." And we get a better perspective on all the functions of this Spirit of Jesus: to teach us everything, to remind us of all that Jesus taught, to give witness to the truth within us, to lead us in the way of all truth. Indeed if faith in Jesus leads to salvation, then the all-inclusive work of his Spirit is to teach us all truth. For the disciples, that meant the Paraclete would "guide [them] to all truth," even that which "[they] cannot bear now." For us, that means the Paraclete "will take from what is mine and declare to you the things that are coming"; that is, the Spirit will deepen our understanding of Christ's teaching and help us apply it to whatever comes.

C. The Paraclete

In the New Testament, the word "paraclete" is found only in Johannine writings. It seems to be a Greek loan word, rather than a true Hebrew title.[2] Etymologically, *parakletos* means "one called alongside to help." It is a verbal adjective found in classical Greek and has a passive sense. It might be translated as "defending counsel" or "advocate." The active sense of this word is secondary; it can refer to an intercessor, a mediator, a consoler. Other New Testament writings do use a related word, *para/klesis*, to describe the exhortation and encouragement found in the preaching of the apostolic witness: for example: "with the consolation of the holy Spirit, [the church] grew in numbers." (Acts 9: 31; see also: Acts 13:15; 1 Thess. 3:2; Rom. 12:8; Heb. 13:22) No one translation of paraclete captures its various functions, for in the texts below the paraclete functions as a witness in defense of Jesus, a prosecuting attorney proving the world guilty, a teacher and guide for the disciples and thus their helper, a consoler of the disciples who takes the place of Jesus among them. We will simply keep the term "paraclete" as a unique and consistent term, rather than vary the translation according to the particular function.

Where does the concept of Paraclete come from? What is the background for the elements that make up John's picture of the Paraclete?

Three Old Testament concepts contribute to the Johannine delineation of the Paraclete. First, the spirit of God comes upon the prophets that they may speak God's word; the spirit is the divine power and inspiration for the prophets to speak God's word faithfully and even boldly. Similarly in John's Gospel, the Paraclete teaches the disciples, so that they can testify to Jesus and testify against the world. Second, the Spirit is similar to the personified Wisdom that comes from God to dwell with God's people and give them the gift of understanding; wisdom teaches God's faithful people but is rejected by others. In John's Gospel, the Paraclete will guide the disciples into all truth and declare to them the things that are coming. Third, the Old Testament offers examples of a great leader, about to die, who passes on some of his spirit to a disciple who will take his place. Thus Moses laid hands on Joshua so that he might be filled with the spirit of wisdom (Deut. 34:9) and Elijah gave Elisha a double portion of his spirit (2 Kings 2:9, 15). So John presents Jesus, just before his death, giving his Spirit to the disciples who will carry on his work ("if I go, I will send him to you"); this "other Advocate" will take the place of Jesus; so powerful will this Spirit of Jesus be for his followers that it is no exaggeration to say, "It is better for you that I go"!

Thus John's presentation of the Paraclete makes use of three Old Testament traditions: the spirit of God inspiring the prophets; personified Wisdom that dwells with God's people and brings the gift of understanding; the passing on of the spirit of a great leader to one who is to carry on his work. In those three Old Testament examples, the functions of the spirits are those of witnessing, teaching, guiding, and accusing; these are the same functions that John mentions to describe the Paraclete. So while the term paraclete is unique to John, the functions of the Paraclete have strong foundations in the Old Testament.

D. The Five Paraclete Texts

The five texts are all found in chapters 14 through 16 in John's Gospel. They are amazing descriptions of the work of Jesus' Spirit. In them, Jesus promises that he will not leave the disciples orphans—without a personal guide to dwell with them—but will send them "another Advocate," his own Spirit of truth to "guide them in the way of all truth." The Spirit of Jesus is clearly a personal presence—the ongoing presence of Jesus for all Christians. The Spirit will perform the same functions that Jesus did: to teach them, to be their advocate in trials, to intercede for them with God, to guide them, to encourage them. These five passages contain the most profound teaching about the Spirit of Jesus in all of Scripture. In this section, we want to give a careful exegesis and indicate in general what this profound teaching means for us. In parts 2 and 3 of this book, we will try to see the implications of these passages for our prayer and for our life in Christ.

1. John 14:16–17

"I will ask the Father, and he will give you another Advocate to be with you always, the Spirit of truth, . . . it remains with you and will be in you."

Notice, first, the immediate context here; Jesus has just promised that the prayers of the disciples will always be heard: "If you ask the Father anything in my name I will do it" (vv. 13–14); he then mentions the gift of the Paraclete (vv. 16–17). In Luke we noticed the same sequence: "Ask and it will be given to you. . . . How much more will my Father in heaven give the holy Spirit to those who ask him." (Luke 11:9–13) In both Gospels Jesus promises their prayers will be heard and he connects that with the Spirit. Second, John calls the Spirit "another Advocate." In John's First Epistle, Jesus himself is called the Advocate (1 John 2:1), inasmuch as he is their heavenly intercessor in the Father's presence after the resurrection. Here then, the Spirit is the "other Advocate" as their internal intercessor in prayer to the Father. Third, Jesus assures them that his Spirit will "dwell with [them] always." Just as God in the Old Testament was "God with us" (Isa. 7:14), so now God's Spirit is to remain with them always. Fourth, in the very next verse Jesus assures the disciples: "I will not leave you orphans; I will come to you." (v. 18) He means he will come to them and abide with them in his Spirit.

What all this means for us is most engaging. In this first Paraclete saying, Jesus establishes the foundation for the entire work of the Paraclete. He assures us that the Paraclete dwells with us permanently as the new presence of Jesus in each one individually. When Jesus lived among the early disciples, he was limited to a definite time and place. Now the Paraclete is not limited by time or place but exists in all believers permanently. The Paraclete is just as present in each Christian today as he was in the first generation of Christians.

This first Paraclete saying already establishes what John's Gospel means by the divine indwelling, especially as it relates to the Spirit of Jesus. John's theology of immanence makes constant use of the Greek expression *manein en*. He uses this expression nineteen times in his Gospel (and twenty-two times in 1 John). It can be translated as "to remain," "to abide," or "to dwell." Biblically, this is almost exclusively a Johannine expression. What he means by it in general is that our relationship to God is not just a series of encounters but a stable way of life, for God actually "remains in" us individuals by his Spirit.

In chapters 14 to 16 and especially in John 14:15–24, there are three types of divine indwelling: in vv. 15–17 the Spirit will dwell within the disciples ("another Advocate to be with you always, the Spirit of truth"); in vv. 18–21 Jesus will dwell within the disciples ("I will come to you . . . [and be] in you"); in vv. 23–24 the Father will come to them along with Jesus ("we will come to him and make our dwelling with him"). Perhaps these three types of divine indwelling had independent origins, but they are woven together here in the final stage of John's Gospel so that all three indwellings are accomplished through the Spirit.[3] To paraphrase John's theology here: the Spirit/Paraclete is the presence of Jesus after Jesus has gone to the Father ("another Advocate to be with you always"); so Jesus can say, "I am coming back to you," by means of the Spirit that he will send. And since the Father and Jesus are one ("I am in the Father and the Father is in me," 14:10–11), they both dwell in the disciples by means of the Spirit ("we will come to him and make our dwelling with him," 14:23).

We might summarize John's theology of immanence this way. By sending us the Paraclete, Jesus makes possible a divine presence abiding within each one who believes. The model for this immanence is the intimate relationship between Father and Son

(14:10–11). The agent of this immanence is the Paraclete (14:26). The meaning of this immanence is that there is a permanent spiritual status for all who believe in Jesus. And John's way of describing all this is by appropriating this immanence to the Spirit/Paraclete.

2. John 14:25–26

"The Advocate, the holy Spirit, that the Father will send in my name—he will teach you everything and remind you of all that I told you."

First, Jesus tells the disciples that the Advocate "will teach you everything." "To teach" in John is practically a verb of revelation. The Spirit will not bring a new teaching or revelation: "He will not speak on his own, but he will speak what he hears." (16:13) The teaching of Jesus contains all that they need to know, all the revelation of God; so the Spirit "will not speak on his own, but he will speak what he hears. . . . He will take from what is mine and declare it to you." (16:13–14) In John, Jesus asks more than once that his followers abide in his word: "If you remain in my word, you will truly be my disciples." (John 8:31; also see 15:7) This is exactly the proper function of the Spirit: to make the teaching of Jesus enter into their hearts fully, to make them understand internally the words of Jesus.

Second, Jesus promises that the Advocate "will remind you of all that I told you." Often in John's Gospel, Jesus promised that later (after the resurrection) the disciples would remember what he told them and come to understand and believe:

> 2:22: [W]hen [Jesus] was raised from the dead, his disciples remembered that he said this, and they came to believe . . . the word Jesus had spoken.

> 12:16: His disciples did not understand this at first, but when Jesus had been glorified they remembered that these things were written about him.

> 13:7: "What I am doing, you do not understand now, but you will understand later."

13:19: "From now on I am telling you before it happens, so that when it happens you may believe that I AM."

14:19–20: "In a little while the world will no longer see me, but you will see me. . . . On that day you will realize that I am in the Father and you are in me and I in you."

14:29: "I have told you this before it happens, so that when it happens you may believe."

15:20–21: "Remember the word I spoke to you . . . they will do all these things to you on account of my name."

15:26: "When the Advocate comes . . . he will testify to me. And you also testify."

16:4: "I have told you this so that when their hour comes you may remember that I told you."

16:12–13: "I have much more to tell you, but you cannot bear it now."

Why was it necessary for the Holy Spirit to remind the disciples of what Jesus told them? Why couldn't he do that himself? Because, prior to the deep mystery of his passion, death, and resurrection, they didn't know what he was talking about; they did not know the whole truth of his passion; even though he gave them some sense of his future suffering and death, the specific details were a later insertion into the Gospels, so they were still more or less in the dark about his passion, death, and resurrection. Jesus added another reason why he could not explain everything to them before the coming of the Holy Spirit, when he told them they could not bear the terrible truth: "I have much more to tell you, but you cannot bear it now. But when . . . the Spirit of truth comes, he will guide you to all truth." (16:12–13) Jesus had a perfect solution for helping them in their coming confusion when he promised them the Spirit of Truth. Along with their remembering what Jesus said, they would be guided by the Spirit to grasp fully the deep meaning of the mystery of redemption.

These functions of the Spirit of Jesus, teaching and reminding, are also meant for us. That is, Jesus' promise is not only intended for his disciples but also for the future believers. The First Epistle of John clarifies this; it refers to the Holy Spirit as "the anointing that . . . remains in you, so that you do not need anyone to teach you. But his anointing teaches you about everything." (I John 2:27) Pope John Paul II affirms this also:

> The promise is not limited to the apostles and their immediate companions. . . . It extends to the future generations of disciples and confessors of Christ. The Gospel is destined for all nations and for all the successive generations which will arise in the context of diverse cultures and of the manifold progress of human civilization.[4]

Let us examine how these first two functions of the Paraclete apply to us. "To teach you everything" is our assurance that the Spirit will make the teaching of Jesus ever more internal with an ever increasing faith. John's entire Gospel stresses the necessity of letting Jesus' teaching enter into our hearts so that his teaching might attain its full effect. The Spirit is given to us precisely to make Jesus' way ever more personal and inspiring.

"To remind you of all that I told you" means that the Paraclete will help us recall what Jesus had said and done, so that we can be continually aware of his teaching and make them live again for us. Pope John Paul II describes this work of the Spirit:

> "By recalling" the words, deeds and the entire salvific mystery of Christ, the Spirit of truth makes him continually present in the church. The Spirit ensures that he takes on an ever new "reality" in the community of salvation.[5]

In the previous chapter, we reflected on Jesus' all-inclusive new commandment: "Just as I have loved you, you also should love one another." (13:34) We need to be constantly reminded how that example of love should be carried out in our lives. The Paraclete is sent particularly to remind us of the example of Jesus, our model for living.

3. John 15:26–27

"When the Advocate comes, whom I will send you from the Father, the Spirit of truth that proceeds from the Father, he will testify to me. And you also testify, because you have been with me from the beginning"

Jesus offers two reasons for the disciples' confidence in witnessing to himself. His second reason is: "you will testify, because you have been with me from the beginning." That is, the disciples have heard Jesus' teaching and seen him with their own eyes, so they can testify reliably as eyewitnesses. The prologue of John's First Letter continues in this same confident tone: "What was from the beginning [of Jesus' public life], what we have heard, what we have seen with our eyes . . . and touched with our hands . . . we testify to it and proclaim to you." (1 John 1:1–2) After all, what is more reliable than the immediate experience of the disciples?

However, Jesus' main emphasis is on the first reason here: "the Advocate . . . whom I will send you from the Father . . . will testify to me. And you also testify." Notice in this quote that Jesus sends the Holy Spirit; in 14:26 Jesus tells his disciples that the Father will send the Holy Spirit. Both remarks are true, for in John, Jesus and the Father are one in their works (10:30). So Jesus asserts that the Spirit "will testify to [me]. And you also testify." Yet this will not be two sources of testimony but only one; that is, the Spirit will encourage them internally to witness to Christ and they will do so with a new and internal assurance.

Compare this with Jesus' assurance in the synoptics and in Acts. In Mark, Jesus' assurance reads: "say whatever is given to you when the time comes, because it is not you who will be speaking; it will be the holy Spirit" (Mark 13:11). In Acts, Jesus' promise is similar: "You will receive power when the holy Spirit comes down upon you; and you will be my witnesses . . . to the ends of the earth." (Acts 1:8) In John, however, there are subtle differences in the witness aspect to which the synoptics and Acts refer. That is, when Jesus promises that the Spirit "will testify to me," he means that the Spirit will testify first to the disciples; his role will be internal—to enlighten the disciples in the midst of adversity and to strengthen them in their own faith so that they can testify as external witnesses. And even the testimony

John has in mind is different from that of the synoptics. For in the synoptics the testimony in which Jesus promises the help of the Holy Spirit has to do with human tribunals, as when the apostles are delivered to the Sanhedrin or brought before political leaders. But in John there is no mention of judicial trials, but rather of their bearing witness to the person of Jesus in order to induce people to believe in him. Their struggle will be similar to that of Jesus in his life when he experienced the great conflict of opposition from the world. Just as the works of the earthly Jesus had borne witness before the unbelieving world, so too will the Spirit bear witness through the preaching of the disciples after Jesus' departure. Jesus assures the disciples that the Paraclete will strengthen them in their similar trials of two camps—for or against him. When the disciples experience opposition from the world, the Spirit of Truth will work within their hearts to strengthen them in their own faith and provide them with unshakable confidence. The very next verse (16:1) continues in the same vein; Jesus says, "I have told you this so that you may not fall away" [or "lest you be scandalized"]; he is concerned that they not be scandalized or fail in faith. John's mention of scandal might refer to the great problem of the Johannine community and the consuming dispute in the Epistles of John: the scandal of the secessionists. The point of Jesus' assurance for the Johannine community is that the Paraclete will not let them "fall away" if they are open to his help.

In our contemporary society, the world in which we live is one of scientific materialism that rejects anything spiritual or supernatural; it tends to treat faith as fantasy and religion as myth. These are our modern scandals that require constant internal guidance from the Spirit of Jesus.

Even though the primary action of the Spirit is to give internal witness to Jesus, we may still wonder how we ordinary Christians can also give witness to Jesus externally. One way we may give witness to Jesus is by our daily acts of kindness and compassion. Even though we are not conscious of giving witness to Jesus, Jesus himself makes the connection for us: "Whatever you did for one of these least brothers/sisters of mine, you did for me." (Matt. 25:40) Now realistically, such acts of kindness give public witness to Jesus only if the people we serve know that we are Christians. As long as they have any sense that we are acting from our general Christian commitment, we are giving witness to Jesus. One final note: giving witness to Jesus occurs even if there is no positive effect on anyone. Even when a person rejects our witness, it is still offered in the name of Jesus.

Another way of giving witness to Jesus involves practicing the difficult virtues that Jesus exemplified: loving the outcasts, the sinners, the poor, the disturbed; forgiving those who offended him. These are virtues not commonly practiced by people in our society. When we mirror these virtues of Jesus in our actions, we give witness to him and to his way. For example, we can show acceptance of people with repellent illnesses, or AIDS sufferers, or offensive people; and we can forgive those who hurt us, even severely, when they ask forgiveness.

4. John 16:8–11

"[W]hen [the Advocate] comes, he will convict the world in regard to sin and righteousness and condemnation; sin because they do not believe in me; righteousness because I am going to the Father and you will no longer see me; condemnation, because the ruler of this world has been condemned."

This passage has to do with giving witness to Jesus similar to the previous one (15:26–27). Again the Spirit's witness is directed first to the disciples and through them to the world. Notice the verse immediately preceding this: "I will send him to you." Ultimately there will be some witness against the world, but prior to that will be the Spirit's strengthening the disciples interiorly in the face of doubts or attacks on their faith. In the synoptics Jesus declares that the disciples will be subject to actual trials; they will be delivered before the Sanhedrin and brought before public officials (Matt. 10:17–18; Mark 13:9). However, in John there is no mention of such formal public trials and judges; rather his concern is for the same theological conflict that characterized the public life of Jesus in John's Gospel, namely, the great opposition between Jesus and the world, the struggle for or against Jesus. De la Potterie describes well the witness that the Spirit of Jesus will bear interiorly for the disciples:

> In this momentous religious trial in which Jesus and the world confront one another, the witness of the Paraclete will have its true

meaning: before the world's hostility, Jesus' disciples will be continually exposed to scandal, will experience doubt and discouragement, and will be tempted to give up the fight. At this very time the Spirit of truth, the defender of Jesus, will intervene. Within the conscience of the disciples, he will bear witness to Jesus; he will strengthen them in their faith and provide them with the assurance that is properly Christian.[6]

Jesus continues to mention three elements of the Spirit's witness against the world among the disciples. First, the Paraclete will prove to the disciples that the world is guilty of **sin**—the basic sin which consists in refusing to believe in Jesus. This sin is described often in John's Gospel (3:19; 9:41; 12:37; 15:22–24). For John this basic sin of disbelief culminated in putting Jesus to death. The disciples will continue this legal contest against the unbelieving world, and the Paraclete will be their "counsel for the defense" and prove the world guilty of disbelief in God and his Word. Another element of the Spirit's witness against the world is to prove the world wrong about righteousness or **justice**, by showing that Jesus, whom it adjudged guilty, was really innocent and just. The Jews had judged Jesus' claim of oneness with the Father as arrogant, blasphemous, and gravely sinful (5:18; 7:12; 9:24; 10:33). But the Paraclete will demonstrate to the disciples that this same death sentence really showed that Jesus was what he claimed, for after his death, Jesus was raised and glorified by the Father (17:5). And the presence of the Paraclete in the disciples is itself a proof that Jesus is with the Father and sends the Spirit to them (14:16–20; also v. 7 here: "if I go, I will send him to you"). The final element in the Paraclete's witness against the world is "**condemnation**," that is, proof that in condemning Jesus the world itself was judged. For in the Paraclete, Jesus is still present after his death; so if Jesus' passion represented the confrontation of Jesus and the Prince of this world (12:31; 14:30), then Jesus' victory over death is also his victory over the Prince of this world; because Jesus stands justified before the Father, the power of Satan has lost the essential struggle (notice 1 John 4:4 and 5:4).

Today, our unbelieving world takes different stances that threaten our witness to Jesus, our steadfastness in faith: the "enlightened" mockery of some scientists, the disregard for human life, the philosophical rejection of God because of pervasive human suffering, the modern attacks against the historical Jesus, the skepticism of some scriptural approaches. These are our modern scandals. In such an atmosphere, we can rely on the witness of the Spirit of Jesus to strengthen us in our faith and provide us with rocklike confidence.

5. John 16:12–13
"The Spirit of truth . . . will guide you to all truth . . . ; he will speak what he hears, and will declare to you the things that are coming."

The functions of the Paraclete here are also similar to those in 14:26, that is, to teach and to call to mind, but they are further developed here, especially by the addition of the phrase "guide you to all truth." For this phrase seems to include more than a deeper intellectual understanding; it also involves teaching a way of life in conformity with Jesus' teaching. The reason for saying this is bound up with the whole Johannine understanding of "the way of truth." For John's Gospel thinks of truth not as an abstract system of faith but as a sphere of action, similar to the Old Testament notion of "the way of truth" as a way of life in conformity with the Mosaic law, and also similar to the notion of "the way" in the Acts of the Apostles.[7]

The phrase "declare to you the things that are coming" does not involve any new revelation, for he adds, "he will speak what he hears"; rather, as Raymond Brown expresses it well:

> [It] consists in interpreting in relation to each coming generation the contemporary significance of what Jesus has said and done. The best Christian preparation for what is coming to pass is not an exact foreknowledge of the future but a deeper understanding of what Jesus means for one's own time.[8]

Or again, the Paraclete, who is present to every time and culture, will not bring a new revelation but will supply new insights into the revelation taught by Jesus, so that Christians of every era will find authentic responses to their own period of history. So when Jesus, who was about to die, promises, "I will not leave you orphans," he meant that his Spirit would continue his work and his presence. Or finally, parallels. First, from the parallels in their work (number 3 above), John teaches that the Paraclete continues the **work of Jesus**. That is, John presents a tandem relationship or a parallelism between the ministry of Jesus and that of the Paraclete. Second, the whole complex of parallels above leads Raymond Brown to a more profound conclusion: the Holy Spirit continues **the presence of Jesus**. Thus the one whom Jesus calls "another Paraclete" is in many ways another Jesus, one who continues the same work of Jesus in us now:

> Since the Paraclete can come only when Jesus departs, the Paraclete is the presence of Jesus when he is absent [after his departure]. Jesus' promises to dwell within the disciples are fulfilled in the Paraclete. . . . John insists that Jesus will be in heaven with the Father while the Paraclete is on earth in the disciples; and so the two [from then on] have different roles.[10]

When we compare this section F with E, above, we see how closely John unites the work of Father, Jesus, and Paraclete. Such parallels lead us to four summary statements: during his public life, Jesus does the work of the Father on earth; how we relate to the human Jesus determines our relationship to the Father; once Jesus returns to the Father, the Paraclete is the new presence of Jesus in us; the Paraclete, the Spirit of Jesus, continues the work of Jesus for Christians in every age.

G. The Spirit in the First Letter of John

There are two passages in the First Letter of John that connect the witness of the Holy Spirit to the summary of whole faith and life in Christ. The first passage is 1 John 3:23–24:

> his commandment is this: We should believe in the name of his Son, Jesus Christ, and love one another just as he commanded us. Those who keep his commandments remain in him, and he in them, and the way we know that he remains in us is from the Spirit that he gave us.

Raymond Brown makes an incisive parallel between this "commandment" and the double commandment of the synoptic tradition. He starts with this famous quote in Mark: when Jesus is asked, "Which is the first of all commandments?" his response is now sacrosanct: "The first is this: . . . 'you shall love the Lord your God with all your heart . . . with all your strength.' The second is this: 'you shall love your neighbor as yourself.'" (Mark 12:28–31) Then he concludes:

> The double commandment of the synoptic tradition offers a parallel attempt to say what is crucial: love of God and love of neighbor as yourself. I John offers instead belief in Jesus and love of one another. . . . [So] Jo. 3:23 might serve very well as the New Testament sentence that best expresses the essence of Christianity.[11]

Then v. 24 connects the Holy Spirit to this essential norm of Christianity: "the way we know that he remains in us is from the Spirit that he gave us." That is, the Spirit is a type of criterion or pledge. What does 1 John mean when he asserts that God abides in us "from the Spirit that he gave us"? How does an invisible Spirit show that God abides in us? Raymond Brown explains:

> The answer may be found in the next unit in I Jo. 4:2: "Now this is how you can know the Spirit of God: Everyone who confesses Jesus Christ come in the flesh reflects the Spirit which belongs to God." One may know that God abides in Christians from the fact that they profess a true faith about his Son, and they can do that only if the Paraclete has taught them.[12]

That is, the proof that we are God's children and God abides in us is shown when we profess faith in Jesus, and we do that only by means of the Spirit who bears witness through us. Recall that in John's Gospel it is the Paraclete who bears witness to our faith in Jesus: "When the Paraclete comes . . . he will bear witness on my behalf." (John 15:26–27) Also compare the Pauline test for the Holy Spirit: "No one can say, 'Jesus is Lord' except the holy Spirit." (1 Cor. 12:3) In all three quotes here, the Spirit is critical to our faith and witness to Christ.

The second passage is from the next chapter in 1 John:

> if we love one another, God remains in us, and his love is brought to perfection in us. This is how we know that we remain in him and he in us, that he has given us of his Spirit. (1 John 4:12–13)

We need to examine each clause separately. The first clause is straightforward: if we love other Christians, then God remains in us. In the second clause, "his love" most likely means God's love for us because it follows the phrase: "God remains in us." Also, the phrase "is brought to perfection in us" seems to refer to the love of Christians for each other, because it follows "if we love one another." So the whole second clause can be paraphrased: God abides in us and the love that comes from him reaches perfection in our love for others. The third clause explains **how** we know that God abides in us. The criterion for this divine indwelling is "that God has given us of his Spirit"; we already saw this very criterion in 1 John 3:24, the parallel passage quoted above. To paraphrase this whole passage, then: If we love one another, God abides in us, and his love becomes effective in us; we are assured that God dwells with us because he gave us his Spirit, and we profess faith in his Son. Here the Spirit is the bond of love and the assurance that God dwells in us.

Schnackenburg adds an insightful connection of these two passages:

> The disciples . . . "know" [the Spirit] because they possess him inwardly and have a direct insight into him and certainty of him. This knowledge that they have of the Spirit is a knowledge of community with God based on their possession of that Spirit. This knowledge is referred to in an almost formal catechetical way in I Jo. 3:24; 4:13. The "spiritual" experience of the community and . . . its consciousness of having been chosen, which are supported by that experience, are all included in the promise of the Paraclete.[13]

Schnackenburg captures the complex interconnectedness that John expresses in the Gospel and in 1 John: possessing and knowing the Spirit, faith in Christ, belonging to the community of disciples, and being chosen by God. The entire First Epistle of John connects these elements and the Spirit in diverse ways. I believe that the key to his thinking can be found in John 14:17: "the Spirit of truth, which the world cannot accept, because it neither sees nor knows it. But you know it, because it remains with you, and will be in you." That is, the unbelieving world has no organ or faculty to grasp the Spirit; but those who believe have the faculty to know the Spirit; they know they belong to the community of God because they possess that Spirit.

Finally, let us situate these two passages about the Holy Spirit. The First Letter of John is a mighty effort of the Johannine school to correct the mistaken belief of the secessionists that nothing else is necessary for salvation except to believe in Jesus Christ. To do that, 1 John repeatedly makes the essential point that Christians must also "love one another as he commanded us." (3:23; cf. also: 2:3–4, 7–10; 3:11, 14, 16–17; 4:7, 11, 19–21; 5:1–3) In the following two passages considered below, the criterion for us to know that we love one another and have God dwelling in us is that he gave us his Spirit.

These same two passages offer a background for the unique contribution of the Johannine writings: that we are really children of God. Previously, in Paul, we saw that "The Spirit itself bears witness with our spirit that we are children of God!" (Rom. 8:16; see also Gal. 4:6) There Paul bases our wonderful relationship to God as his children on the fact that we possess the "Spirit of his Son." But, both in Romans and Galatians, Paul uses the term *huiosia*, which means "adoptive sonship"; still he rightly exclaims: "We are children of God!"

The First Letter of John, however, calls us simply "children of God": "See what love the Father has bestowed on us that we may be called the children of God. Yet so we are. . . . Beloved, we are God's children now; what we shall be has not yet been revealed." (1 John 3:1) The word for "children," here, is *tekna* (singular, *teknon*). Raymond Brown explains how this term is even more realistic and significant:

> *Teknon* is the technical Johannine term covering divine sonship/daughterhood, since *huios*, son, is reserved for Jesus in relationship to God. . . . John's language of begetting by God makes more realistic the imagery of "children of God" than if he spoke of adoption; it also brings the status of Christian children close to that of Jesus, God's Son.[14]

In this passage, John does not connect our status as children of God with the Holy Spirit. But he does imply that connection twice in the context, as we just saw above (1 John 3:24; 4:13). There John affirms: "This is how we know that we remain in him and he in us, that he has given us of his Spirit." His reasoning is something like this: We know that God abides in us from the fact that we profess a true faith about his Son, and we can do that only if the Spirit has taught us (see John 14:26; 16:13–14). And God's abiding in us by his Spirit is a permanent abiding, establishing our intimate relation to God our Father, "that we might be called children of God." (3:1) Notice, finally, how John's Gospel uses a similar reasoning: "to those who did accept him, he gave power to become children of God, to those who believe in his name." (John 1:12) All throughout the First Letter of John, profession of true faith, God's abiding in us, our abiding in God, and the gift of the Spirit are joined in multiple ways. To say all this quite simply: we who profess faith in Jesus have God abiding in us constantly as our Father by means of his Spirit, so that "we may be called the children of God."

Notes

1. Council of Trent, Session 8, *De Baptismo*, canon 2.
2. Raymond Brown, *The Gospel According to John, 13–21*, Anchor Bible, vol. 29A (New York: Doubleday, 1966), 1136–37.
3. This insight is from Brown, *The Gospel According to John, 13–21*, 643.
4. Pope John Paul II, *The Spirit, Giver of Life and Love* (Boston: Pauline Books and Media, 1966), 22.
5. Ibid.
6. Ignace De la Potterie and Stanislaus Lyonnet, *The Christian Lives by the Spirit* (Staten Is., NY: Alba House, 1971), 71–72.
7. Brown, *Gospel According to John, 13–21*, 628–29.
8. Ibid., 716.
9. Ibid., 1135.
10. Ibid., 1140–41.
11. Raymond Brown, *The Epistles of John*, Anchor Bible, vol. 30 (New York: Doubleday, 1982), 481–82.
12. Ibid., 483.
13. Rudolph Schnackenburg, *The Gospel According to St. John*, vol. 3 (Kent England: Burns and Oates, 1992), 75–76.
14. Brown, *The Epistles of John*, 388–89.

CHAPTER FOUR

Other New Testament Writers

∞

A. The Gospel of Mark

We begin with Mark, the earliest evangelist. Together with all four evangelists, Mark describes Jesus' baptism as his endowment with the Holy Spirit:

> Jesus . . . was baptized in the Jordan by John. On coming out of the water he saw the heavens being torn open and the Spirit, like a dove descending upon him. And a voice came from the heavens, "You are my beloved Son; with you I am well pleased." (Mark 1:9–11)

For Mark, the repose of the Spirit upon Jesus, together with the word of the Father, authenticates Jesus as the Messiah. Mark opens his Gospel by indicating that John the Baptizer is the fulfillment of Old Testament prophecies: "Behold I am sending my messenger ahead of you; he will prepare your way." (1:2; the whole quote here is a combination of Isaiah 40:3 and Malachi 3:1) That is, John the Baptizer is the messenger who prepares the way for the Messiah. Mark affirms that now the age of fulfillment has dawned in Jesus, who is the unique bearer of the Spirit. He is equipped with the Spirit for his tremendous task of announcing the kingdom of God and what it means for God's people. Jesus expresses that conviction in his first recorded words: "Jesus . . . proclaiming the gospel of God: 'This is the time of fulfillment. The kingdom of God is at hand.'" (1:14–15) Then throughout his Gospel, Mark indicates that Jesus alone is the man of the Spirit; no one else is empowered by the Spirit before Jesus' death and resurrection.

One hint is given by Mark that after Jesus' death, the Spirit will equip the apostles for bearing witness to Jesus. When he tries to prepare the apostles for the persecution that will certainly come, he assures them:

> "You will be arraigned before governor and kings because of me, as a witness before them. But the gospel must first be preached to all nations. When they hand you over . . . say whatever will be given to you. . . . For it will not be you who are speaking but the holy Spirit." (13:9–11)

In a word, in Mark's Gospel Jesus alone is the unique bearer of the Holy Spirit. He adds only a hint that after Jesus' resurrection, the apostles will know the power of the Spirit in their witnessing to Jesus.

B. The Gospel of Matthew

Matthew also presents Jesus as the focus for the Spirit's activity. In keeping with all the evangelists, Matthew describes Jesus' endowment with the power of the Spirit at his baptism: "the Spirit of God descend[ed] like a dove. . . . And a voice came from the heavens, saying, 'This is my beloved Son, with whom I am well pleased." (3:16–17)

However, for Matthew, the influence of the Holy Spirit on Jesus begins earlier, with his conception: "this is how the birth of Jesus Christ came about. When his mother Mary was betrothed to Joseph . . . she was found with child through the holy Spirit" (1:18–19); also Joseph is told, "it is through the holy Spirit that this child has been conceived in her." (1:20) Thus Matthew affirms that Jesus was endowed with the Spirit from the first moment of his existence.

Matthew later quotes Isaiah 42:1–4, with reference to Jesus, God's chosen one:

"Behold my servant whom I have chosen, my beloved in whom I delight; I will place my spirit upon him, and he will proclaim justice to the Gentiles. A bruised reed he will not break . . . until he brings justice to victory." (Matt. 12:18–20)

In this passage, Matthew describes Jesus as the meek servant of the Lord and the spirit of God as the energizing principle in Jesus' healing ministry. But Matthew does not indicate the inspiration of the Spirit in anyone else during Jesus' public ministry. The only other reference to the Spirit is similar to Mark; Jesus predicts that after his death the apostles will suffer persecution from both Jewish and civil authorities; but he tells them: "do not worry about . . . what you are to say. . . . It will not be you who speak but the Spirit of your Father speaking through you." (10:19–20)

C. Ephesians

We consider Ephesians separately from the authentic works of Paul because most critical exegetes (perhaps 80 percent) deny that Paul is the author of Ephesians.[1] Still, it deserves our consideration, because it adopts Paul's image of the body of Christ and develops it in a new way by identifying his body as the universal church with Christ as its head (1:22–23; 5:23). As head of the body that is the church, all life and growth proceed from him (4:15–16); all the gifts and charisms of ministry are given by him (4:11–13). Christ nourishes and cherishes his church (5:29) and "handed himself over for her" (5:25), so that a goal of Christ's life and death has become the church (1:22–23); and together with his church he gives all glory to God (3:19).

But Ephesians also identifies the work of the Spirit in this universal church:

> [T]hrough [Christ] we both [Jews and Gentiles] have access in one Spirit to the Father. So then you are . . . fellow citizens with the holy ones and members of the household of God, built upon the foundation of the apostles and prophets, with Christ Jesus himself as the capstone. Through him . . . you also are being built into a dwelling place of God in the Spirit. (2:18–22)

The author points out that the one Spirit gives all people common access to the Father; all have the Spirit as their intercessor in God's presence. The rest of this quote emphasizes the "household of God" and "the dwelling place of God in the Spirit." The material of this "dwelling place of God" consists of God's faithful; the building becomes a temple by the indwelling presence of the Holy Spirit (see also 1 Cor. 3:16–17). That is, God dwells in his people by means of his Spirit; that is why this dwelling can be called a temple.

In sum then, Ephesians builds on the creative Pauline notion of the church as the body of Christ; it adds the wonderful image of Christ as the head who animates and nourishes his church. But it also teaches that the church depends on the Holy Spirit as the powerful intercessor with God and as the constant presence of God in his temple.

Another primary text regarding the Spirit is in chapter 3: "the mystery of Christ, which was not made known to human beings in other generations as it has now been revealed to his holy apostles and prophets by the Spirit." (3:4–5; cf. also 1:8–10) The thrust of this passage is that the Holy Spirit is the revealer of God's wisdom. Paul says this even more clearly in 1 Corinthians:

> we speak God's wisdom, mysterious, hidden . . . this God has revealed to us through the Spirit . . . no one knows what pertains to God except the Spirit of God. We have received . . . the Spirit that is from God, so that we may understand the things freely given us by God. And we speak about them . . . with words taught by the Spirit. (I Cor. 2:7–13)

When we studied this text in Paul's pneumatology, we concluded that only one who has received the Spirit of God can understand and believe his revelation. God's eternal plan of redemption can be known to us only through revelation, and the Spirit of God is the bridge between God and us, so that we learn the mystery that only God knew before then. In a word, the Spirit is our only way and means of revelation.

This same Pauline teaching is affirmed here. Ephesians 3:5 affirms that God's entire plan of redemption in Christ is made known to us "through the Spirit"; or to say this another way: the mysteries of Christ were not known to other generations, but only to his prophets now by means of the inner working of the Spirit. Elsewhere Ephesians identifies the Spirit as "a Spirit of wisdom and revelation" (1:17), who disposes us to accept revelation and communicate it to others (3:16). That is, the Spirit is our teacher of God's whole revelation who effectively confirms our faith.

Ephesians 3:4 teaches that without the Spirit, the apostles could not have revealed this "secret of the Messiah." (This is how the Anchor Bible translates this phrase.)[2] What does the author mean by the secret of the Messiah? The whole context is speaking primarily of the inclusion of the Gentiles along with the people of the promise, that is, the Jews. But Ephesians says simply, "the secret of the Messiah" without limitation; that is, the secret **is** the Messiah in all his messianic work: the revealer, the savior, the high priest, the one who unites Jews and Gentiles into God's people, and the head of the church; for revelation, salvation, and unification are all identified in Christ our Messiah. All of the mystery of Christ is revealed to us "through the Spirit." This whole passage then proclaims the Spirit as the source of our understanding all the wisdom and revelation of God.

Also, Ephesians speaks forcefully about the seal of the Holy Spirit: "In [Christ] you also, who have heard the word of truth, the gospel of your salvation, and have believed in him, were sealed with the promised holy Spirit." (1:13; see also Eph. 4:30; cf. 2 Cor. 1:21–22) Historically, sealing referred to a stamped impression in wax on a letter or document that showed ownership and authenticity. Figuratively as used here, sealing with the Holy Spirit refers to God's marking the Ephesians with the Holy Spirit as God's own possession. How is that sealing done? What does the sealing refer to? Exegetes give two answers to these questions: **baptism itself**: that is, sealing is baptizing; or **baptism with a public purpose**: that is, sealing is not just the rite itself but also the designation, appointment, and equipment for public ministry. (See the excellent discussion by Markus Barth in the Anchor Bible.)[3] All agree that sealing with the Spirit includes baptism, but some add the sense that the sealing is a public certification. This latter opinion seems more likely for three reasons: the sealing involves our existing "for the praise of [God's] glory" (vv. 12 and 14); the sealing involves publicly living the new life in Christ so as not to "grieve the holy Spirit of God" but give "edification" to others (Eph.

4:30); and Ephesians in general stresses the public unity of the community and the world mission of the church.

Finally, Ephesians encourages all Christians to rely on two powerful helps of the Spirit: "take . . . the sword of the Spirit, which is the word of God . . . [and] pray at every opportunity in the Spirit." (Eph. 6:17–18) These two verses conclude the famous metaphor to "put on the armor of God" (vv. 11–17) and is reminiscent of similar Pauline metaphors to "put on Christ" (Rom. 13:14; cf. Gal. 3:27), or "put on the new self" (Col. 3:10; cf. Eph. 4:24), or "put on [the virtues of Christ]" (Col. 3:12–14). The Spirit inspires and is the source of both the "word of God" and prayer. In v. 17, the sword is the word of God that is given by the Spirit. The word itself is the inspired word of God (especially the "mystery of Christ," Eph. 3:4–5), which is "sharper than any two-edged sword." (Heb. 4:12) All Christians can wield the sword of the word because they are inspired by the Holy Spirit. In v. 18, prayer is empowered by the Spirit (cf. Eph. 5:18–20), as Paul himself insists (Rom. 8:26–27). The Spirit will help us pray with assurance and perseverance. These two verses assure us that we have strong defenses against any threat to our faith, for the Spirit inspires courage through the gospel and through prayer. We might summarize here what Ephesians teaches about the Holy Spirit. The Spirit is the source of our understanding all the wisdom and revelation of God (3:4–5). By our baptism we are sealed and marked by the Spirit as God's own possession. By the inspiration of this Spirit we possess the word of the gospel and the effective intercession with God. The whole church becomes a temple of God by the indwelling presence of the Holy Spirit.

Notes

1. Raymond Brown, *The Churches the Apostles Left Behind* (New York: Paulist Press, 1984), 47.

2. Markus Barth, *Ephesians, 1–3*, Anchor Bible, vol. 34, (New York: Doubleday, 1974), 331.

3. Ibid., 143.

CHAPTER FIVE

Descriptions of New Testament Pneumatologies

Introduction

Now we want to describe the pneumatologies of Paul, Luke, John, and the Pastoral Epistles. Each one has a unique theology of the Spirit (pneumatology). First, we will describe the particular emphases each one gives to the work of the Holy Spirit; second, we will point out some distinctive strengths of each; finally, we will note some weaknesses. Each one of these four views of the Holy Spirit was written for particular communities, but the strengths and weaknesses can also be instructive for our church today. No one view offers a complete theology of the Holy Spirit for all times and places. Yet all of them together give us a more rounded view of the Spirit of Jesus. We can choose which one is more life-giving for us, as long as we respect the other pneumatologies.

A. The Spirit in the Pauline Church

1. General Description

Paul's pneumatology can be roughly described under five headings. First, regarding individual Christians, Paul teaches that the Holy Spirit establishes our intimate relationship to God; we become children of God and can address God familiarly as "Father": "As proof that you are children, God sent the Spirit of his Son into our hearts, crying out '*Abba*, Father.'" (Gal. 4:6) He means that the Spirit animates and activates Christians, making them children of God; their status is initiated through faith and baptism (see Gal. 3:26–27) but is activated and realized through the indwelling Spirit. In Romans, Paul is even more emphatic; he tells us that the gift of the Spirit constitutes our sonship/daughterhood: "All those who are led by God's Spirit are children of God." (Rom. 8:14) That is, the Spirit of Jesus, the Son, establishes us as sons/daughters of God, so that we can cry out with the very words of Jesus himself: "*Abba*, Father."

Second, Paul describes the church as the body of Christ and the Holy Spirit as the source of its unity: "As . . . the parts of the body, though many, are one body, so also Christ. For in one Spirit we were all baptized into one body." (1 Cor. 12:12–13) Most likely, Paul is the originator of this wonderful description of the church; it represents his mature thinking about the church; by it he expresses the profound union of Christ and the church through the power of the Holy Spirit. What this means is that each of us who is united to the body of Christ and permeated with the Spirit through faith and baptism is really a member of Christ and forms a life with him on the level of a son or daughter. The indwelling of the Spirit and incorporation into the body of Christ is the rationale or basis of our intimacy with Christ. We belong to Jesus by his Spirit and he dwells in us by that same Spirit.

Third, the Spirit is the proof and the medium of the outpouring of God's love: "The love of God has been poured out into our hearts through the holy Spirit that has been given to us." (Rom. 5:5) Here, the love of God means "God's love for us," as v. 8 makes clear: "God proves his love for us, in that . . . Christ died for us." For us Christians, the very nature of God is love; in giving us love he imparts something of his own nature—which in Pauline language is his Spirit. This inestimable and transcendent God is also the God who loves us and dwells intimately in us by his Spirit.

Fourth, Paul describes the Holy Spirit as dwelling in us as our personal intercessor: "The Spirit itself intercedes for us with inexpressible groanings." (Rom. 8:26) This idea of the Spirit as intercessor is unique to Paul. As intercessor, first "the Spirit too comes to the aid of our weakness; for we not know how to pray as we ought"; that is, because weakness is characteristic of our human condition, we do not know for what we should pray or how we should pray, so the Spirit intercedes for us and gives us confidence in our prayer. By "inexpressible groanings" Paul is not clearly referring to charismatic gifts such as speaking in tongues or extraordinary Pentecostal activities, but rather the praying of the Spirit, which cannot be expressed in human terms. So with the Spirit praying within us and for us, our Christian prayer can be quite genuine despite our not knowing how to pray. Also, as intercessor the Spirit "intercedes for the holy ones according to God's will." (8:27) What we learn from all the Gospels is that we can have great confidence that God will always answer our prayers as long as any request includes the notion "if it be according to your will." Here Paul tells us that if we rely on the Spirit as our intercessor, then our prayers will necessarily be according to the will of God.

Finally, Paul's church is a charismatic church. In 1 Corinthians 12:8–10, Paul mentions nine "charisms," or gifts, of the Holy Spirit; the first two seem to be primary concerns of the Greeks (wisdom and knowledge); the next five are extraordinary phenomena (faith, healing, miracles, prophecy, discernment); and the last two relate to glossolalia (speaking in tongues and interpretation of tongues). These are all charisms of the Spirit (vv. 4–8); they are extraordinary external manifestations. Paul spends most of chapters 12 and 14 in affirming these gifts and also cautioning about their use, because they sometimes interfere with the order and unity of the church at Corinth.

Paul also regularly refers to the experience of the Holy Spirit, especially at the time of baptism; he seems to mean more than an internal light or the actual rite of baptism; he reminds his converts of this initial experience as a proof that they belong to Christ. In Paul's church, these external experiences were powerful proofs of the presence of the Holy Spirit. They were used to solve the primary problem of his church: How can Jews and Gentiles exist equally in the church? He answers, that if the Spirit has so obviously manifested acceptance of Gentiles as well as Jews, then we must do the same.

Throughout the history of the church, the charismatic gifts of the Spirit have varied greatly in kind and degree of presence. Gifts such as prophecy, healing, and courageous witness to Christ seem to be more common in the recent church.

2. Strengths
This section will point out a couple of strengths of Paul's pneumatology. The first strength in Paul's description of the Spirit is that it is multifaceted; it includes so many functions of the Holy Spirit, both for individuals and for the church community. He relates some of the Spirit's functions to individuals. He teaches that the Spirit dwells within us and causes us to become sons/daughters of God; he tells us that the Spirit's presence makes us temples of the Holy Spirit; he informs us that the Spirit is the source of the love of God in our hearts; and he makes the Spirit known as our personal intercessor with God in prayer. But Paul also affirms that the Spirit is a powerful force within the church as a community; thus he develops the wonderful image of the church as the body of Christ, united by the Holy Spirit; and he affirms all the charisms of the Holy Spirit in the churches. In a word, Paul adds so many dimensions to the work of the Holy Spirit. Without the pneumatology of the Pauline church, we would not know the Spirit of Jesus as the driving force of the church community; we would not know the intense unity that God clearly intends for his church by means of his Spirit; we would not be able to understand or evaluate the various charisms of the Spirit.

The second strength of Paul's theology of the Spirit is to make us comfortable with our transcendent God. The Old Testament was most forceful in teaching the transcendence of God: God was known as the all-powerful creator of the whole world; his faithful were taught to avoid even the mention of his name, Yahweh; they believed that if they saw God, they would die. Paul and his church inherited this profound reverence for the totally transcendent God. But Paul himself transformed their notion of such an ineffable God by his creative and inspired way of addressing God: As proof that you are children, God sent the spirit of his son into our hearts, crying out, *Abba*, Father. (Gal. 4:6) For Paul this new relationship to

God by means of the Holy Spirit meant that this infinite, unimaginable God could now be addressed in this warm and familiar way, "Father."

In the twenty-first century, our new cosmology makes God even more transcendent and unimaginable. Scientists have described the evolution of our universe in staggering figures.[1] The universe is over fifteen billion years old; our solar system was formed about five billion years ago; our Milky Way galaxy contains billions of stars; our Earth is not the center of this galaxy; our sun is only one of billions of other suns and planets; other galaxies number in the tens of billions (each one with millions or billions of stars); finally, human beings have only existed on earth for a couple of million years. For scientists of the last century, this teaching about the evolution of our universe is the only probable theory.

Understanding reality in this way leads some Christians to a great crisis of faith; they have a hard time incorporating such a cosmology into their religious worldview, so they reject this modern cosmology and as a result their worldview becomes outdated and unreal. They fear the answers to many questions that arise within them in terms of God's creation, Christ's redemption, and scriptural truth.

Paul's view of the universe does not demand a rejection of modern cosmology, and his view of the transcendent God is not the whole story. For Paul assures us that our transcendent God is also our indwelling God and Father, who will help us face all these questions. We can then live in even greater awesome wonder in our relationship to God; we can grow in awareness of the mystery of God's constant presence; we can begin to see a beautiful symbiosis between this cosmology and the wondrous presence of God's Spirit at the heart of our existence.

3. Weaknesses

On the other hand, Paul's pneumatology can become problematic for us today. For Paul's description of the church in Corinth is filled with charisms of the Spirit, while those charisms are not so evident in our modern church. This apparent disparity between Paul's church and ours is problematic for many Christians today, especially for Pentecostal and charismatic churches. Some Protestant scripture scholars try to give evidence for the charisms of the Spirit in ordinary Christian life today. One fine example is Gordon Fee's book *God's Empowering Presence*.[2] Also Michael Green in his recent book, *I Believe in the Holy Spirit*, spends the last third of his book on the charismatic gifts of the Spirit; his position is forthright:

> Christians in the main line of both Catholic and Protestant traditions have for a long time been very scared of allowing that these gifts of the Spirit . . . might be expected to occur today. They are supposed to have died out in the apostolic era. . . . [T]hese gifts did not die out, though they were often viewed with great suspicion by church authorities.[3]

Catholic scholars also have some difficulty in dealing with Paul's charismatic church at Corinth. In *The Spirit of Life*, Luis Bermejo, S.J., asserts: "Since the call [to Christian vocation] is universal, applicable to all Christians, so are also the charisms connected with it."[4]

These authors are quite right, of course, when they point out that the presence and power of the Spirit of Jesus is evident in our Christian church today in terms of moral renewal, spiritual illumination, understanding of Scripture, and sacramental grace; this inspiration of the Spirit of Jesus is present in every church and every age, in every Christian country or culture. Such an assurance is the major premise of this book as well. But all that does not add up to the same kind of supernatural charisms manifested in Paul's church of Corinth. Nor should we expect that the activity of the Holy Spirit must be the same in all churches, in all times and places.

Paul's wonderful image of the church as the body of Christ can also lead to an ideal image of the church—one without defects. Throughout the twentieth century, this image of the body of Christ and of our being members of him was the primary metaphor of the church. Pope Pius XII, in his encyclical *Mystici Corporis*, profoundly affected our sense of church and our union with all Christ's members. This was a most positive and inspiring image.

Yet even this wonderful image of church could be corrupted by a lack of realism and balance. For it was so easy to emphasize this exalted image of the church as the body of Christ, that the hierarchy and most of us ignored or tried to hide the very human aspect of the church: its failures, injustices, inadequacies, and sins. It took the second Vatican Council to remind our universal church that it is also "the People of God"; that the church consists of all the men and women of faith who are all somewhat deficient and somewhat sinful, who will always be imperfect. If we see the church only as the "divine" body of Christ, what happens to our faith in the Spirit when scandals rock the church in terms of authoritarian leaders, rigid and arrogant members, pedophile priests, and divisive groups? We need to remember that the Mystical Body is made up of the "People of God," who are all necessarily human and imperfect.

B. The Spirit in the Lukan Church

1. General Description

At the end of Luke's Gospel, he relates the promise of Jesus to his apostles: "I am sending the promise of my Father upon you; but stay in the city until you are clothed with the power from on high." (Luke 24:49) Then in the beginning of Acts, Jesus explains: "wait for the promise of the Father about which you have heard me speak; for . . . in a few days you will be baptized with the holy Spirit." (Acts 1:4–5) Thus, Jesus teaches that the Spirit is the power to be given to the apostles and the dynamic principle of their role as witnesses in the third phase of salvation history (after the Old Testament phase and the Jesus phase). Then Jesus summarizes the whole mission of the apostles and the powerful work of the Spirit in them: "you will receive power when the holy Spirit comes upon you, and you will be my witnesses in Jerusalem, throughout Judea and Samaria, and to the ends of the earth" (Acts 1:8); that is, the Spirit is the power behind all the apostles do and proclaim; they are to be witnesses inspired by the Spirit; the commission given them starts in Jerusalem and continues "to the ends of the earth." Luke continues to follow this paradigm throughout Acts; he characterizes the Spirit as the power to witness (Acts 1:8; 4:31; 5:32).

Thus Luke gives massive importance to the Spirit in the early church; the Spirit takes the place of Jesus on earth in this third phase of salvation history. Lukan ecclesiology, then, is based on the constant presence of the Holy Spirit in terms of giving impulse and guidance to the apostles, encouraging them to speak openly and confidently, choosing additional missionaries, and helping them to decide crucial issues.

Two additional notes. Luke's pneumatology is deeply rooted in the Old Testament, both in the range of prophetic and charismatic activity he attributes to the Spirit and in the vocabulary he uses (the Spirit as the manifestation of the divine presence and power, the Spirit as filling or inspiring prophetic speech). Second, Luke does not connect the Holy Spirit to any office as the permanent power of that office; rather he commonly describes the Spirit as the inspiration for individual people to give witness, to preach, and to decide what direction to take.

2. Strengths
One strength of the Lukan theology of the Spirit concerns the ability to give witness to Christ. Throughout Acts the primary action of the Spirit of Jesus is to help the missionary church give witness to Christ. The first instance of this is at Pentecost; the Spirit inspires many disciples to speak in tongues and make it possible for people of all languages to understand their witness. Then, when they accepted the message and asked Peter, "What are we to do?" Peter answered them: "Repent . . . be baptized . . . and you will receive the gift of the holy Spirit." (2:37–38) This response became the paradigm for Luke throughout Acts: faith, conversion, baptism, gift of the Spirit. We see this repeated again and again as the Spirit inspires the main characters of Acts: Peter, Stephen, Philip, Paul, Barnabas, and Timothy. So in Luke's church, the Spirit functions mainly in individuals, both those who witness to Christ and also those who accept their message and then receive the Spirit. Consistently then in Acts, the Spirit's activity in the apostles is internal but directed to giving witness to others; and the Spirit's action in the converts is also within them but directed toward conversion. To say it all simply, in the Lukan church the work of the Spirit of

Jesus is totally missionary—to constantly increase the community of believers "in Jerusalem . . . to the end of the world."

In our day, whatever we do as individuals that has anything to do with witnessing to Jesus—whether we are leaders in the church or ordinary faithful Christians—we can do with confidence in the Spirit of Jesus who will continue to inspire our witness to Christ.

The other strength of Lukan pneumatology concerns the work of the Spirit in the church community. That is, Luke describes the Spirit as the dominant force, the primary guide of the church. Peter and Paul are clearly instruments of the Spirit, and all the missionaries of the early church are inspired by the Spirit. This means that, for Luke, the guidance and power of the Spirit relativizes the work of individual leaders. Luke does not hide the disputes, imperfections, and failures of this church, because he is confident of the unfailing guidance of the Spirit. He knows that the Spirit will never let the church down. To say this another way, no matter what disputes arose in the early church, and no matter what the failures of the leaders, Luke gives assurance that the powerful influence of the Spirit will not fail the church.

Today, we have endless disagreements among various groups in the church: between the local church and the Roman authority, between the traditional church and the post–Vatican II church, between the conservative and the liberal wings of the church. All of us get distressed at times—some even leave the church—because of such disappointing church leadership or very painful antagonisms. In the spirit of Luke's church, we might take comfort in saying, "Thank God the church is directed by the Holy Spirit, who will pull us through." That is, the Spirit does not destroy the failures of individual leaders or the divisiveness of some groups, but he never ceases to guide and inspire all of us.

One glorious example of the Spirit's guidance in our lifetime was that of Pope John XXIII, who was inspired to call the Second Vatican Council; he never wavered from the Spirit's inspiration, despite hesitations and objections from the Roman Curia. When the council convened, the assembled bishops rejected many of the prepared articles and schemata and were led in ways that were quite different from what some church officials wanted. They seemed to be directed by the onrushing Spirit of Acts. The influence of this Spirit-inspired council has been muted in many instances recently. But the work of the council and the surprises of the Spirit are not finished.

3. Weaknesses
This same sense of the constant presence and direction of the Holy Spirit in the church can lead to a weakness in the church, by fostering a triumphal picture of the church and a false optimism. Whenever the church relies entirely on the power and inspiration of the Holy Spirit and fails to recognize widespread human deficiencies or corruption, the church is vulnerable to grave divisions. For example, in the time of the Reformation, one-half of Europe was lost to the Catholic Church; in the seventeenth century almost all of China was lost because of poor decisions by Rome; in many countries today the church is losing believers and practicing Catholics. We cannot be passive and expect the Spirit to accomplish everything; we all need to cooperate with the Spirit of Jesus. For the Spirit never forces leaders of the church, even when they are wrong-headed; and the Spirit never takes away our free choice, even if some choose to abandon his church. Certainly we can be confident of the Spirit's presence and inspiration in guiding the church; but we can be just as sure that the leaders of the church and all of us will always be human and free and so notably imperfect.

C. The Spirit of the Johannine Church

1. General Description
In John's church, the Spirit/Paraclete constantly dwells within the individual disciples (14:17) as their constant companion. This "new Advocate" takes the place of Jesus; that is, what Jesus was to the disciples while he was with them on this earth, the Paraclete is to all Jesus' followers once he has gone back to the Father (15:26; 16:7–8).

The Spirit of Jesus will teach them everything (14:26), guide them along the way of all truth (16:13), bear witness about Jesus

(15:26–27), remind the disciples of all that Jesus told them (14:26), and explain further only what Jesus has revealed (16:13). This teaching about the Paraclete as the new Advocate was the answer to the critical question for the Johannine community: What would happen to the community once the last of the eyewitnesses of Jesus had died? Their preoccupation with this question led to a rumor that "the beloved disciple" would never die (John 21:21–23); and once he did die, they would be bereft. What a powerful answer Jesus offered them in the Paraclete, who offers an immediate and direct continuity between believers and Jesus:

> [T]he lengthening time gap between John and the historical Jesus . . . [does] not mean a steadily increasing distance between each generation of Christians and the Christ. On the contrary, each generation is as close to Jesus as the last—and the first—because the Paraclete is the immediate link between Jesus and his disciples in every generation. . . . The vitality of Christian experience does not cease because the historical Jesus has faded into the past . . . ; it retains its vitality because the Spirit is at work here and now as the other Paraclete.[5]

In a word, in John's church the Paraclete makes the person and work of Jesus present to the church and to the individual Christian. This all-encompassing work of the Spirit is carried out by teaching us the complete truth about Jesus, by strengthening our faith in the face of a cynical society, a hostile world.

2. Strengths

Johannine theology of the Paraclete is amazingly internal and individual; this quality constitutes its strength. All five Paraclete passages tell the disciples that they will have a new Advocate dwelling within them constantly as their teacher, guide, and support. In the first passage, which is the foundational one, Jesus simply affirms that the Advocate will "be with you always." Clearly, the primary activity of the Paraclete is individual and internal. The amazing promise of Jesus is that each disciple—each Christian—will have the presence and power of the Spirit of Jesus within them. John expresses this quality above all: that all Christians possess the Spirit of Jesus to help them in prayer, to teach them the way of Jesus, to deepen their spiritual life in Christ.

Another outstanding strength of the Johannine church is its egalitarianism, that is, the sense of equality among all the members of the community. In John's church, the most important category is not that of apostle or church authority but simply that of disciple; there are no second-class citizens; neither charisms nor office gives status. Because the Spirit is given to all Christians to lead them in the way of Jesus, all can be assured of their individual worth in Christ. In every society, precedence is equated with value; in every religion, some people are set over others because they are elite in some way. Jesus' religion is the first world religion in which there is no preference, no status, no elite ones, no superiority. And in the Johannine church, the individual presence of the Spirit of Jesus in each disciple is the assurance of the unique value and personal dignity of each in Christ.

The third strength of John's church is that it is most conducive to a loving relationship with Jesus. This aspect is of profound significance for us and for our Catholic Church. Let us approach it this way: simple membership in the church of Christ is not a sufficient goal to attract many people; wonderful church doctrine will not inspire membership; engaging liturgy by itself does not hold members; scriptural learning does not win over hearts. The church of Christ must do more for us, if we are to dedicate our lives to it. Above all, it must lead to a loving relationship with Jesus; it must bring people into personal contact with Jesus; it must lead us to encounter the real person, Jesus. Beyond everything else, the church of Jesus must lead people to encounter Jesus, to have a personal love of Jesus, to become a friend of Jesus (15:14–15). And this is the very task of the Spirit of Jesus in John's Gospel: to remind us of who Jesus is for us, to teach us the love of Jesus our friend, to lead us to follow in the way of Jesus, to love Jesus as he loved us, to "love one another as [he has loved us]." In John, all of this is the summary of the work of the Spirit who dwells with us personally as our constant teacher.

This loving relationship to Jesus, fostered by the Holy Spirit, also leads us to the heart of our religion and morality. That is, we Christians do not follow a rule of law but a rule of love; we are not ultimately bound by obedience to laws but by the love of a person, Jesus. Thomas Merton's insight is very apropos:

> Christianity is a religion of love. Christian morality is a morality of love. [It] is not the religion of a law but the religion of a person. The Christian is not merely the one who keeps the rules imposed on him by the church. He is a disciple of Christ. . . . Jesus himself, living in us by his Spirit, is our Rule of Life. His love is our law, and it is absolute.[6]

Another strength of the Johannine pneumatology is in clarifying our notion of God's providence. During the public life of Jesus, society was still struggling to understand the providence of God; they still saw human suffering and tragedy as a punishment from God. Jesus himself had to correct this false sense of the providence of God. The disciples questioned him about the man born blind: "Who sinned, this man or his parents, that he was born blind?" Jesus answered, "Neither he nor his parents sinned. . . ." (John 9:2–3) Clearly then, Jesus teaches that human tragedies are **not** sent by God as punishment. This false sense of God's providence was a pervading belief in the Old Testament; it probably was not easily corrected among his disciples (Cf. Luke 13:1–5). Allied to this question was the whole problem of evil in terms of the suffering of innocent persons and especially the passion and death of Jesus.

In John's Gospel, Jesus tells his disciples again and again that they will not be able to understand so many things about his life and death and about his teaching, until the Spirit comes to remind them and explain to them the meaning: "I have much more to tell you, but you cannot bear it now. When he comes . . . the Spirit of truth, he will guide you to all truth." (16:12–13) After Jesus' death and resurrection, the disciples came to understand much more about Jesus and about God's providence (12:16; 13:7, 19; 14:29; 16:4). With the guidance of the "new Advocate" they began to understand the seeming tragedy of his passion and the contradictions of sin and evil in the world.

Even in the twenty-first century, many seem to have just as much confusion over the problem of evil, either in the personal form—"How could God do this to me?"—or in the universal form: "How could a good and merciful God permit such horrific evils as the Holocaust or the ethnic cleansing of whole nations?"

As I write these words in September of 2001, our whole nation is shocked and confused by the worst domestic tragedy ever to strike our country: the terrorist attacks on the twin World Trade Towers in New York and on the Pentagon in Washington, D.C. Many are asking: What did our country do to deserve this? What did we do wrong to be punished in such an unspeakable way?

Modern theologians expand on Jesus' teaching that sickness and tragedy are not sent by God as a punishment for sins. For example, they teach that

> God works through secondary causes. God does not 'intervene' in the world in the sense that God interrupts and interferes with the normal course of human events. . . . Our actions remain completely free, but they are at the same time grounded in the grace or presence of God.[7]

That is, they teach that God is the ultimate cause of our world but leaves us totally free. My sense of this is that we are not marionettes on a string manipulated by God, so that when we sin, he punishes us, or when we follow his way, he rewards us. **No!** There simply are no strings on us at all. Nature acts according to its nature, and we humans are really free to act any way we choose (otherwise we would not be free human beings). So the answer to all such questions about human evil has nothing to do with God directly, but everything to do with the ways of nature and the free will of human beings. Such is the general thrust of all of Christ's teaching about evil in general and about his own totally unjust and tragic end. And the Holy Spirit is the one Jesus sent to dwell with us and teach us about the deep mysteries of human freedom and the evil in our world: "the holy Spirit will remind you of all that I told you." (14:26)

3. Weaknesses
The Johannine Spirit theology was so comforting and freeing for individual believers, for each individual possessed the Spirit of Truth

as his/her personal guide: "the Spirit of truth will guide you to all truth." (16:13) But the last chapter of John's Gospel, a later addition, gives evidence of a major flaw that threatened the whole community; that is, this wonderful personal dependence on the Spirit of truth could be easily abused by individuals. For they could reject any external direction or authority from anyone else in the church, since they had their own divine guide in the person of the Paraclete.

So within a short time, the Johannine church was gravely split over the question of any authority in the church. And many members—probably the majority—of the Johannine church soon seceded from the rest of the church. This situation required the addition of the twenty-first chapter to John's Gospel; for only with some authoritative leadership from Peter could the church maintain its unity. Those who relied exclusively on the personal inspiration of the Spirit soon disappeared from the church.

Throughout history, including our modern times, so many individuals and groups have split off from the various Christian churches to form Pentecostal or Spirit-guided charismatic churches, without the acceptance of any form of human authority or church direction. All Christian churches need to reflect on the experience of the Johannine church; for even this church of the Paraclete could not maintain its unity without some form of community direction and authority.

D. The Spirit in the Church of the Pastoral Epistles

1. Description

The Pastoral Epistles (1 and 2 Timothy and Titus) need to be included here, for they contain the most formal treatment of the later continuance of the church in the New Testament. Even though they are nonauthentic Pauline writings (One reliable estimate claims "90 percent of critical scholarship judges that Paul did not write the Pastorals")[8], still they are so important for anyone who wants to study the way the church chose its leaders after the apostles died, and how it began to structure itself. They also try to capture Paul's mind as he nears his death: "the time of my depature is at hand. I have competed well; I have finished the race. . . . From now on the crown of righteousness awaits me." (2 Tim. 4:6–8) We will follow convention and refer to the author of the pastorals as "Paul."

These letters (written sometime between 80 and 100) focus on how the churches are to survive after all the apostles have died. They are appropriately called "pastoral" because they are concerned with tending the flock of Christ, with church life and practice, and with church structure. In general, Timothy and Titus are to appoint leaders for the individual churches; these leaders include *episcopoi* (overseers) (see 1 Tim. 3:1–7; Ti. 1:7–9), *presbyteroi* (elders) (see Titus 1:5–6; 1 Tim. 5:17–20), and *diaconoi* (deacons) (see I Tim. 3:8–13). A main function of all these leaders in the church is to assure that "sound doctrine" is preached; more than a dozen times these letters mention sound doctrine, divinely revealed faith, the deposit of faith, or similar terms meaning orthodox teaching.

To be honest, there are not many Spirit texts in these letters. In 1 and 2 Timothy there are four notable passages. In these, Paul reminds Timothy to rely on the Spirit, for the Spirit is the origin of his life in Christ and of his call to ministry. The first reminder is admittedly vague: "I entrust this charge to you, Timothy . . . in accordance with the prophetic words spoken about you." (1 Tim. 1:18) That is, Timothy is to be mindful of his calling to be a prophet for Christ for missionary service, and the Spirit is the agent who singled out Timothy (as indicated in 2 Tim. 1:13–14). The second counsel seems to refer to the Spirit as the "gift" of God that is in Timothy: "Do not neglect the gift you have, which was conferred on you . . . with the imposition of hands of the presbyterate." (1 Tim. 4:14) Again Paul reminds Timothy of his Spirit-directed call to ministry; this gift of the Spirit includes the grace to carry out his ministry. Paul's third reminder is to "stir into flame the gift of God that you have through the imposition of my hands; for God did not give us a spirit of cowardice, but rather of power and love and self-control." (2 Tim. 1:6–7. Here the laying-on of hands should lead Timothy to courage and endurance because of the gift of God. This gift of God is the Holy Spirit, as indicated clearly at the end of this passage (vv. 13–14).

The final counsel is the most explicit: "Take as your norm the sound words that you heard from me . . . Guard this rich trust with the help of the holy Spirit that dwells within us." (2 Tim. 1:13–14) Clearly Paul urges Timothy to keep to sound teaching by the power of the indwelling Spirit. In the context he is asked to stay loyal to the gospel in the face of considerable hardship (2 Tim. 1:9–12). In these four passages the gift of the Spirit is connected with Timothy's commissioning as a leader in order to help him complete his assigned task. This commissioning is not an ordination, but it does mean that Timothy can lay hands on others to commission them in the Spirit (see 1 Tim. 5:2).

One passage from Titus needs to be included here: "[God] saved us through the bath of rebirth and renewal by the holy Spirit, whom he richly poured out on us." (Titus 3:5–6) The words here are trenchant. "[God] saved us through the bath" means that God is the principal agent who saves us through a sacramental baptism. "Rebirth" and "renewal" are not only internal but also visible and experiential; they are specifically the work of "the holy Spirit." The description of the Holy Spirit "poured out on us" echoes the prophecy of Joel (Joel 2:23–24), the preaching of Peter on the day of Pentecost (Acts 2:17–18, 33), and the baptism of Cornelius (Acts 10:45).

2. Strengths

The Pastorals place a great emphasis on the power and guidance of the Holy Spirit for the leaders of the church. They give one of the clearest pictures of the way the church developed after the death of the apostles, especially in terms of a more structured church. They give us some sense of Paul's recommendations for continuing the work of Christ in teaching sound doctrine and relying on the power of the Spirit. What a great source of encouragement they offer for priests and bishops. For no matter how burdened they feel with the responsibility of serving God's people, no matter how troubled they are when they see society becoming increasingly indifferent or antagonistic to religion, they can be ever confident that they are not alone, that they have the help of the Spirit that was promised them by the laying on of hands.

Throughout history, then, leaders of the church have used these inspired writings to instill confidence in bishops, priests, and other ministers of the church. How effective it is for a bishop to encourage his priests: "Stir into flame the gift of God that you have through the imposition of my hands . . . Guard this rich trust with the help of the Holy Spirit that dwells within us." In terms of the institutional church, it is hard to find better counsels for those who are entrusted with the care of God's people. This kind of reliance on the Holy Spirit is so much in keeping with the main emphasis of this book: that the Spirit of Jesus is the immediate source of all the grace, inspiration, guidance, and spiritual power for all of us in God's church.

3. Weaknesses

This wonderful source of encouragement for the leaders of the church has, often in history, led to an exaggerated sense of authority and dominance by those same leaders. Because the Pastorals so emphasized the inspiration of the Holy Spirit in their pastoral work and did not give equal stress to the rest of the church, it became easy to ignore the work of the Spirit in the ordinary members of the church. We must never forget that this same Spirit is promised to all Christ's followers as our inspiration, our spiritual guide, our personal advocate. We must remember that it is true for **all** God's people: "*Spiritus spirat ubi vult.*" (the wind/Spirit blows where it wills; John 3:8) Failing to remember this is a grave weakness that can understandably result from the Pastoral Epistles.

Second, consider the movements in the Catholic Church in the last century, such as the formation of priest councils and religious leadership councils, pastoral councils in the parish or diocese, base communities, lay leadership in so many areas of parish work, men and women as liturgical ministers. Surely many of these developments are due to the inspiration of the Holy Spirit. Yet the impetus for some of these came from the grass roots of the church. The leaders did not always encourage these movements; it took many years for the center to embrace some of them.

Even Pope John XXIII's proposal to convene Vatican Council II was first greeted with skepticism by some in Rome, who tried to control the council with outdated agendas.

Now, forty years after the council, some of the hierarchy have not completely accepted the reforms or trusted collegial procedures in the various levels of church living. Recently, we have seen the mistrust of bishops' national conferences, the criticism of liberation theology, the rejection of inclusive-language texts, the requiring of a *mandatum* for theologians, and the refusal to dialogue about the ordination of women.

Certainly these matters are not easily solved; but we all need to be more open to the inspiration of the Spirit of Jesus.

Notes

1. Michael Morwood, *Tomorrow's Catholic* (Mystic, CT: Twenty-third Publications, 1997), 27–28.

2. Gordon Fee, *God's Empowering Presence: The Holy Spirit in the Letters of Paul* (Peabody, MA: Hendrickson, 1994), 270.

3. Michael Green, *I Believe in the Holy Spirit* (Grand Rapids, MI: Eerdmans, 1989; reprint 1998), 249–50.

4. Luis Bermejo, S.J., *The Spirit of Life* (Chicago: Loyola University Press, 1989), 356.

5. James D. G. Dunn, *Jesus and the Spirit* (Philadelphia: Westminster Press, 1975), 351.

6. Thomas Merton, *The New Man: Life in Christ* (New York: Farrar, Straus and Giroux, 1961), 106–7.

7. Richard McBrien, *Catholicism* (San Francisco: Harper and Row, 1981), 339. He has a fine treatment on God's providence and human freedom on pp. 321–40; his treatment is based on Karl Rahner, *Foundations of Christian Faith* (New York: Seabury Press, 1978), 86–89.

8. Raymond Brown, *The Epistles of John*, Anchor Bible, vol. 30 (New York: Doubleday, 1982) introduction, chap. 5; esp. 69–71, 110–11.

9. Raymond Brown, *The Churches the Apostles Left Behind* (New York: Paulist Press, 1984), 47.

CHAPTER SIX

Comparisons between the Work of the Spirit of Jesus in Paul, in Luke, and in John

∞

Introduction

Almost any comparison of the work of the Spirit in the pneumatologies of Paul, Luke, and John is worth considering. The similarities are potentially quite numerous; many of them could be studied by comparing chapters 1, 2, 3, and 5 above. But some topics deserve more extensive treatment, either because they are so critical to our life in Christ or because such a comparative study yields some surprising insights.

When we describe the similarities that are found in Paul, Luke, and John, we will also note their variations. That is, they describe similar functions of the Holy Spirit but use different phraseology and different paradigms. We do not need to reconcile all the variations or cover over their differences but merely take notice of the general agreements. Hopefully, these reflections on their similarities may give us new insights into those functions of the Holy Spirit and strengthen our convictions.

A. The Spirit Is the Successor to Christ

1. In Paul

Romans 8:9–11 introduces Paul's formal treatment of the influence of God's Spirit in Christian life:

> 9 You are in the Spirit if only the Spirit of God dwells in you. Whoever does not have the Spirit of Christ does not belong to him. 10 but if Christ is in you . . . the spirit is alive because of righteousness. 11 If the Spirit of the one who raised Jesus from the dead dwells in you, the one who raised Christ from the dead will give life to your mortal bodies also, through his Spirit that dwells in you.

V. 9 presents the Spirit as the new principle of Christian life that comes from God. Christians who belong to Christ have the internal vitalizing influence of the Spirit, here referred to as "Christ's Spirit." Then in v. 10 "Christ in you" is shorthand for "if Christ dwells in you by his Spirit." Paul uses various ways to express the basic union of Christians with Christ. So Christ is said to dwell in Christians as his Spirit becomes the source of new life empowering them in a new way.[1] Then, v. 11 adds that the Spirit dwelling within them is the same Spirit that "raised Christ from the dead," and so will be the source of eternal life for all Christians.

In the context (Rom. 8:1–4), Paul stresses that salvation is wrought by Christ through his death and resurrection. Here he adds the essential point that this salvation effected by Christ is now realized in the life of the believer by the Holy Spirit, who is the vitalizing power of God in individual believers. The indwelling Spirit, then, is the source and the driving force of new life in Christ. It is another significant way in which Paul describes the permanent union of a Christian with Christ by means of his Spirit. So his speaking of the "Spirit in us" (Rom. 5:5; Rom. 8:16; Gal. 4:6) is almost synonymous with talking about our being "in Christ." Many times Paul speaks about the Spirit dwelling in us, but he never says that Jesus "dwells in us" (Eph. 3:17 is the only exception, and it is not authentically Pauline). For Paul then, Christ is present in us through his Spirit; therefore, these are almost identities for him: the Spirit of God dwells in you = you have the Spirit of Christ = Christ is in you.

So now that Christ is no longer physically present among us, we can still be united with him by means of his Spirit. For Paul, then, the Spirit is the successor of Jesus in the sense that Jesus dwells within us by his Spirit and our new life in Jesus is now the work of the Spirit.

2. In Luke

At the end of Luke's Gospel, Jesus' final promise to the apostles points to the critical presence of the Spirit in the future church:

> Thus it is written that the Messiah would suffer and rise from the dead on the third day and that repentance . . . would be preached in his name to all the nations, beginning from Jerusalem. . . . And behold I am sending the promise of my Father upon you. (Luke 24:46–49)

In the very beginning of Acts, Luke refers to this "promise of my Father" (Acts 1:4–5) and quotes the words of Jesus: "you will receive power when the holy Spirit comes upon you, and you will be my witnesses . . . to the ends of the earth." (Acts 1:8) Then throughout Acts, the Spirit is mentioned fifty-seven times: as the one who inaugurates the period of the church by powerful manifestations at Pentecost, who drives the early missionary preaching, and who again and again inspires, directs, and strengthens the members of the early church.

It seems that Luke presents the Holy Spirit as the one who inspires the early missionaries at decisive moments of preaching, decision making, and witnessing, but not as one who acts as the permanent successor of Jesus or as the new presence of Jesus. At the most, Luke presents the Spirit of Jesus as the power sent by Jesus to continue his work of salvation.

3. In John

John's teaching about the Paraclete as the new presence of Christ is rich and inspiring; all by itself it gives us a powerful pneumatology. Raymond Brown astutely summarizes John's theology for us:

> [T]he one whom Jesus calls 'another Paraclete' is another Jesus. Since the Paraclete can come only when Jesus departs, the Paraclete is the presence of Jesus when he is absent [after his departure]. Jesus'

promises to dwell within the disciples are fulfilled in the Paraclete. . . . John insists that Jesus will be in heaven with the Father while the Paraclete is on earth in the disciples; and so the two [from then on] have different roles.[2]

In many ways, whatever Jesus was for his disciples while he was with them, the Holy Spirit will be for them later. Just as Jesus spent all his public life with the disciples (13:33), so the Holy Spirit will dwell with them for the rest of their lives (14:16). Just as Jesus taught and formed the disciples (13:13–14), so the Spirit will "remind them" what Jesus taught them and "teach them all truth." (14:26) Just as Jesus was known by his disciples and they accepted his testimony (14:9; 8:14), so the Spirit will be known by them, and they will receive his testimony (14:17; 15:26). Just as Jesus prepared the disciples by telling them what would come (14:29; 16:4), so the Spirit will "declare to you the things that are coming." (16:13) In all these ways, then, the Paraclete is given by the risen Jesus as a way to make permanent his glorious presence among his disciples. This permanent presence of the Spirit of Jesus is such an amazing gift for each of them that Jesus could truthfully say, "It is better for you that I go." (16:7)

The same is true for us. The Paraclete is not confined only to charismatics, to administrators, or to preachers; rather the Spirit is the possession of every believing Christian. Therefore, there is no such thing as a second-class Christian: the Spirit is for the ordinary Christian as well as those who hold some office; the Spirit is for the twenty-first-century Christians as well as for those in the first century.

This Johannine teaching about the Spirit of Jesus taking the place of Jesus in the lives of individual Christians is a cosmic truth for me. That is, when Jesus makes the extraordinary claim, "It is better for you that I go," he means that the Spirit of Jesus will continue Jesus' presence in all his followers individually in at least three ways: the Spirit will deepen our faith by helping us personally understand the life and message of Jesus (John 14:16–17, 25–26); the Spirit will strengthen our faith in terms of witness against the attacks of the world (15:26–27; 16:7–11); the Spirit will disclose to us the lasting content of Jesus' teaching and open our hearts to know how to follow Jesus in all future world situations. This teaching should be a great source of confidence in our prayer and our spiritual life in general.

B. The Spirit of Jesus Reveals the Whole Truth About God

1. Paul

When Paul preaches the message of the gospel, he insists that his proclamation of the mystery of God and the understanding of that mystery does not depend on human wisdom but on the Spirit of God, who alone knows the mind of God:

> [W]e speak God's wisdom, mysterious, hidden, which God predetermined before the ages. . . . This God has revealed to us through the Spirit . . . [for] no one knows what pertains to God except the Spirit of God. But we have received . . . the Spirit that is from God, so that we may understand the things freely given us by God. (1 Cor. 2:7–12)

Paul clearly asserts in the above that God revealed his truths to us through the Spirit. In the context he denies that his own excellence of speech and persuasive words are sufficient; rather his words are suggested and governed by the Spirit. And he implies that human hearing and ordinary understanding are not enough for a person to believe God's message of salvation. Only the Spirit knows the mind of God and can reveal it to us.

2. Luke

The Acts of the Apostles begins by recalling how Jesus, before "he was taken up" to God, gave "instructions through the holy Spirit to the apostles whom he had chosen." (Acts 1:2) That is, Jesus made use of the Holy Spirit to instruct the apostles. Through this instruction, the apostles came to understand the mystery of redemption and became the official transmitters of the gospel that Jesus had preached. Luke does not clarify how the Spirit instructed the apostles, but we get some notion of that from the rest of Acts.

Jesus; we need to depend on his Spirit who is given to us precisely to know Jesus, to possess him, to be his friend. Jesus has made that all possible for us by giving us his Spirit, along with the Spirit-inspired Scripture and the action of the Spirit in our sacraments.

This unique work of the Spirit of Jesus in his community is essential for our complete dedication to Christ. Even when we admit the terrible failures of the church throughout history or notice the defects of some church leaders or the deficiencies of our fellow Christians, we can still be confident that the Spirit of Jesus will never desert his church. Our church is very human and deficient; it will never be perfectly just or loving; for the leaders of our church—and all of us—will often be inadequate in our following of Jesus our model. Despite all this, our Christian Church is the one source for his word and sacrament, and the Spirit of Jesus abides in this human church.

C. The Spirit of Jesus Is Our Source of New Life in Christ

1. Paul

In chapter 8 of Romans, Paul introduces the formal treatment of the Spirit's influence in Christian life; in this chapter, he mentions the Spirit nineteen times. He describes the Spirit as the powerful source of new life in Christ:

> You are not in the flesh; . . . on the contrary, you are in the spirit, if only the Spirit of God dwells in you. Whoever does not have the Spirit of Christ does not belong to him. . . . If the Spirit of the one who raised Jesus from the dead dwells in you, [he] will give life to your mortal bodies also, through his Spirit that dwells in you. (Rom. 8:9–11)

We see that Paul first describes God's Spirit as the powerful source of new life in Christ; and he actually dwells with us as a permanent influence. Second, notice the different ways Paul expresses our relationship to the Spirit: we are "in the Spirit" or in union with his Spirit; "the Spirit dwells" in us as a person; we have "the Spirit of Christ" so that we belong to Christ; "Christ is in us" by his Spirit;

"[God] who raised Christ . . . dwells in us." All of these highlight the reality of the new life we have in Christ through his Spirit. Finally, the Spirit is presented as the manifestation of the Father's presence and life-giving power once Christ has risen from the dead.

Whenever Paul speaks of the individual Christian as a "temple of the holy Spirit," he means that the Holy Spirit's permanent presence makes one's body or person holy; for example: "your body is a temple of the holy Spirit within you, whom you have from God." (1 Cor. 6:19) That is, the Christian has a new life from God by means of the Spirit permanently present within. That new life in Christ is so real for Paul that he argues strongly: "If we live in the spirit, let us also follow the Spirit." (Gal. 5:25)

2. Luke

After his first speech on the day of Pentecost, Peter responded to the question, "What are we to do?" His answer was: "Repent and be baptized, every one of you . . . and you will receive the gift of the holy Spirit." (Acts 2:38) In Acts, Luke is concerned with the Spirit both as the dynamic principle of testifying to Christ and as the source of new life and spirituality. Later in Acts, Peter explained to his Jewish believers how the Gentiles were baptized with the Holy Spirit:

> [T]he holy Spirit fell upon them as it had upon us at the beginning, and I remembered the word of the Lord [Jesus] . . . "John baptized with water but you will be baptized with the holy Spirit." [So] God gave them the same gift he gave to us when we came to believe in the Lord Jesus Christ. (Acts 11:15–17)

Peter's argument here is not that the Gentiles received a momentary gift but "the same gift he gave us when we came to believe." Rather the gift of the Spirit is permanently given in baptism and connected with their growth in faith.

3. John

Let us begin with the question of Nicodemus:

> "How can a person once grown old be born again?" . . . Jesus answered, "Amen amen I say to you, no one can enter the kingdom of God without being born of water and Spirit." (John 3:4–8)

Jesus' response is based on a simple parallel: a man enters the world because his father begets him; so also, a man can enter the kingdom of God only when he is begotten by the heavenly Father by means of "water and the Spirit." Here a man is "born again" or "born from above" by means of the Spirit. If this passage is based on a historical scene, it must be admitted that Nicodemus could not have understood Christian Baptism or the theology of rebirth. But on the secondary level—which we often find in John—the likely reference is to baptism.

However, in the first Paraclete saying, Jesus promises that the Paraclete will be the "new advocate" to dwell within his disciples always: "I will ask the Father and he will give you another Advocate to be with you always, the Spirit of truth . . . [who] will be in you." (John 14:16–17) So the Spirit of Truth is a Paraclete precisely because he carries on the earthly work of Jesus who is the first Paraclete (1 John 2:1). And Jesus immediately indicates that the Paraclete will be a permanent presence: "I shall not leave you orphans." (v. 18) Jesus' whole point in this first saying is simply to promise the permanent dwelling of the Spirit of Truth within the disciples as their new teacher in his way. In the other four Paraclete sayings, Jesus describes what the new life of the Spirit will mean to all his disciples.

D. The Spirit of Jesus Is Our Individual Guide to Christian Living

1. Paul

We begin with Paul's Letter to the Romans. In chapter 8 Paul affirms, "Whoever does not have the Spirit of Christ does not belong to him." (8:9) For Paul, if Christ Jesus has made possible the new life for Christians to be lived in him and for God (objective redemption), it is the Spirit of Jesus that is the dynamic and vital principle of that life (subjective redemption). Through this Spirit we are justified (8:2), so that the Spirit dwells permanently within us (8:11); through the Spirit we become children of God (8:14); through the Spirit the love of God is poured out into our hearts

(5:5); and through the Spirit we learn how to pray effectively (8:26–27).

Let us add just two quotes from Paul's other letters here, by way of summarizing the work of the Spirit in us: "If we live in the Spirit, let us also follow the Spirit" (Gal. 5:25); that is, the gift of the Spirit is meant to help us live in the Spirit of Jesus; to walk in the Spirit means to serve one another in love, to follow in the way of Christ; "No one can say, 'Jesus is Lord,' except by the Holy Spirit" (1 Cor. 12:3): that is, even the simplest expression of faith is spoken with the aid of the Spirit. Perhaps it is not too much to say that, for Paul, the agent of all grace and of subjective redemption is the Spirit of Jesus.

When we compare Paul's teaching about the Spirit of Jesus to that of Luke and John (as below), it seems clear that Paul is the outstanding teacher of the Spirit as the vital and dynamic principle of our life in Christ. He assures us that we can depend on the Spirit of Jesus, dwelling within us, to guide us in living the way of Jesus and in following him as our model.

2. Luke

The Spirit is much more prominent in Luke's Gospel than in the other synoptics; he mentions the Spirit at least seventeen times. But in most instances, Luke depicts the S/spirit as he appears in the Old Testament. Thus, in the Old Testament, *pneuma*, "spirit," is a dynamic entity by which God accomplishes his ends—either as transient power (rather like an impersonal force) that raises up leaders and inspires prophecy, or as a permanent charism for kings (and eventually for the coming messianic king).

Luke is unique among the evangelists in presenting the grand plan of salvation, consisting of three periods, each of them initiated under the influence of the Spirit. The first period is that of preparation or the period of **Israel**; thus John the Baptizer is "filled with the Holy Spirit" (1:15), as were Elizabeth (1:41) and Zechariah (1:67). The second period is that of **Jesus**; the Spirit is the power mentioned at his conception and birth (1:35) and at his presentation (three times regarding Simeon; 2:25–26); then the Spirit comes permanently on Jesus, making him God's "beloved Son." (3:22–23) The third period is that of the **church**; at the ascension and most dramatically at

Pentecost (Acts 2:1–4) Jesus sends "the promise of the Father upon" the disciples; that promise is the Holy Spirit (Acts 1:4–5; 2:8).

Comparing Luke's Gospel to those of Matthew and Mark, we see the Spirit as more influential and even dominant in Luke. But the Spirit is still somewhat impersonal and only appears as a temporary power for people other than Jesus himself. In section D, below, we will consider the influence of the Spirit in the church. Here, we might note that this same power of the Spirit appears often in Acts as the inspiration for several individuals in the early church: Peter (4:8), the apostles (4:33), the seven assistants (6:3), Stephen (6:10), Philip (8:29, 39), and Barnabas and Saul (13: 2–4). So in Luke, in general, the Spirit is the power and guide for the recognized leaders in the church.

As regards the Spirit coming down on the ordinary Christians at the various Pentecosts found in Acts, we can be confident that this same Spirit will guide us who have also received the Spirit of Jesus through baptism and confirmation.

3. John

The five Paraclete sayings in chapters 14 through 16 deal with the Spirit of Truth; in an unparalleled treatise, John describes the Paraclete as the "new Advocate" who takes the place of the ascended Christ. The primary work of that Spirit, as we saw extensively, is to teach us the whole truth about Jesus. But in the fifth saying, Jesus tells the disciples, "the Spirit of truth . . . will guide you to all truth." (John 16:13) This seems to include more than a deeper intellectual understanding of the truth; that is, it also involves teaching a way of life in conformity with Jesus' teaching. The reason for saying this is bound up with the whole Johannine understanding of the way of truth. For John's Gospel thinks of truth not as an abstract system of faith but as a sphere of action, similar to the Old Testament notion of the way of truth as a way of life in conformity with the Mosaic law, and also similar to the notion of the way" so prominent in Acts.[3]

> Also as we saw above (61–62), the First Letter of John asserts that if we keep God's commandments and love one another, God remains in us, and "the way we know that he remains in us is from the

Spirit that he has given us." (1 John 3:23–24) Thus, the presence of the Spirit within us is the necessary principle for our living as a Christian. So the Johannine writings also encourage us to rely on the Spirit as a practical guide for living the way of Christ.

E. The Spirit of Jesus Is the Soul of the Church

1. Paul

St. Augustine is the originator of the title given to the Spirit here: "the soul of the church": "What the soul is for the human body, that the Holy Spirit is for the body of Christ, which is the church; what the soul works in all the members of the one body, that the Spirit works in the whole body of the church."[4] Augustine is not speaking ontologically but rather functionally, to describe the Holy Spirit as the life force of the church. The scriptural foundation for this description of the Spirit is found especially in Paul. He offers three principal reasons for that assertion.

First, Paul teaches that the people of God form a holy temple of God: "you are the temple of God, and the Spirit of God dwells in you . . . for the temple of God, which you are, is holy" (1 Cor. 3:16); in the context Paul is clearly speaking about the church at Corinth: "you are God's field, God's building." (1 Cor. 3:9) He means that the Corinthians are a building filled with the Spirit, built by the Spirit. The Letter to the Ephesians adds a famous image about the church as the temple of God:

> [Y]ou are . . . members of the household of God, built upon the foundation of the apostles . . . with Christ Jesus himself as the capstone. Through him the whole structure is held together and grows into a temple sacred in the Lord; in him you are also being built together into a dwelling place of God in the Spirit. (Eph. 2:19–22)

In these passages the temple is formed by the Spirit and is made holy by the indwelling of the Spirit. That is, the church is a new temple, the place of God's dwelling in the midst of his people; in fact, the Holy Spirit dwelling in the community is the way God is present to his people.

Second, Paul describes the church as the body of Christ and the Holy Spirit as the source of that unity: "As . . . the parts of the body, though many, are one body, so also Christ. For in one Spirit we were all baptized into one body." (1 Cor. 12:12–13) Apparently, this wonderful description of the church as the body of Christ is original with Paul; it is distinctly Pauline and represents his mature thinking about the church. He means that the unity of Christians has no parallel in the natural realm, for the "body of Christ" is a profound union of Christ and the church through the power of the Spirit. So, each believer is incorporated into the body of Christ and permeated with the Spirit by means of faith and Baptism. We are not just individual members of Christ, we are all joined together by the Holy Spirit into the one body of Christ. Because of this unity in the body of Christ, all distinctions—"whether Jews or Greeks, slaves or free persons"—lose their validity and importance, for we are all one in Christ. Because of this unity in the Spirit, we can be intimate with Jesus as members of his body.

Paul's third reason why the Spirit is the soul of the church springs from his teaching on the gifts of the Spirit within the body of Christ; he affirms that the church is charismatic because of the extraordinary gifts of the Spirit. Here is the famous passage from 1 Corinthians:

> There are different kinds of spiritual gifts but the same Spirit; . . .
> To each individual the manifestation of the Spirit is given for some benefit.
> To one is given the expression of wisdom . . . through the Spirit;
> to another the expression of knowledge according to the same Spirit;
> to another faith by the same Spirit;
> to another gifts of healing by the same Spirit;
> to another mighty deeds; to another prophecy;
> to another discernment of spirits; to another varieties of tongues;
> to another interpretation of tongues.
> But one and the same Spirit produces all of these, distributing them individually to each person as he wishes. (1 Cor. 12:4–11)

Paul affirms here that the charisms that mark the members of the church are all the result of the Spirit's gifts. They are not natural abilities that people possess from birth but charismatic gifts given for the life of the church. These charisms are quite diverse; they are freely given to individuals by the Spirit. But in every case, they are given for the common good of the church; notice the frequent repetition of "the same Spirit"; this is Paul's way of emphasizing the unifying power of the Spirit in the church; by this emphasis Paul hopes to correct the individualism and division plaguing the Corinthian church.

Because the Spirit is the soul of the church, he can be the source of its unity even for those possessing such extraordinary spiritual gifts. Paul spends all of chapters 12 and 14 (and perhaps 13) in affirming these gifts of the Spirit but also cautioning about them, for these charisms were not only evidence of the power of the Spirit but also became very problematic for the church because of individualistic pride and divisive manifestations.

In our contemporary church, there are not so many evident charisms in the church, though there are some; surely the Spirit inspired Mother Theresa and Pope John XXIII. Pope John Paul II affirms that the Spirit is the soul of the church also in our day:

> The Holy Spirit is the vital principle of the church. . . . He is the Giver of life and unity to the church, along the lines of the efficient cause, that is, as the author and promoter of divine life in the Body of Christ. [The Second Vatican] Council . . . states that . . . "his Spirit . . . gives life to, unifies and moves the whole body. This he does in such a way that his work could be compared by the Fathers with the function which . . . the soul fulfills in the human body."[5]

2. Luke

As noted before, *pneuma*, "Spirit" is mentioned seventy times in Acts, which is almost one-fifth of all the references to the Spirit in the whole New Testament. Indeed, the distinguishing feature of Luke's ecclesiology is the constant presence and power of the Holy Spirit. Thus, Luke presents the Spirit as the constant guide and power for the church; the Spirit is promised to the apostles to empower them to give witness to Jesus (Acts 1:8); this same Spirit inaugurates the church at Pentecost (2:1–4) and expands the church after Peter's first sermon (2:38–41), and significantly to the Gentiles (10:44–48; 19:5–7); again the Spirit directs the leaders of the church: Peter (10:19), Barnabas and Paul (13:2–4), Paul often (16:6–7; 20:22–23); and most decisively the Spirit is the inspiration for the crucial decision at the so-called Council of Jerusalem: "It is the decision of the Holy Spirit and of us." (15:28)

We can summarize all this work of the Spirit in Acts by affirming that the Spirit is the driving force from the very beginning of the church, responsible for the instruction and guidance of the apostles, and the dynamo that continues the work of Jesus himself through those who follow the way of Jesus. This is how Luke presents the Spirit as taking the place of Christ on earth by being the primary guide of his church. Luke's development emphasizes the Spirit as guiding the missionary church in giving witness to Jesus.

Compared with Paul, Luke presents the Spirit, even more than Paul, as the director and guide of the church. Compared with John, Luke presents a powerful Spirit in the church as a whole as well as in its leaders, while John emphasizes the individual guidance of the Spirit for all believers.

3. John

For me, the five Paraclete sayings of Jesus are unequaled in all of Scripture in terms of the Spirit's profound influence on the individual Christian. But when we look for John's teaching about the Spirit's influence on the church, we will likely be disappointed. In John's Gospel there are two clear indications that those who believe in Jesus form a community; they are the metaphors of the sheepfold (John 10:1–18) with Jesus himself as the good shepherd (10:14–16), and the metaphor of the vine and the branches (15:1–8). But in both of these, the Spirit is not mentioned as the source of that unity. Also in chapter 21 (which was added by a redactor as a necessary ecclesial chapter for the Johannine church,)[6] Peter is given the role as shepherd of the sheep; this important addition certainly deals with church life and affected the relation of the Johannine community to the church at large; but again there is no direct reference to the Spirit.

One passage in the Gospel that does deal with the Spirit and the community directly is John 20:22–23. After the resurrection, Jesus appears to the disciples and formally commissions them: "Receive the holy Spirit. Whose sins you forgive are forgiven them, and whose sins you retain are retained." Here the eleven disciples are given power to forgive sins for the whole community (through baptism or penance), and that power is related to their receiving the Holy Spirit. This giving of the Spirit consecrates the disciples with power over sin and evil, with power to forgive the sins of the community.

Also, while the emphasis in the five Paraclete sayings is on the Spirit's influence on individuals, at least the third saying refers also to the community: "the Spirit of truth will testify to me. And you also testify." (John 15:26–27) These two verses conclude the section on the world's hatred and persecution (15:18–25); they assure the Spirit's help in witnessing to Jesus for as long as the disciples experience the world's hatred. And if that witness is to be effective, the Spirit must work in the disciples as a body; therefore, the Paraclete must be promised to the entire community of disciples and to the church in general.

As we turn to the First Letter of John, we find one reference to the Spirit's influence on the church. The entire letter is in response to a grave situation in the Johannine community; that is, many who were a part of the Johannine community from the beginning believed that faith in Jesus was the only criterion for salvation, that there was no need for following the commandments or living according to the way of Jesus by loving one another. For them, eternal life consists in knowing God and the one whom he sent (John 1: 3), so that intimacy with God was gained by "knowing" him, without emphasis on behavior; they claimed that they could believe in God without depending on any external authority or any external rites. Because of their rejection of all external authority, there was no way to keep them in the Johannine church, so they eventually seceded from it. John responds to them throughout his letter, insisting again and again that they must follow the commandments, love the brethren, and take part in the ways of the community. In one passage particularly, John refers to the Spirit and to their reception of the Spirit in Baptism: "you have the anointing that comes from the holy one." (1 John 2:20)

Scripture scholars have struggled with this passage. After an extended exegesis of this passage, Raymond Brown concludes: "the author was referring to an anointing with the Holy Spirit, the gift from Christ which constituted one a Christian. This anointing . . . was probably connected with entry to the Community."[7] Having said all this, we must admit that John's direct teaching on the work of the Spirit in forming the church is not very strong or clear.

F. Christ Fulfills His Promises through the Work of the Holy Spirit

Throughout Jesus' public life, he made numerous promises that are brought to fulfillment by means of the **Holy Spirit**. But the fulfillment was often surprising or unexpected. Paul, Luke, and John each have different methods of dealing with these promises and their fulfillment; however, they all point to the Spirit's involvement for their solution.

1. Paul in Acts

Promise: In this instance, the promise is from God to Ananias regarding Saul/Paul. The Lord told Ananias to find Saul and cure his blindness, so that he could be a witness to the Gentiles: "this man is a chosen instrument of mine to carry my name before Gentiles." As Ananias met Saul, he told him: Jesus helped you recover your sight "and be filled with the holy Spirit." (Acts 9:15–17)

Fulfillment: After his conversion and healing, "Saul grew all the stronger and confounded the Jews . . . proving that this is the Messiah." (Acts 9:22) Then the Holy Spirit directed Paul's ministry to the Gentiles: "the Holy Spirit spoke to them: 'Set apart Barnabas and Paul for me to do the work for which I have called them.'" (Acts 13:2)

Result: When Paul reached Ephesus, his witness resulted in the conversion of many Gentiles: "When Paul laid his hands on them, the holy Spirit came upon them, and they spoke in tongues and prophesied." (Acts 19:6) This event might be seen as the Pauline Pentecost motif. The rest of Acts continues to describe the ministry of Paul, who was "filled with the holy Spirit" as the apostle to the Gentiles.

2. Luke

Promise: Luke mentions Jesus' promise again and again—each time with more clarity regarding the Holy Spirit. First, Jesus promises his help in the coming persecution: "[you will be led] before kings and governors in my name. . . . I will give you a wisdom in speaking that all your adversaries will be powerless to resist or refute. (Luke 21:12–15). Then after the resurrection, Jesus assures them that the "promise of the Father" will give them "power": "I will send down on you the promise of my Father . . . with power from on high." (Luke 24:49) In Acts, Jesus clarifies that this "promise of my Father" is the Holy Spirit: "Wait for the fulfillment of my Father's promise. . . . in a few days you will be baptized with the holy Spirit." (Acts 1:4–5) Then finally, Jesus promises that the Holy Spirit will be their individual power for giving witness to him: "you will receive power when the holy Spirit comes upon you, and you will be my witnesses. . . ." (Acts 1:8)

Fulfillment: "When the time for Pentecost was fulfilled . . . they were all filled with the holy Spirit and began to speak in different tongues, as the Spirit enabled them to proclaim." (Acts 2:1, 4) Immediately Peter testifies to the fulfillment of Jesus' promise: "This is what was spoken through the prophet Joel . . . I will pour out my spirit on all mankind . . . your sons and daughters shall prophesy" (Acts 2:17), and then Peter declares that this is all accomplished now by means of the Holy Spirit: "Jesus received the promise of the holy Spirit from the Father and poured it forth, as you see." (Acts 2:33)

Result: The power of the Holy Spirit is poured out on them visibly: "When the time for Pentecost was fulfilled . . . they were all filled with the holy Spirit and began to speak in different tongues, as the Spirit enabled them to proclaim." (Acts 2:1–4) This Lukan Pentecost event conferred the power of the Holy Spirit on the Jerusalem community. That power of the Spirit of Jesus showed itself immediately by their speaking in tongues, having visions, and performing miracles. It continued from that day forward as a power for continuing witness: "you will be my witnesses in Jerusalem . . . and to the ends of the earth." (Acts 1:8) Throughout Acts, there is frequent evidence of the power of the Spirit working through the apostles, so that this permanent power of the Spirit became the force for the widespread growth of the Christian Church.

3. John

Promises: Jesus promises the coming of the Paraclete: "I will ask the Father, and he will give you another Advocate to be with you always, the Spirit of truth." (John 14:16–17) And he explains that this Spirit of truth can only come to the disciples after Jesus has returned to the Father: "It is better for you that I go, for if I do not go, the Advocate will not come to you. But if I go, I will send him to you." (John 16:7) Then he makes explicit the work of the Spirit: "The holy Spirit will instruct you in everything and remind you of all that I told you" (John 14:26); and again, "The Paraclete, the Spirit of truth will testify to me. And you also testify." (John 15:26)

Fulfillment: On the very day of Easter, Jesus tells the disciples: "Receive the holy Spirit. Whose sins you forgive, they are forgiven them." (John 20:22) Here Jesus imparts the Holy Spirit to the disciples; this is the Johannine Pentecost. So the disciples immediately "receive the holy Spirit," apparently as a permanent presence and power; the explicit power mentioned here is to forgive sins. Then the First Letter of John attests to this Spirit dwelling within the members of the Johannine community: "The way we know that God remains in us is from the spirit that he gave us." (1 John 3:24); and again: "This is how we know that we remain in him and he in us, that he has given us of his Spirit." (1 John 4:13)

Result: The Spirit of truth dwells within all those who believe, and testifies to Christ: "Everyone who believes that Jesus is the Christ has been begotten of God. . . . It is the Spirit who testifies to this, and the Spirit is truth." (1 John 5:1, 6) Thus the Paraclete takes the place of Christ in us; the Spirit of Jesus reminds us of all that Jesus taught, bears witness to Jesus in us, and leads us in the way of all truth.

G. The Eschatological Spirit

Paul, Luke, and John all present the Spirit of Jesus as the eschatological gift of God. The Greek word *eschaton* means "last," so eschatology is the theology about the last things. It refers principally to the end of the world, judgment, and resurrection; but occasionally it refers to the time after Christ ascends to the Father and before his second coming, the final age of God's plan of salvation or the age of the church. Paul, Luke, and John each present the Spirit of Jesus as the eschatological Spirit, but they approach this teaching differently.

1. Paul

Paul speaks of the Spirit as the "first installment" (*arrabon*): "the one who gives us security with you in Christ and who anointed us is God; he has also put his seal upon us and given the Spirit in our hearts as a first installment." (2 Cor. 1:21–22; also 5:5) As we saw before, Paul means that the gift of the Spirit in us is God's down payment of our inheritance, the first installment or pledge of the glory that is assured us in heaven. In Romans, Paul gives us a sense of our life now in Christ as both "already" assured of salvation and "not yet" attained: "we ourselves, who have the first fruits of the Spirit . . . groan within ourselves as we await . . . the redemption of our bodies." (Rom. 8:23) In both cases Paul instills a sense of eschatological expectation—awaiting the glory of eternal life; that is, the gift of the Spirit is our beginning of salvation and also our guarantee of future inheritance. For Paul, then, the gift of the Spirit in us inaugurates the *eschaton* by being our first payment and pledge of eternal life.

2. Luke

In Acts, Peter gives his first sermon on the day of Pentecost; he quotes from the prophet Joel:

> "It will come to pass in the last days," God says, "that I will pour out a portion of my spirit upon all flesh. Your sons and daughters shall prophesy, your young men shall see visions, your old men shall dream dreams . . . and it shall be that everyone shall be saved who calls on the name of the Lord." (Acts 2:17, 21)

Luke heightens the eschatological character of this quote by adding "in the last days" and by the remark, "everyone shall be saved." The whole tenor of chapter 2 of Acts is that the outpouring of the Spirit at Pentecost marks a new epoch of God's dealings with humankind; for Luke this is the third phase of salvation history (the first, the Old Testament; the second, the time of Christ). Fitzmyer expresses this well:

> The Spirit poured out on Pentecost inaugurates a new age—that is the whole point of the Pentecost-experience narrated in Acts 2. That is also the reason why one must reckon with a three-phase view of salvation-history in Lukan theology. The role of the Spirit . . . has become the initiator of a new era of salvation-history, when the Spirit becomes God's presence to his people anew.[8]

For Luke, then, the Spirit at Pentecost inaugurates the new age, the third phase of salvation. In Acts, this third phase is marked by the Spirit offering consistent guidance to the church and inspiration for witness to the apostles as well as to individual followers.

C. John

In John, Jesus is presented during his earthly ministry as the unique, once-and-for-all revelation of God. So John presents the moment of judgment **now**; he teaches that the revelation of God is fulfilled in Jesus; he urges all to make their decision now: "Whoever believes in [Christ] will not be condemned, but whoever does not believe has already been condemned, because he has not believed in the name of the only Son of God." (John 3:18; see also 3:35–36; 5:24–25; 12:44–48) These are clear examples of John's realized eschatology; he means that "now is the time of judgment" (John 12:31), because "everyone who believes in [God's Son] might not perish but might have eternal life." (John 3:16)

Later, in all five Paraclete sayings, John makes it clear that after the ministry of Jesus, another period will begin, the period of the Paraclete/Spirit; perhaps Jesus' most explicit expression is this: "I have told you this while I am with you, The Advocate, the holy Spirit that the Father will send in my name—he will teach you everything and remind you of all that I told you." (John 14:25–26) Notice how all the verbs in this passage are in the future tense, for the sending of the Spirit can only take place after Jesus has departed. This was John's assurance for the members of the Johannine community who came later and had no direct contact with Jesus; they would receive the revelation of God, not through Jesus, but through the action of the Spirit. This period of the Paraclete would not bring a new revelation: "he will not speak on his own, but he will speak what he hears . . . he will take from what is mine and declare it to you." (John 16:13–14) In fact, those who live in the period of the Spirit and come to believe in God's Son are not at a disadvantage; they too can already realize salvation so that they "might not perish, but might have eternal life." (John 3:16)

John is famous for his "realized eschatology." In his Gospel, the singular agent of this period is the Spirit; those who live in the era of the Paraclete are not at a disadvantage: "Blessed are those who have not seen [the earthly Jesus] and have believed." (John 20:29)

Notes

1. Joseph Fitzmyer, *Romans*, Anchor Bible, vol. 33 (New York: Doubleday, 1993), 490.

2. Raymond Brown, *The Gospel According to John, 13–21*, Anchor Bible, vol. 29A (New York: Doubleday, 1996), 1140–41 (emphasis added).

3. Ibid., 628–29.

4. St. Augustine, sermon 267, #4.

5. John Paul II, *The Spirit, Giver of Life and Love* (Boston: Pauline Books and Media, 1996), 321; the quote is taken from *Lumen Gentium*, par. 7.

6. Raymond Brown, *The Epistles of John*, Anchor Bible, vol. 30 (New York: Doubleday, 1982), 1077–82.

7. Ibid, 342–48, for the extended exegesis. The quote is found on 348, and the emphasis is in the original.

8. Joseph Fitzmyer, *The Gospel According to Luke, 1–9*, Anchor Bible, vol. 28 (New York: Doubleday, 1981), 230.

SECOND PART

THE SPIRIT OF JESUS IN PRAYER

CHAPTER SEVEN

Luke

∽

A. Spirit and Jesus

The power of the Holy Spirit, in Luke, is dominant in Jesus' ministry. More than the other synoptic Gospels, Luke makes the Holy Spirit the constant guide of Jesus as well as the source of his power. Throughout Jesus' public life, Luke presents him as the unique bearer of the Spirit. His public life begins with his baptism: "Jesus also [was baptized] . . . and the holy Spirit descended upon him. . . . And a voice came from heaven, 'You are my beloved Son, with you I am well pleased.'" (Luke 3:21–22) For Luke, Jesus' receiving the Spirit symbolizes the preparation for his public life. The very next verse (v. 23) notes the formal beginning: "Jesus began his ministry." In the next chapter, Luke notes: "filled with the holy Spirit, Jesus . . . was led by the holy Spirit into the desert." (Luke 4:1) Then at Nazareth, Jesus reads from Isaiah, "The Spirit of the Lord is upon me" (Isa. 61:1–2), and continues, "Today this scripture passage is fulfilled in your hearing." (Luke 4:18–21) Here Jesus is presented as consciously aware of the influence of the Spirit on him. And he asserts that what Isaiah had announced, Jesus is now doing: "he has anointed me to preach the good news." (v. 18) Typically, Luke turns this quote from Isaiah "into a prediction, the fulfillment of which is found in the person, words and deeds of Jesus."[1]

One other characteristic of Luke's Gospel is the way he presents Jesus as praying before or during many of the major episodes of his ministry. Thus, Luke presents Jesus praying at his baptism (3:21), before choosing the twelve apostles (6:12), before his first announcement of the passion (9:18), at his transfiguration (9:28), before he teaches the Our Father (11:2), at the Last Supper (to strengthen Peter's faith, 22:32), during his agony in the garden (22:41), and on the cross itself (23:46). This is an evident attempt by Luke to highlight Jesus' dependence on God and the Spirit.

We might summarize Luke's description of the influence of the Holy Spirit on Jesus by saying Jesus was driven, inspired, and empowered by the Spirit. Two messages for us seem to follow naturally from Luke's description of Jesus and the Holy Spirit: to depend on the guidance of the Spirit in our important personal decisions; to recognize the prayerful Jesus as our model for prayer.

B. The Our Father

Luke introduces the Our Father by noting: "[Jesus] was praying . . . and when he had finished, his disciples said to him, 'Lord, teach us to pray.'" (11:1) Luke's immediate connection of Jesus' prayer and the apostles' request seems to reveal their desire to pray as their master does. Jesus responds: "When you pray, say: Father, hallowed be your name, your kingdom come. Give us each day our daily bread and forgive us our sins as we ourselves forgive everyone in debt to us, and do not subject us to the final test." (Luke 1:2–4) Luke's form of the Our Father has only five petitions (not seven as in Matthew). His five petitions are probably closer to the wording of Jesus himself, for Matthew often adds phrases to Jesus' speech. Also we should note that here in Luke the Our Father seems to be presented as a **model** prayer for Christians.

"Father" is the frequent way that Jesus addressed God (as in 10:21 and 22:42). Such an intimate form of address is never used by an individual in the Old Testament in speaking to God and seems to be original with Jesus; he wants us to pray to God not merely as transcendent Lord but also as a loving Father who is near to his children. His whole prayer is one of direct simplicity and familiarity, one in which he encourages us to have his own personal attitude toward the Father.

The first petition, "hallowed be your name," asks that God himself be vindicated and recognized as holy. The second petition, "your kingdom come," is a prayer that God's kingdom on earth might be brought to its full realization. As spoken to the apostles, these first two petitions probably referred immediately to the work of Jesus and the apostles as a means of vindicating God and realizing his kingdom. As Luke now teaches it to the Christians of his day, he hoped that they would have some part in furthering God's work.

The second group of petitions expresses a humble reliance on God and confidence to be heard. Here in Luke these petitions are more concerned with our **present** condition, while in Matthew they emphasize the end-time or eschatological need for help. The third petition, "Give us each day our daily bread," probably refers to material bread or food (not directly to the Eucharist). And it asks for food one day at a time, similar to the Exodus experience (Exou. 16:4). The fourth petition, "forgive us our sins as we ourselves forgive everyone in debt to us," is not to be considered as a *do ut des* attitude (i. e., I forgive others so that God may forgive me); that is, our own forgiveness of others is not **a condition** for God's forgiveness. Rather this petition impels us to realize that God's forgiveness cannot be expected if we withhold forgiveness from others when we are asked. Another observation about forgiveness is only hinted at here. Notice that for God to forgive us any sin, no matter how serious, we need only have real sorrow and ask God's forgiveness; if we are not contrite and refuse to ask his forgiveness, he does not forgive our sins. So God himself requires that we ask for forgiveness. Now it seems clear to me that we are certainly not expected to be more merciful than God. So we are required to forgive others only when they ask it of us or show in some way that they are sorry. The final petition, "do not subject us to the final test," hides an Old Testament protological way of thinking; that is, in the Old Testament all things were seen as effected by God—both the good and the bad; God was seen as the direct cause of everything. However, in the

New Testament Jesus corrects that early belief and teaches that evil is not sent by God as a punishment for sin; nor does God "lead us into temptation." So the sense of this petition is: give us your grace that we may resist all temptation and sin.

Admittedly, none of Luke's Our Father refers explicitly to the Holy Spirit. We have to appeal to St. Paul in order to make a connection between the Holy Spirit and the Our Father. In Galatians, Paul teaches, "As proof that you are children, God sent the Spirit of his Son into our hearts, crying out, '*Abba*, Father.'" (Gal. 4:6) That is, Paul clearly connects our addressing God so intimately as "Father" with the fact that we possess the "Spirit of his Son." Our Christian prayer then flows from our filial relationship with God, which we possess by the gift of the Spirit of his Son. So Luke's model Christian prayer, then, is based on the reality of our possessing the Spirit dwelling with us.

C. Confidence in Prayer

Each synoptic writer has a passage encouraging confidence in prayer. Luke's treatment is longer and more forceful than Matthew's and Mark's, and it concludes with an assurance that God will grant the supreme gift of the Holy Spirit. Luke begins with an engaging parable that is unique to him:

> Jesus said to them, "Suppose one of you has a friend to whom he goe at midnight and says, 'Friend lend me three loaves of bread, for a friend of mine has arrived at my house from a journey and I have nothing to offer him, and he says in reply within, 'Do not bother me; the door has already been locked and my childen and I are already in bed. I cannot get up to give you everything.' I tell you, if he does not get up to give him the loaves because of their friendship, he will get up to give him whatever he needs because of his persistance." (Luke 11:5–8)

Luke's whole point here is about persistence in prayer. The friend comes to his neighbor at an inopportune time, asking for a favor. The friend acts as if he has no one else he can appeal to in his need.

The neighbor does not renounce their friendship but insists this is most inopportune and too much to ask of him. Still the friend will not take no for an answer; he is persistent. Finally, the neighbor realizes how relentless the friend is, so that he and his family will get no sleep unless he yields to his relentless request. He grants the unreasonable request not out of friendship, but because of persistence.

For Luke, the neighbor represents God, not in the sense of one who is unwilling to help or needs to be cajoled into giving us what we need, but as one who will be especially moved by requests that are persistent. This kind of persistence, which is even relentless, shows how much one relies on God and values the particular gift asked for.

Immediately after this forceful parable, Jesus continues to teach persistence in prayer by directly urging us to pray with great confidence that God will hear our prayer:

> [A]sk and you shall receive; seek and you will find; knock and the door will be opened to you. For everyone who asks, receives; and the one who seeks, finds; and to the one who knocks, the door will be opened. What father among you would hand his son a snake when he asks for a fish? If you then . . . know how to give good gifts to your children, how much more will the Father in heaven give the holy Spirit to those who ask him? (Luke 11:9–13)

Jesus urges confidence in prayer in three modes of petition (asking, searching, knocking); by repeating this three times, Jesus is encouraging us to unwearying prayer. He bolsters his argument by a profoundly human argument: no father would deceive his son or give him something harmful; such a response is unthinkable! But God's bounty transcends that of any earthly parent, so that even more certainly will God our Father respond to our persistent prayer. His conclusion then, in v. 10, sounds like a universal law, so that each of these three actions meets with a corresponding response from God. My understanding is that this **is** a universal promise as long as we ask properly. What spiritual writers mean when they speak about asking properly is explained in various ways: if what we ask for is in keeping with the will of God, if it furthers the kingdom of God, if it reflects the spirit of Jesus' prayer. These conditions are quite similar; they all promise this: whatever we pray for, if the bottom line of our prayer is that God's will be done, God will always help us to fulfill his will.

This proper attitude in prayer is so critical, and Luke's Gospel helps us to understand it. For Luke not only presents Christ as praying often, he offers Jesus' attitude in prayer as a **model** for us. And Luke describes this model forcefully in Jesus' supreme moment of trial; in the agony in the garden, Jesus' prayer could not be more clear: "Father if you are willing, take this cup away from me; still, not my will but yours be done." (Luke 22:42) What this model means, then, is that we can ask for anything in our prayer with great confidence, as long as the bottom line of our petition is that God's will be done in us.

Luke's final conclusion in this whole section on perseverance in prayer is: "How much more will the Father in heaven give the holy Spirit to those who ask him." This is a different conclusion from Matthew: "How much more will your heavenly Father give good things to those who ask him." (Matt. 7:11) That is, of all the things we might ask God for, to seek the gift of the Holy Spirit is most in keeping with his will; he will certainly grant such a petition for it must be a part of God's will and in keeping with Jesus' own prayer. In all our prayer, then, we can be most confident when we seek the help of the Holy Spirit to progress in prayer or follow in the way of Jesus.

Note

1. Joseph Fitzmyer, *The Gospel According to Luke, 1–9*, Anchor Bible, vol. 28 (New York: Doubleday, 1981), 529.

CHAPTER EIGHT

Paul

A. The Holy Spirit Intercedes for Us

"[God] who searches hearts knows what is the intention of the Spirit, because it intercedes for the holy ones according to God's will." (Rom. 8:27) Paul's description of the Spirit as an intercessor is not found in the Old Testament. He is the first scripture writer to describe the Spirit as our personal intercessor with God. This seems to be another result of God's Spirit "that dwells in you." (Rom. 8:11) Paul's point here is that the Spirit can "intercede for [us] according to God's will" so that God will certainly hear us; that is, because the Spirit intercedes for us in a divine manner, God shares the Spirit's intention on behalf of his holy ones. Notice that the Spirit does not necessarily intercede to give us exactly what we pray for, but rather to help us fulfill the will of God in whatever happens. The reason we need the Spirit in our prayer is that we can never be sure what is the will of God for us. Perhaps the deepest cause of our uncertainty and lack of confidence in prayer is our ignorance of the divine will. However, the Spirit of God overcomes such diffidence by interceding for us and presenting our prayer so that it is in keeping with God's will.

B. Power in Weakness

"[T]he Spirit too comes to the aid of our weakness; for we do not know how to pray as we ought, but the Spirit itself intercedes with inexpressible groanings." (Rom. 8:26) This assurance goes together with A, above (the Spirit as intercessor). Here Paul tells us that God's Spirit not only makes known to us our weakness but also comforts and strengthens us despite our inability. The particular weakness to which Paul refers is that we do not know what we should pray for or how we should pray. The Spirit pleads our cause with the Father, helps us present our needs, adds his own "inexpressible groanings." These sighs or groanings of the Spirit do not refer to charismatic prayer or speaking in tongues, but to sighs of the Spirit that cannot be expressed in human terms.

In the Old Testament, there is a tradition in which patriarchs and prophets make intercession for the people before God (see Tob. 12:12–15; Job 33:23–26). The most famous example of this is Abraham's pleading with God—even boldly bargaining—for the city of Sodom (Gen. 18:22–32). Here in Romans, the Spirit acts as a superintercessor, much more forceful than any other.

In chapter 1, we saw how Paul dealt with his own weakness (2 Cor. 12:9). He learned one of the supreme lessons of his life by facing his weakness. His very sense of ineptitude, of his poverty before God, became the occasion for the intervention of the Spirit: "when I am weak, then I am strong." God taught him: my power is actualized by your weakness; your deep sense of need and helplessness is the condition for my special graces. That is, the vacuum created by his weakness permits the powerful action of the Holy Spirit. In our own prayer, especially more advanced prayer, everything depends on our learning this lesson: "power is made perfect in weakness."

C. Child of God

"[T]hose who are led by God's Spirit are children of God. For you did not receive a spirit of slavery to fall back into fear, but you received a spirit of adoption, through which we cry out, 'A*bba*, Father!' The Spirit itself bears witness with our spirit: we are children of God!" (Rom. 8:14–16)

Paul's first point here is that the Spirit animates and activates us Christians; being "led by the Spirit" is Paul's way of expressing the active influence of the Spirit in our lives. Then, Paul shows how this contrasts with the "spirit of slavery"; for the attitude of a slave is one of anxiety and fear before his master, while the attitude of a child of God is one of confidence as belonging to God, as a member of his family. He means that because we are sons/daughters of God and know it, we can cry out with confidence, "Father." Paul adds that the Spirit establishes our new relationship to God as daughters/sons of God. In fact, the gift of the Spirit constitutes sonship/daughterhood. That is, this new status is initiated through faith and baptism (Gal. 3:26–27) and is activated and realized through the indwelling Spirit (Rom. 8:14). Notice, finally, that here and in Galatians 4:6, Paul preserves the Greek transliteration of the Aramaic *Abba*, which Jesus used to address God in his moment of supreme confidence in God (Mark 14:36). Many New Testament commentators regard this Aramaic word, *Abba*, as the *ipsissima vox Jesu* (the precise word Jesus used) in his prayer to God the Father. This mode of addressing God is not found in the Old Testament for any individual Jew. Yet Paul tells us to use it confidently as an actual child of God. Finally, "the Spirit itself bears witness" means that we pray this way not out of presumption or boldness, but because the very word, "Father," is given to us by the Spirit, who moves us to pray in this way to God our Father.

D. Our Internal Teacher in Prayer

"[W]e speak God's wisdom, mysterious, hidden, which . . . none of the rulers of this age knew. . . . But as it is written: 'What eye has not seen, and ear has not heard . . . what God has prepared for those who love him,' this God has revealed to us through the Spirit." (1 Cor. 2:7–10)

Then in v. 11, Paul argues that "no one knows what pertains to God except the Spirit of God." So the Spirit becomes our link between God and us. The Spirit is the key to our understanding the gospel itself, the source of our knowledge about the hidden wisdom of God: "We have received . . . the Spirit that is from God, so that we may understand the things freely given us by God." (v. 12) This hidden wisdom is primarily the mystery of God's redemption by means of a crucified Christ; there is no end to our further understanding of this mystery. The Spirit is given to us just for that purpose and teaches us most effectively in meditation.

E. God's Love in Us

"[T]he love of God has been poured out into our hearts through the holy Spirit that has been given to us." (Rom. 5:5)

Paul is not speaking about our own love for God, as many older commentators thought, but about God's love for us, as the following sentence makes clear: "God proves his love for us, in that while we were still sinners Christ died for us." (5:8) For Paul, the gift of the Spirit in baptism and in our experience is not only a proof of God's love for us (Gal. 4:6) but also the medium of the outpouring of God's love (Rom. 8:15–17). This love of God is poured out in the human "heart," precisely because his Spirit resides there. God and his love are present by means of the Spirit; because the very nature of God is love, God pours out his nature, his Spirit, as our permanent possession. Most of our prayer can be centered on God's love for us; with the help of his Spirit we can "know him more clearly and love him more dearly."

CHAPTER NINE

John

∞

A. The Paraclete as the New Presence of Jesus

In chapters 14 through 16 of John's Gospel, Jesus tells the disciples that the Spirit is to come from God after Jesus has returned to the Father.

Jesus can no longer be with them, but the Spirit of Jesus will dwell with them forever. As such, the Spirit is clearly a personal presence—the ongoing presence of Jesus. Indeed, the Spirit will perform the same functions as Jesus did: to teach them, to be their advocate in trials, to intercede for them with God, to guide them, to encourage them.

All Jesus' references to the Paraclete are found in five passages. They present us with the most profound teaching about the Spirit in all of Scripture. Let us study each passage with the emphasis on what the Paraclete means for us in our own personal prayer.

B. "Another Advocate to Be with You Always"

Jesus promises here that this Advocate will be "with you always . . . will remain with you and will be in you." (14:16–17) This is what Jesus means when he tells the disciples, "I will not leave you orphans;

I will come to you" (14:18); that is, "I will come to you" in the person of the Spirit. Jesus can no longer be with them, but the Spirit of Jesus will dwell with them forever. In this first saying about the Paraclete Jesus establishes only the foundation for the whole work of the Paraclete: that the Spirit will dwell with them and in them as their own personal guest; the Spirit will be with them permanently as the new presence of Jesus.

In this first saying, then, we know very little beyond this amazing promise: the Paraclete will be our own internal presence, the new presence of Jesus, and will act as "the Spirit of truth." But that in itself is most important for our prayer life: to know that the same internal presence of the Spirit of Jesus will be within us and within every believer; the Paraclete is our own personal possession; the very Spirit of Jesus is with us always. Though we never saw Jesus in the flesh, we now possess him and know him in his Spirit. We can relate to this Spirit just as we would relate to Jesus. In terms of our prayer, then, we should not only imagine Jesus as the risen Lord, far removed from us, but we can pray to this Spirit of Jesus as intimately and individually present within us. What a powerful gift this is for our prayer life! Our whole spirituality can be described simply as a personal, intimate relationship to Jesus as "the Way, the Truth and the Life"; and this one assurance of Jesus tells us that this Spirit of Jesus is the real, personal, intimate link with Jesus himself.

C. "The Advocate Will Teach You Everything."

Very clearly, Jesus tells us here (14:26) that a primary function of his Spirit is to help us understand more and more the great mystery of Jesus' word and work; his very purpose is to make the teaching of Jesus penetrate our hearts so that it becomes ever more a part of us. This teaching function of the Spirit has two parts to it: to "teach you everything," and to "remind you of all I told you." The first function, **teaching**, in John's Gospel is practically a verb of revelation. And his whole Gospel stresses the necessity of making Jesus' teaching internal with an ever increasing faith. Note, for example, in the chapter following this (chap. 15), Jesus teaches the strong metaphor of the vine and the branches: "I am the vine, you are the branches. Whoever remains in me . . . will bear much fruit. Anyone who does not remain in me, will be thrown out like a branch and wither." (John 15:5–6; see also John 8:31 and 2 John 9) This is exactly the work of the Spirit here: to teach what Jesus taught and cause it to enter into our hearts so that Jesus' teaching attains its full effect in us.

The work of the Spirit is also one of **reminding**, as John explains in a couple of passages. Only after the resurrection did the disciples grasp what Jesus had said to them earlier; that is, they remembered or were reminded of what Jesus had told them and now understood the real meaning of it. For example, in 2:22: "when [Jesus] was raised from the dead, his disciples remembered that he said this, and they came to believe the scripture and the word Jesus had spoken." (See also 12:16; 13:7; 14:29; 16:4.) In these cases the disciples remembered what Jesus had said to them and were able to grasp the meaning of them in the light of faith.

The Spirit can do much the same for us; Jesus' words also relate to us and to the Spirit helping us to understand more deeply what Jesus taught us in Scripture. And he can help us remember certain words of Jesus as they relate to our own struggles to follow in his way. Much of the time that deeper understanding comes primarily through our meditating on Jesus' life; so in all our prayer and meditation we can confidently depend on the Spirit to "teach [us] everything and remind [us] of all" that Jesus taught.

D. "[The Spirit] Will Testify to Me."

"When the Advocate comes, whom I will send you from the Father, the Spirit of truth that proceeds from the Father, he will testify to me. And you also testify, because you have been with me from the beginning." (John 15:26–27)

This saying mentions a very different function of the Spirit of truth: to testify, to help bear witness to Jesus. This activity of the Paraclete is very much in keeping with his title, "Paraclete," for both the Greek word and the Latin equivalent, *Advocatus*, have a legal connotation. But here in John, the Spirit's witness is not directed primarily to the world, but rather to the disciples themselves ("The Advocate whom I will send you"); specifically, the work of the Spirit is to preserve them from scandal and doubt, to enlighten them in the midst of adversity, and to strengthen them in their faith in the face of the world's hostility (see John 15:18–25; 16:1–4). In all of this, Christ promises that the Spirit will provide them with strong assurance in their Christian faith.

Today, we experience similar struggles in our unbelieving world, such as a multicultured society, the holding of different sets of values, the "enlightened" mockery of some scientists, the philosophical rejection of God because of pervasive human suffering, the modern attacks against the historical Jesus, the skepticism of some radical scriptural approaches. These modern scandals seem to imply that our faith in Jesus is naive or simplistic or not worthy of our enlightened age. A weak faith can be easily threatened or undermined by the opinions of science, of philosophy, of extreme scriptural approaches. In such an atmosphere, we can rely on the witness of the Spirit of Truth to strengthen us in our faith and provide us with rocklike assurance. Such witness by the Spirit is an internal strengthening in our deepest center. And since much of our serious reflection on the life and meaning of Jesus comes to us during our prayer, we can rely on him to testify for us about Jesus in our prayer: "the Spirit of truth will testify to me. And you also testify."

E. "The Advocate . . . Will Convict the World."

"[W]hen [the Advocate] comes he will convict the world in regard to sin and righteousness and condemnation: sin, because they do not believe in me; righteousness, because I am going to the Father . . . condemnation, because the ruler of this world has been condemned." (John 16:8–11)

Jesus promises again that the Paraclete will fulfill his appropriate role as Advocate. However, as we saw above, the primary work of the Paraclete will not be public but rather within the personal conscience of the disciples, for here too Jesus makes this promise of the

Spirit's help for the disciples. (See the context: John 16:1–7, for example, "that you may not fall away.") He means that the Spirit will strengthen the disciples interiorly and give them the confidence that the truth is on Jesus' side. In particular, the Paraclete will show them that sin is on the side of the world, justice is on the side of Jesus, and the one to be condemned is the prince of this world.

In our lives today, Jesus' promise means that the Spirit will testify within us by helping us overcome any confusion or doubt in our prayer, so that we may believe wholeheartedly in this kind of Savior: one who does not wipe out the evils of the world but instead overcomes them by his suffering and death and his promise of eternal life. The Spirit's very presence will assure us that Jesus is victorious over sin and death and that all the horrible evils of the world do not contradict the goodness and love of God. In addition, the Spirit will give us confidence that no sin is beyond the forgiveness of God, that "nothing shall separate us from the love of God." These are the kinds of considerations that naturally come to mind at times in our prayer; with the Spirit of Jesus we can face them with confidence.

F. "The Spirit . . . Will Guide You along the Way of All Truth."

"[T]he Spirit . . . will guide you to all truth. He will not speak on his own, but he will speak what he hears, and will declare to you the things that are coming." (John 16:13)

The last saying about the Paraclete is similar to that in 14:26; it also mentions the functions of teaching and calling to mind. But it develops them somewhat differently in two ways. First, the phrase is v. 13 is slightly different: "[the Spirit] will guide you to all truth." Notice that in Johannine terminology, "spirit," "way," and "truth" seem to have some of the Old Testament implication of a moral path. Second, Jesus adds: "[the Spirit] will declare to you the things that are coming." So the Spirit's guidance seems to involve more than a deeper intellectual understanding; it also involves a way of life in conformity with Jesus' teaching. This does not relate to any new revelation, but rather to interpreting the significance of what Jesus has said and done for each coming generation. The more we understand the way of Jesus, the more we understand things that "are to come" from a Christian perspective.

This final Paraclete saying seems ideally suited to our prayer, especially meditation on the life of Jesus. For when we meditate on Jesus' life and teaching, we don't stop at knowing Jesus; we also ask the Spirit to help us follow in the way of Jesus. Also, we want our prayer to be related to the world around us and its effect on us. The Spirit is given to us particularly to help us apply Jesus' teaching as we give witness to our world and manifest a Christian attitude toward all these changing times, values, and life situations.

G. "Whatever You Ask the Father in My Name, He Will Give You."

"Amen, amen, I say to you, whatever you ask the Father in my name he will give you. Until now you have not asked anything in my name; ask and you shall receive. . . . The hour is coming . . . when you will ask in my name." (John 16:23–26)

This quote is part of a longer passage (vv. 20–28) that follows immediately after the five Paraclete sayings. All of vv. 20–26 deal with what will happen to the disciples "on that day" (vv. 23a and 26) after Jesus has risen and sent the Paraclete. According to Raymond Brown, this entire section came to be understood in the Johannine Gospel context as relating to the privileges of Christian existence after the resurrection: "in Johannine thought . . . the Paraclete is given by the risen Jesus precisely as a way to make permanent his glorified presence among his disciples, now that his place is with the Father."[1] Jesus mentions four privileges, all interconnected, which flow from the intimate presence of Jesus in the Paraclete. The first (vv. 20–22) promises lasting joy: "a little while and you will see me . . . [and] your grief will become joy"; the second (v. 23a) promises knowledge: "On that day you will not question me about anything"; the third (vv. 23b, 24, 26) promises the granting of all their petitions: "whatever you ask the Father in my name, he will give you"; and the fourth (v. 25) promises clear knowledge of the Father: "I will no longer speak to you in figures but I will tell you clearly about the Father."

The entire passage has a definite connection to John's treatment of the Paraclete. That is, after Jesus' resurrection, the disciples will have the continued presence of the Spirit of Jesus, and because of the new presence of the Spirit of Jesus, they will experience joy, deeper knowledge, and confidence in prayer.[2] The direct connection with the Paraclete is very obvious in the second and fourth promises of Jesus, regarding fuller knowledge; for that is exactly the main function of the Paraclete: "He will teach you everything." (14:26)

Let us look only at the third privilege (vv. 23–26, above), which deals directly with our prayer life:

V. 24: "Until now you have not asked anything in my name." Jesus has not been their intercessor with the Father while he was with them. After Jesus' resurrection and the sending of the Paraclete, the disciples will be united with the risen Jesus by means of the Paraclete and can then "ask anything in [Jesus'] name."

V. 23: "On that day [after the Paraclete comes] . . . whatever you ask the Father in my name he will give you." That is, the disciples will be so intimately united with the Spirit of Jesus that their requests will surely be granted. The connection between the coming of the Paraclete and the prayers of the disciples being heard is clearer in chapter 14.

In that parallel passage, Jesus promises that the prayers of the disciples will always be heard: "If you ask [the Father] anything in my name, I will do it." (14:13–14) Then he immediately mentions the gift of the Spirit (14:16–17), apparently so that they can "do the works that I do" (14:12), have their prayers answered in Jesus' name (14:14), and possess the new presence of Jesus in his Spirit (14:16–18).

V. 26: "On that day you will ask in my name." Notice that in v. 13, Jesus promises the disciples "Whatever you ask in my name I will do"; there he explicitly promises that their petitions would be granted. Here in v. 26 the promise is implicit, but now based on the new presence of the Spirit of Jesus. Only when they are so intimately united with the Spirit of Jesus can they have such confidence with the Father.

To paraphrase vv. 23–26 then: Once the Paraclete comes, the disciples will have the Spirit of Jesus as intimately present to them. Though Jesus will still be their Advocate in heaven (cf. 1 John 2:1), now they also have the new Advocate, the Paraclete, who dwells within them and unites them even more intimately with Jesus and with the Father. Therefore, anything that the disciples ask of the Father in Jesus' name will be granted.

Notice the similarity between John's teaching here and Paul's teaching in Romans. Paul assures us that "the Spirit intercedes for the holy ones according to God's will." (Rom. 8:27) That is, the Spirit "comes to the aid of our weakness" and makes our prayer to the Father effective. Here, John tells us "whatever you ask the Father in my name he will give you," because of the new Advocate who dwells within us.

Notes

1. Raymond Brown, *The Gospel According to John, 13–21*, Anchor Bible, vol. 29A (New York: Doubleday, 1966), 730.

2. See the incisive comments of Raymond Brown, ibid., 731–35.

CHAPTER TEN

The Spirit of Jesus and the Stages of Prayer

∞

A. Introduction

One of my favorite stories is about a priest who was visiting Ireland. As he walked along a country road one cloudy evening, he met an old man who was also enjoying the evening air. They walked and talked together for a while, until a sudden downpour of rain made them take shelter. As their conversation ran out, the old Irishman reached into his hip pocket for his little prayer book and bowed his head in prayer. The priest gazed at him for a long while, then quietly said: "You must be very close to God." With a smile he answered the priest: "Yes! the Father is very fond of me."[1]

To be a Christian in more than name means to be personally committed to Christ, to believe wholeheartedly in Christ, as well as to follow his way of living. We can never do that with a mere rational assent to certain truths or with a mere acceptance of laws and morality. Commitment to Jesus Christ means relating to him as a real person, as one to whom we are attracted personally, as one whom we love as a friend. One of the best ways to allow this to happen is to have personal contact with him in prayer, for it is in prayer that we can personally experience his human appeal.

Jesus' very purpose of sending us the Holy Spirit is that his Spirit might "teach us everything": "The Advocate, the holy Spirit . . . will teach you everything and remind you of all that I told you." (John 16:26) From what we already explained about Scripture, we can expect the Spirit of Jesus to be our guide in all our praying. Whatever our prayer life has been or is now, we can depend on the help of the Spirit of Jesus.

The various kinds of prayer and stages of prayer, developed below, may help us to understand how the Holy Spirit can "lead [us] into all truth." What Scripture tells us about the Spirit and prayer is universally applicable to any stage of prayer. But some graces of the Spirit are more helpful in vocal prayer, while other gifts are more necessary in meditation or contemplation. So when we mention some Scripture quote about the Spirit of Jesus at one stage of prayer, we are merely choosing to emphasize that particular saying as very fitting in that case; we do not intend to limit its application in any way.

B. Vocal Prayer

Vocal prayer, especially prayer of petition, is most familiar to us. In all the Gospels, Jesus assures us that God will hear our prayer when we ask him for help. In Luke he is most emphatic:

> I tell you, ask and you will receive; seek and you will find; knock and the door will be opened to you. For everyone who asks, receives; the one who seeks, finds; and to the one who knocks, the door will be opened. . . . If you . . . know how to give good gifts to your children, how much more will the Father in heaven give the holy Spirit to those who ask him? (Luke 11:9–13)

In this and other quotes, Jesus seems to promise a universal answer to our prayers of petition; that is, whatever we ask for in prayer properly will be granted. But only Luke adds the final clause: "how much more will God give the holy Spirit to those who ask him?" Surely we can have even more trust that God will answer our prayer if what we ask for is to receive the grace of the Spirit.

Richard Rohr comments on this passage in Luke with a similar insight:

> Pray for bread, fish or egg, pray for whatever you want. God might give you these things, but what God promises is that you will always receive the Holy Spirit. That is God's answer to every prayer and to every question.[2]

Paul also connects the Spirit with confidence in prayer: "the Spirit too comes to the aid of our weakness; for we do not know how to pray as we ought [but the Spirit] intercedes for the holy ones according to God's will." (Rom. 8:26–27) Paul's point is that the Spirit can "intercede for us according to the will of God" so that God will certainly hear us, not necessarily by giving us exactly what we pray for, but by helping us fulfill the will of God above all.

Pope John Paul II notes that the Holy Spirit can help us know our weaknesses and strengthen our desire to serve God:

> In prayer . . . with God our Father, we can discern better where our strengths and weaknesses are, because the Spirit comes to our aid. The same Spirit speaks to us and slowly immerses us in the divine mysteries, in God's design of love for humanity, which he realizes through our willingness to serve him.[3]

Probably the most frequent form of praise and worship is that done by the Christian community at prayer, especially our weekly Eucharistic liturgy. When Paul encourages the Corinthians to use the charisms of the Spirit for the good of the church, he refers especially to their common worship. He reminds them that "in one Spirit we were all baptized into one body" (1 Cor. 12:13) so "when you meet as a church" (1 Cor. 11:18), each must use whatever charism the Spirit gives him/her for the common good (1 Cor. 12:7). Even with such wondrous gifts of the Holy Spirit, they can only worship God worthily if they maintain their unity in his Spirit. What Paul might say to us in this period of history is that whatever ministry each of us carries out with the help of the Spirit in Sunday worship, we should carry out that ministry in such a way as to build up the body of Christ.

C. Mental Prayer in General

Most Catholics also practice one or another kind of mental prayer. Many of us pray our own personal reflective prayer during mass or after communion. Others have spent years of their lives in formal meditation: those who have been in a seminary or religious order or who have read books on prayer studied and practiced specific forms of meditation. Whatever our history of prayer, let us consider Christian prayer specifically as aided by the Spirit of Jesus.

Spiritual writers have traditionally described seven stages of mental prayer. As we review them, you may recognize yourself in some of these stages at different moments in your life. The classical spiritual writer, Lehodey, offers this incisive summary of these stages of mental prayer:

> [T]he ways of mental prayer exhibit an admirable progression. Vocal prayer consists altogether in formulas and words, recited however with attention and devotion . . . ; meditation is more interior, but still it requires quite a din of reasoning; affective prayer simplifies the work of the mind; the prayer of simplicity simplifies even that of the will; and prayer ends [in the later stages] by becoming at least occasionally, hardly anything more than a loving attention to God, and the soul has become a most silent sanctuary; God, who fills this sanctuary, makes his presence mysteriously felt. . . . His action at first affects only a portion of the soul's faculties, afterwards it affects all of them. . . . Such is the logical development and the ordinary order of ascent in the ways of prayer.[4]

As we take a closer look at each stage of prayer, our focus will be very limited; that is, a succinct description of that form of prayer will be given, followed by some comments on how the Holy Spirit can encourage or inspire us in that particular form of prayer. Some of these stages will include a suggested example of prayer, which might help us see the connection between the particular Scripture quote about the Spirit and that particular stage of prayer.

D. Meditation

The first stage of mental prayer is called simply meditation. It consists of considerations, affections, petitions, and resolutions on some spiritual topic: a short passage of Scripture, an incident in the life of Christ, one particular Christian virtue, or the example of a saint. Some refer to this stage of prayer as discursive prayer, or prayer of reasoning, because considerations and reasoning play a major part in it.

Meditation has many forms. We may already have our own personal form of reflection that suits us well. Whatever method we use, we might recall Paul's reminder: "Do you not know that your members are the temple of the holy Spirit, who is in you, whom you have from God?" (1 Cor. 6:19) Our meditation can be more intimate if we concentrate on the one dwelling within us; the Spirit is able to teach us the way of Jesus because he is our permanent, loving guest. St. Augustine tells us that this Holy Spirit is *"intimior intimo meo"* (more intimate than my own conscious self); that is, the Spirit is the intimate presence of God who wants to teach and inspire us. Such is the description of mental prayer given by St. Teresa of Avila: "Mental prayer in my opinion is nothing else than an intimate sharing between friends; it means taking time frequently to be alone with Him who we know loves us."[5]

The emphasis in this stage of prayer is definitely on using our reasoning powers, on trying to learn the truth about Christ our model and learning more and more about his way. Christ himself tells us that all of this is precisely the work of the Spirit of Jesus: "The Advocate, the holy Spirit . . . will teach you everything and remind you of all that [I] told you." (John 14:26) Our confidence in mental prayer comes not from our own abilities alone but from the promises of Jesus about his Spirit, who is our personal teacher.

What should be the object of our meditation? What topics should we choose? One answer is: anything at all—Scripture, spiritual books, saints, virtues, truths of our faith, personal challenges. However, there comes a time for each of us when our prayer quite naturally tends to center more and more on Jesus himself. For Jesus—in his life, his teaching and his person—is the entire revelation of God for us. As Colossians describes him: "He is the image of the invisible God. . . . Christ, in whom are hidden all the treasures of wisdom and knowledge." (Col. 1:15; 2:3) And John repeatedly presents Jesus as the very person of truth (John 8:26, 32; 14, 6), the Word of God (John 1:1–14). Therefore, in meditation there is nothing greater that the Spirit can teach us than Jesus, who is the entire revelation about God for us.

There are many books on meditation and numerous methods from which to choose. We are free to choose whatever works for us. Our goal is to choose a style in which we eventually focus on Jesus. One caution, however, from St. John of the Cross, the Mystical Doctor, is that we not set our hearts on supernatural charisms, or private revelations, or visions from God. John of the Cross has a wonderful answer to those seeking visions or private revelations. One suggestion for our meditation is to use his strong counsel:

Suggestion for Prayer
Any person questioning God or desiring some vision or revelation would be guilty . . . of foolish behavior . . . by not fixing his eye entirely upon Christ. . . . [To such a person] God could respond as follows: If I have already told you all things in my Word, my Son, and if I have no other word, what answer or revelation can I now make that would surpass this? Fasten your eyes on him alone, because in him I have spoken and revealed all, and in him you shall discover even more than you ask for or desire. Since that day when I descended upon him with my Spirit on Mount Tabor proclaiming, "This is my beloved Son in whom I am well pleased, hear him," . . . he is my entire locution and response, vision and revelation . . . ; behold him well, for in him you will uncover all these revelations already made, and many more besides.[6]

E. Affective Prayer

As the will and affections become dominant in our mental prayer, we are experiencing another stage of mental prayer, called affective prayer. Ordinarily, we first begin to meditate by using our reasoning powers to gain knowledge and convictions about Christ and his way. Once those convictions grow and take root, we tend to spend less prayer time on them, and we naturally turn to affections, desires, and acts of love. As we gain knowledge of Christian truths and have reasoned through all the truths of our faith, we need less time for careful reasoning in order to find Christ. St. Francis de Sales, the great spiritual director, is very helpful here regarding affective prayer. He is aware that many people who meditate follow some definite method, involving much rational thought and considerations. If they find a growing difficulty doing such discursive prayer, he suggests they might follow their inclinations and pray more simply with their affections:

> Many deceive themselves thinking that to pray well, much method is necessary; and they . . . seek a system which they think is indispensable. . . . What I say is that the soul should not be completely tied to them, as happens to some who never think they have made their prayer well if they do not go through the considerations before the affections the Lord gives them.[7]

St. Teresa of Avila describes this form of prayer simply: "with great humility speak to Him as to a father. Beseech Him as you would a father; tell him about your trials; ask him for a remedy against them."[8]

Suggestion for Prayer
Lord God, Paul teaches us to pray as your son/daughter; we know that we are your children because we have the Spirit of your own Son in our hearts who cries out "*Abba*, Father." How can you not hear your children? How can you not hear the Holy Spirit "who intercedes for [us] as God wills?" How can you not hear us who echo the cry of Jesus himself, "*Abba*, Father?" You, Lord, have shown us the whole truth in your Son. You have no other wisdom or revelation to give us than Jesus, who is your Word. I look for no other answers, no other expression of who you are, no other truth to believe than Jesus. To see the Son is to see you, the Father; to know him is to know you; to believe in him is to gain eternal life with you.

Another Suggestion for Affective Prayer

The sequence for the feast of Pentecost is one long affective prayer. At this stage of prayer, it can be particularly appropriate and helpful:

> Come, Holy Spirit, come!
> And from your celestial home
> Shed a ray of light divine.
>
> Come, Father of the poor!
> Come, source of all our store!
> Come within our bosoms shine!
>
> You, of comforters the best;
> You, the soul's most welcome guest;
> Sweet refreshment here below;
>
> In our labor, rest most sweet;
> Grateful coolness in the heat;
> Solace in the midst of woe.
>
> O most blessed Light divine,
> Shine within these hearts of thine,
> And our inmost being fill!
>
> Where you are not, we have naught,
> Nothing good in deed or thought,
> Nothing free from taint of ill.
>
> Heal our wounds, our strength renew;
> On our dryness pour your dew,
> Wash the stains of guilt away.
>
> Bend the stubborn heart and will;
> Melt the frozen, warm the chill;
> Guide the steps that go astray.
>
> On the faithful who adore
> And confess you evermore
> In your sev'nfold gifts descend.
>
> Give them virtue's true reward;
> Give them your salvation, Lord;
> Give them joys that never end.
> Amen. Alleluia.

F. Prayer of Faith

Simple prayer or the prayer of faith is the third stage of mental prayer. Many other forms of prayer happily flourishing today seem to belong to this stage of prayer. Some examples are: centering prayer, praying with an oft-repeated mantra or sacred word, and attentive or receptive prayer, or so-called acquired contemplation. Any one of these methods can be most helpful at this stage of prayer. This simple prayer of faith is a natural development to our prayer, because once we have meditated for some time on the truths of our faith, we have no need to continue in the same fashion. Rather, our prayer becomes naturally more simple, with less and less intellectual work or affective response.

For many, this can be a difficult period, for we are no longer in control of our own reflections or filled with the delightful affections of beginners. The romantic stage of our prayer has almost disappeared. Spiritual writers try to assure us that this is an entirely normal development of prayer.

> In the early stages of the interior life, considerations occupy a large place, because we have need to strengthen our faith; later on . . . considerations progressively diminish, and end by giving place to a simple thought, to a simple attentive look.
> On the other hand, affections . . . go on increasing; they gain all the ground that considerations lose; they, too, are after a time simplified . . . and the soul ends by attaching itself to a few affections only, which suffice for its needs and attractions.[9]

I personally found this prayer of faith a dark one, for once my rational efforts of prayer became insufficient, I experienced less and less satisfaction in intellectual activity. I needed to be assured that there was nothing wrong with such a state, that everything was developing naturally. It took a long time to realize that only when my reasoning activity became quiet and my affections dried up, could I really listen in silence and be attentive to the Spirit.

This kind of simple prayer prepares us for a new kind of knowledge, a new openness to the Spirit. In fact our very darkness and inability to pray as before is leading us to depend on the Holy Spirit to intercede in our stead: "the Spirit too comes to the aid of our weakness; for . . . the Spirit itself intercedes with inexpressible groanings." (Rom. 8:26) These words of Paul can be particularly encouraging in this stage of prayer. For they tell us we can have much hope, even when we are not able to pray as before. That is, when all is dark, the Holy Spirit prays in our place with great desire for union with God.

Suggestion for Prayer
Spirit of Jesus, my prayer now is void of images, reasonings, and affections. The wonderful insights and affections that were so much a part of my prayers for some time have all deserted me now. Yet I have come to believe that this darkness is my friend, for only in the dark can your new light be seen. You have taught me that this silence is the way to wisdom, for only in quiet can your gentle voice be heard; this emptiness is very receptive, for the more I see my emptiness, the more you will fill it; this weakness is my strength, for only when I know my weakness will you give me your power. So I will try to rest peacefully in this darkness and be attentive to your inspiration. I will remain here; you plead to God for me "with inexpressible groanings." Only your presence within me as my faithful teacher and companion gives me confidence that you will "lead me to all truth."

G. Contemplative Prayer

The first three stages of prayer are considered ordinary or active prayer, because we advance in them with ordinary grace and light of the Holy Spirit. But the last four stages of prayer are called mystical or passive prayer, because we can only pray this way with the special, infused grace of the Holy Spirit. In these four stages of contemplation, we deliberately set aside our own active senses, imaginations, reasoning, and affections and strive to remain attentive and open to the gifts of the Spirit. St. John of the Cross encourages us in several quotes like this:

> The principal agent and guide and mover of souls in this matter [at the beginning of contemplation] is . . . the Holy Spirit. . . . when the

soul achieves emptiness and surrender of [all reasoning, affection, and any natural activity] it is impossible, if the soul as much as in it lies, that God should fail to perform his own part by communicating himself . . . at least secretly and in silence.[10]

For all these forms of contemplation, John of the Cross would encourage us to rely on the Holy Spirit; he urges us to be most confident because "it is impossible . . . that God should fail to [communicate] himself at least secretly and in silence." Here John clearly and simply distinguishes ordinary mental prayer from contemplation: instead of relying on our own rational faculties and efforts, we rely on the infused wisdom of the Holy Spirit, for the Spirit is our "principal agent and guide and mover" in all of contemplative prayer.

Why is it necessary to make this transition to another kind of prayer? Why must we progress from our own activity and knowledge to another kind of knowing, a passive dependence on the Holy Spirit? St. Thomas Aquinas helps to answer such questions by distinguishing two kinds of knowledge—and so two kinds of prayer. One kind of knowledge is **acquired** by the process of scientific inquiry or more simply by our natural experience, understanding, and judging. In this kind of knowledge, there is "nothing in the intellect which was not first in the senses" (as both Aristotle and Aquinas taught). The second kind of knowledge is **infused** by the Holy Spirit; it does not come from our exterior senses but is directly infused by God. This knowledge comes to us *sine medio*, without the mediation of sensible images; that is, God works on the human person directly, infusing into the heart knowledge or love. Notice how Paul connects the love of God and the Spirit: "The love of God is poured into our hearts by the holy Spirit" (Rom. 5:5); Paul means that God's love for us is infused ("poured into our hearts by the holy Spirit"); and God's love, then, naturally causes or infuses our love for him. This quote seems to be the original reason why we call mystical prayer infused contemplation.

John of the Cross also follows Thomas Aquinas in explaining these two kinds of prayer. Again and again he counsels those who can no longer pray in the old way—with images, reasonings, and affections—that they must leave all that behind, because none of those natural activities can act as intermediaries for us with God. Rather we should let the Spirit of Truth take over our prayer and lead us to a knowledge of God without intermediaries. He describes this process from ordinary prayer to infused prayer this way:

> [A]ll the movements and operations and inclinations which the soul had before, and which belonged to the . . . strength of its natural life, are now in this union changed into divine movements. . . . For the soul . . . is moved wholly by the Spirit of God. . . . So the understanding of this soul is now the understanding of God; and its will is the will of God and its memory is the memory of God.[11]

* * * * * * *

In John's Gospel, the five Paraclete sayings of Jesus can help guide us into infused prayer. For the main thrust of Jesus' promise of the Paraclete is that the Spirit will teach us everything we need to know about Jesus and his way; the Spirit will abide with us and guide us to all truth. Certainly that includes the infused wisdom of the Spirit of Truth, which is the most sublime and complete knowledge we can ever learn. Infused knowledge can **only** come to us by means of the Spirit of Truth within us. All of these works of the Paraclete are active and effective during our prayer, especially during contemplative prayer. Every time we begin our prayer—especially contemplative prayer—we can begin by remembering these wonderful promises of Jesus and praying with great assurance.

These promises of Jesus will also help us when we encounter darkness, weakness, or aridity in our contemplation. The very nature of contemplative prayer drives us to rely on the Spirit of Jesus, for the essential nature of this prayer involves the infused wisdom of the Holy Spirit. So the way we prayed before—with images, reasonings, and affections—can no longer be our common way of praying; none of those natural activities can act as intermediaries for us with God. Rather, we need the secret wisdom of the Holy Spirit to take over our prayer, as John of the Cross explains:

This communication [through contemplation] is secret and dark to the work of the intellect and the other faculties. Insofar as these faculties do not acquire it but the Holy Spirit infuses it and puts it in order in the soul, . . . the soul neither knows nor understands how this comes to pass and thus calls it secret.[12]

In time, the Spirit of Truth will take over our prayer and lead us to a knowledge and love of God without the work of our intellect and natural faculties. The Paraclete will open up the door to a whole new world of knowledge and love of God. So in all of the stages of contemplation, our singular effort is to be quiet and attentive; in the early stages, our usual sense of God's presence will be dark and unsatisfying; we will feel weak, helpless, and empty. This is the only way we can learn not to rely on our rational faculties but on the Spirit of Jesus.

Progressively, in the early stages of contemplation (the prayer of quiet and the prayer of union) the Spirit raises us "from the darkness of **natural** knowledge to the morning light of the **supernatural** knowledge of God—not brightly, but darkly, like the night at the . . . rising of the dawn."[13] And finally, "this flame of love . . . which is the Holy Spirit"[14] transforms the soul with the light of knowledge and the warmth of love.

H. The Prayer of Quiet

The prayer of quiet is the fourth stage of mental prayer. The terms "quiet" and "repose" mean that the mind ceases from discursive acts and affections while the spirit remains tranquil, receptive, quietly waiting on God in a dark but open state. Because our mind, will, and affections are not active, we often experience a sense of profound aridity. And since we are just beginning to attune ourselves to the working of the Holy Spirit, we are left with an unsatisfying and obscure recollection. In the early experiences of this prayer of quiet, we have only a vague sense that God is present in an ineffable manner. We need to trust that, as John of the Cross strongly insists, the Holy Spirit is "the chief agent, guide and mover of souls,"[15] especially in contemplation.

When St. Paul reminds us "the Spirit too comes to the aid of our weakness" (Rom. 8:26), his counsel is never more necessary than in this dark beginning of contemplation. Paul himself describes the principal lesson he learned regarding prayer and life in Christ: "a thorn of the flesh was given me. . . . Three times I begged the Lord about this, that it might leave me, but he said to me, 'My grace is sufficient for you, for power is made perfect in weakness.'" (2 Cor. 12:7–10) He came to understand only slowly and painfully that God grants his great graces only to those who know they have no power, no claim on God's mercy. His experience of his weakness and utter need led to his singular trust in the Spirit: "the Spirit comes to the aid of our weakness."

Suggestion for Prayer
Holy Spirit, faithful teacher, like St. Paul with his "thorn of the flesh" I feel a great darkness and inability to pray and beg that this "might leave me." After all these months/years of prayer, I feel like I am standing before a wall; my prayer is more and more simple and dark; I am more and more helpless and weak. Tell me what to do.

RESPONSE: "My grace is sufficient for you, for power is made perfect in weakness"; just because you know your weakness, you are prepared for a new way of prayer. You are not just up against a wall; you are in front of a door in that wall. What you are experiencing now in prayer is not wrong at all; rather it is just where you should be. This experience is entirely natural, following the usual way of simplification of prayer; it is an integral part of development in prayer, a necessary stage. For it is impossible to achieve direct union with God by any natural operation of your senses or intellect. You have come to the point where you can clearly understand that you must suspend these activities. Only then can I begin to infuse a whole new mode of knowledge, a direct experience of God. All you need is to be receptive and open, and I will "lead you to all truth."

I. Prayer of Union

Now we come to the fifth stage, called union or simple union. In this simple union, we neither see nor understand anything clearly but remain united with God. Personal labor is reduced to almost nothing; God himself does almost everything. We are confident of the presence of God within us, but the contact remains subtle and dark. We might define this stage as an intimate union of the soul with God, accompanied by the suspension of all the interior faculties along with a vague sense of God's presence within the soul. God communicates with the soul directly, though tenuously. He infuses himself almost imperceptibly into the soul.

John of the Cross encourages us again and again to persevere in this prayer of union, for the action of the Holy Spirit is so subtle and unsatisfying:

> [T]he blessings this silent communication and contemplation impresses on the soul, without its then experiencing them . . . are inestimable; for they are most hidden unctions of the Holy Spirit and hence most delicate, and they secretly fill the soul with spiritual riches.[16]

Infused contemplation and deep knowledge of God is another facet of Christ's promise to us: "When the Spirit of truth has come, he will teach you everything and guide you to all truth." (John 14:26; 16:13) Certainly "everything" and "all truth" include this wonderful completion of our knowledge and love of God.

John of the Cross now approaches this work of the Spirit from a different angle; he speaks of the Holy Spirit as the forerunner or quartermaster who prepares the soul for Christ's new form of constant presence: "In this breathing of the Holy Spirit through the soul, which is the Holy Spirit's visit of love . . . the Son of God is himself sublimely communicated. He sends his Spirit to act as his quartermaster, to prepare his dwelling."[17]

Suggestion for Prayer
Lord Jesus, fill me with your Spirit, for you want your Spirit "to lead [me] in the way of all truth." Your way of truth leads only into transformation in love. I will wait for this consummation in love with confidence, for you want this more than I do. I do not seek any ecstatic experience, for that can so easily mislead me, and that is not the essence of complete union with you. I do not seek any new revelation,

for you, Lord, are the whole revelation of God. I do not seek intellectual clarity, but only an intimate absorption with you in love. Come, Lord Jesus. May your Spirit lead me "into all truth," and into loving you completely.

J. Full Union

The sixth stage of prayer is called full union, meaning that in this stage the senses are suspended and the soul is fully absorbed in God. The certitude of God's presence attains a wonderful degree of intensity. St. Teresa of Avila prefers the term "ecstatic union," which emphasizes the external ecstasy that often accompanied her prayer. St. John of the Cross uses the term "spiritual espousal," meaning that in this prayer the Holy Spirit actively purifies the soul greatly and prepares it for transforming union with God.

For John of the Cross, spiritual espousal already brings about an outline of Christ, an imperfect sketch of Christ in the soul in terms of her knowledge and love for Christ:

> [T]hese [divine] truths are infused by faith into her intellect. And since knowledge of them is imperfect, she says they are sketched. Just as a sketch is not a perfect painting, so the knowledge of faith is not perfect knowledge. . . . [Similarly] when there is union of love, the image of the beloved is so sketched in the will and drawn so intimately and vividly, that it is true to say that the beloved lives in the lover.[18]

John likes to use terms such as "sketch," "outline," "imperfect image of Christ" in describing this spiritual espousal; for then he quite naturally describes the final stage of spiritual marriage as perfecting the painting or image of Christ in the soul. For me, the best image John of the Cross finds to describe the effects of this spiritual espousal is that of an outline of Christ himself now formed in the soul: "This is the meaning of St. Paul's affirmation: 'I live now not I, but Christ lives in me.' [Gal. 2:20] In saying, 'I live now not I,' he meant that even though he had life, it was not his, because he was transformed in Christ, and it was divine more than human."[19]

Suggestion for Prayer
Loving Jesus, you are the life for me to live, so that with Paul I might say, "I live now, not I, but Christ lives in me." (Gal. 2:20) As you were united with the Father even in your humanity, so you invite me to be transformed into you. As your words and wisdom were only your Father's, so you want me to know and express your words. As your works and power were all dependent on your Father, so any spiritual power I have is yours; without you I can do nothing. As you came only "to do the will of [your] Father," so I want only "your kingdom come, your will be done." As you abided in your Father's love, so you want me to "abide in [your] love." As you were totally united with the Father, so you want me to be transformed into you in love. Without you, Lord, I am nothing; when I surrender to you and depend on your life of grace, I fulfill my whole life.

K. Transforming Union

We come to the final stage of prayer, which spiritual writers call transforming union or spiritual marriage. In this stage, God takes hold of the soul in a more perfect and permanent way. All the powers of the soul feel permanently bound to God in a calm, loving, and abiding union. The soul loves God by means of the Holy Spirit: "in the perfect transformation of this state of spiritual marriage . . . the soul . . . loves in some way through the Holy Spirit who is given [Rom. 5:5] in this transformation of love."[20] That is, God's love is "poured out by the holy Spirit who is given to us"; and this love moves us to love God in return, also by the work of the Spirit. When spiritual writers speak of this stage as a spiritual marriage, they mean a permanent consummation of union in love between the soul and God so that it feels permanently embraced by God. St. John of the Cross adds that in this state:

> [The soul's] entire aim in all her works is the consummation . . . of this state. . . . She finds in this state a much greater abundance and fullness of God, a more secure and stable peace, and an incomparably more perfect delight . . . ; here it is as though she were placed in the arms of her Bridegroom.[21]

Suggestion for Prayer
Lord Jesus, you promised: "the holy Spirit . . . will teach you everything and remind you of all that I told you." May your Spirit teach me now what is the goal of all prayer and living in you. You taught this in your own prayer to the Father. Lord just as you, even in your humanity, lived entirely transformed into God your Father, so you invite us to be totally transformed into you. As you were sent into the world as the complete messenger of your Father, so you send us as your disciples: "As you have sent me into the world, so I have sent them into the world." (John 17:18) As the words you spoke were entirely the Word of the Father, so the words we speak are yours: "The words you have given to me I have given to them." (John 17:8) Just as your works were those of your Father, so our works are done in you: "The Father who dwells in me is doing his works . . . [and] whoever believes in me will do the works that I do." (John 14:10–12) Just as you are entirely dependent on your Father and have no power but his, so we are entirely dependent on you and have no power but yours: "The Son can do nothing on his own" (John 5:19); [and similarly] "without me you can do nothing" (John 15:5). Just as you came down from heaven "to do . . . the will of [your Father]" (John 6:38), so we are to keep your commandments as the essence of our love: "Whoever has my commandments and observes them is the one who loves me." (John 14:21) Just as you and the Father were united in love, so we are united in love with you: "As the Father loves me so I also love you. Remain in my love. (John 15:9) Your union with the Father is our model of union with you: "as you, Father are in me and I in you, that they also may be in us." (John 17:21) You abide in the Father as we are to abide in you; your life is wholly in God as ours is to be in you: "Remain in me as I remain in you [and as I] remain in his love. (John 15:4–10) Without you, Lord, we are nothing; when we surrender totally to you, we fulfill our whole human life and become transformed into you.

Notes

1. Edward Farrell, *The Father Is Very Fond of Me* (Denville, NJ: Dimension Books, 1975), 5.

2. Richard Rohr, OSF, "We Need Transformation, Not False Transcendence," *National Catholic Reporter*, February 15, 2002, 13.

3. Pope John Paul II, *The Private Prayers of Pope John Paul II* (New York: Pocket Books, 1994), 116.

4. Dom Vitalis Lehodey, *The Ways of Mental Prayer* (Dublin: M. H. Gill and Son, 1955), 311.

5. St. Teresa of Avila, *Life*, chap. 8, #5, 67. Please note that all the quotes from St. Teresa of Avila will be taken from *The Collected Works of St. Teresa of Avila*, 3 vols., ed. Kieran Kavanaugh, O.C.D. and Otilio Rodriguez, O.C.D. (Washington, DC: ICS Publications, 1976). The chapter and paragraph reference can be found in any version of St. Teresa of Avila's works; the page number, however, will refer only to these collected works.

6. St. John of the Cross, *The Ascent of Mount Carmel*, Book II, 22, 5; 180. Please note that all the quotes from St. John of the Cross will be taken from *The Collected Works of St. John of the Cross*, ed. Kieran Kavanaugh, O.C.D. and Otilio Rodriguez, O.C.D. (Washington, DC: ICS Publications, 1979). The general reference can be found in any version of John of the Cross's works; the page number, however, will refer only to this critical version of Kavanaugh and Rodriguez.

7. St. Francis de Sales, *Direction of Religious*, chap. 45.

8. St. Teresa of Avila, *The Way of Perfection*, chap. 28, 140–41.

9. Lehodey, *The Ways of Mental Prayer* 14.

10. St. John of the Cross, *The Living Flame of Love*, st. 3, #46; 627.

11. Ibid., st. 2, #34; 608.

12. St. John of the Cross, *The Dark Night of the Soul*, Book II, chap. 17, #2; 368.

13. St. John of the Cross, *The Spiritual Canticle*, st. 14–15, #23; 471.

14. St. John of the Cross, *The Living Flame of Love*, st. 1, #3; 580.

15. St. John of the Cross, *The Living Flame of Love*, st. 3, #46;471.

16. St. John of the Cross, *The Living Flame of Love*, st. 3, #40; 625.

17. St. John of the Cross, *The Spiritual Canticle*, st. 17, #8; 481. Note that E. Allison Peers uses the word "forerunner."

18. Ibid., st. 12, #6 and 7; 455.

19. Ibid., #8; 455–56.

20. Ibid., st. 38, #3; 554.

21. Ibid., st. 22, #5; 498.

CHAPTER ELEVEN

Intimacy with God

A. Introduction

After Jesus returned to the Father, the early church felt the great void of his absence. By the time John's Gospel was written, the early Christians struggled with the death of the last of the eyewitnesses of Jesus. Each of our three scripture writers, Luke, Paul, and John, was confronted with crucial questions such as these: How could the following of Jesus survive after he died? How could Christians be drawn to Jesus once the last of the apostles had also departed? How could love for Jesus be real and wholehearted for those who never personally met him? They realized that future generations needed to be brought into a loving relationship to Jesus. They knew that those who chose to follow "the way" would not remain strong unless they encountered Jesus in the community. They understood that people who had never known Jesus during his lifetime needed to experience Jesus himself in real human contact. Luke, Paul, and John saw that beyond the theological arguments for believing in Jesus and belonging to his church, people could only be loyal to the community if they found a personal love for Jesus there. Paul could confidently assert: "The love of Christ impels me." (2 Cor. 5:14) But he, Luke, and John each found unique ways to inspire such an intimate relationship to Jesus. Let us concentrate on some ways these three scripture writers encourage intimacy with Jesus or God. In each instance we will begin with the words of Jesus. And in keeping with the theme of this book, we will emphasize how the Holy Spirit helps us toward this essential intimacy with Jesus.

B. God's Personal Presence (John)

"[The Father] will give you another Advocate to be with you always, the Spirit of truth. . . .You know it because it remains with you, and will be in you." (John 14:16–17)

Jesus promises here that God will give us another Advocate "that the Father will send" (14:26) to dwell with us personally. This Advocate will take the place of Jesus with us: "I will not leave you orphans; I will come to you." (14:18) More than that, by means of this Spirit of truth both the Father and the Son will dwell with us: "my Father will love [you], and we will come to [you] and make our dwelling with [you]." (14:23) What this means is that the Holy Spirit is the personal presence of God dwelling within us. Jesus comes to us by means of the Spirit: "I will come to [you]" (14:18); and both Jesus and the Father come to us by means of the Spirit: "[we will] come to [you] and make our dwelling with [you]." (14:23) To say this another way: we possess the personal presence of God, Father, Son, and Spirit within us; but Jesus teaches here that we should **appropriate** this presence to the Holy Spirit. This Spirit of Jesus is our teacher dwelling constantly with us, who is *"intimior intimo meo"* (more intimate than my own conscious self).

It might help our understanding of this promise of Jesus if we first looked at his similar promise at the end of Matthew's Gospel: "I am with you always, until the end of the age." (Matt. 28:20) This pledge is so comforting to us Christians that it is repeated time and again, especially by preachers and teachers. The great appeal of this promise is that Jesus will be permanently with his followers "until the end of the age." Matthew's main thrust is on the power of Jesus ("all power in heaven and earth has been given to me"), which will empower Jesus' followers to "make disciples" and "teach." (Matt. 28:18–20) Exactly how Jesus will be with his disciples is not clearly indicated, other than by his power and guidance.

Now compare this first Paraclete saying in John to Matthew 28:20. Similar to that in Matthew, Jesus' promise in John assures his disciples that the Spirit will permanently dwell within his disciples. Throughout chapters 14 to 16 in John's Gospel, John teaches that after his return to the Father, the presence of Jesus is accomplished in and through the Paraclete, who will be their permanent guest.

When we compare Jesus' promise in Matthew with that in John, we realize how much more intimate and engaging is his promise in John:

	MATTHEW	JOHN
1. The gift	Power of Jesus	Spirit of Truth
2. The promise	To make disciples and teach them	Teach, witness, remind, guide to all truth
3. The presence	General: with you always (28:20)	Specific: The Spirit will be in you (16:17)
4. Primary thrust	Communal: make disciples of all nations	Individual: remains with you to teach you

Both in Matthew and John, Jesus' promise is certainly encouraging. But in John, the Paraclete's functions are more inclusive (teach, witness, remind, and guide) and more comprehensive (lead to all truth). And most of all, in John, the Spirit is more personal and intimate: the Spirit is presented as a substitute for Jesus, so that whoever listens to the Paraclete is listening to Jesus.

Finally, in the context, Jesus adds that this divine Spirit will be our constant source of peace (John 14:25–27) and the evidence of God's love for us (John 14:23–24). If we are to take Jesus at his word, we can be assured that his own Spirit is our direct contact with him, so that all our prayer is enlivened by the intimate presence of his Spirit of Jesus. He is forever our loving guest who intercedes for us in our following of Jesus our Lord.

The personal presence of the Spirit of Jesus is the essential foundation for two other intimate relationships described below: God as our Father and Jesus as our friend. According to John and Paul, these two intimacies are only real for us because of the Spirit permanently within us. Let us see how Scripture makes this clear.

C. Father (Paul)

"[T]hose who are led by the Spirit of God are children of God. For . . . you received a spirit of adoption through which we cry '*Abba*, Father!' The Spirit itself bears witness with our spirit that we are children of God." (Rom. 8:14–16)

Paul here uses the very word, *Abba*, that Jesus customarily used in his prayer. He tells us that through the gift of the Spirit, Christians have been taken up into the very family of God. Through faith and baptism they have been adopted into filial relationship with God as their Father and Jesus as their brother. In Galatians 4:6, Paul repeats this same teaching, but here in Romans he is even more direct in the connection between the Spirit and us, for here the gift of the Holy Spirit actually constitutes our status as children of God, it activates and realizes it. He means that the vital dynamism of the Holy Spirit constitutes our status as sons/daughters and bestows the power to recognize this.

For Paul then, our fundamental attitude toward God, especially in prayer, is expressed in this cry, "*Abba*, Father." He implies that we should not see ourselves as creatures who are nothing before God, nor as slaves (Gal. 4:7) who do not belong to God's family, but as children, because we have "the Spirit of his Son" so that we can pray to God as our Father. Paul would have us pray from this supernatural standpoint: we are children of God and can pray with great confidence.

There are two further clarifications which can add to our sense of intimacy with God our Father. First, we need to realize that God our Father is not like our own earthly father (no matter how loving he may have been), so we can happily be most intimate and childlike with him. When we realize that God is the most loving of Fathers, we can have no fear, only boundless trust. Our petitions can be truly boundless as long as we add the final condition that "your kingdom come, your will be done." Then, "how much more will your heavenly Father give the good Spirit to those who ask him." (Luke 11:13)

Second, when we were children, it may have been easy to pray, "*Abba*, Father," because we were children. But now that we are adults, we do not naturally talk to any parents anymore as if we were their little children. By way of response, recall how Jesus himself calls all of us to have the spirit of children before our God:.

> [T]he disciples approached Jesus and said, "Who is the greatest in the kingdom of heaven?" He called a child over, placed it in their midst, and said, "Amen, I say to you, unless you turn and become like children, you will not enter the kingdom of heaven. Whoever humbles himself like this child is the greatest in the kingdom of heaven." (Matt. 18:1–4; see also Mark 10:15)

Scripture scholars offer many different explanations of Jesus' phrase "become like children": humility, simplicity, trust, innocence, complete dependence. It seems we cannot authoritatively settle on one meaning of Jesus' words, but Paul's words in Romans certainly mean that all Christians, no matter what their ages, can happily and boldly pray to God as children who are totally dependent on God for all grace, spiritual help, and eternal salvation. That is, no one can enter the kingdom of heaven without a childlike spirit; so when we pray to God, we need to be as trusting and dependent as children in our prayer, "*Abba*, Father."

D. Friend (John)

"No one has greater love than this, to lay down one's life for one's friends. You are my friends if you do what I command you. . . . I have called you friends, because I have told you everything I heard from my Father. It was not you who chose me, but I who chose you." (John 15:13–16)

In the synoptics (section E, below), one basis for intimacy with Jesus is that we are his brothers or sisters. However, for John, as indicated so strongly here, the basis for our intimacy is that we are his friends. In this one quote, Jesus mentions three proofs of his friendship with the disciples: because he himself gave them the greatest possible proof of his friendship by laying down his life for them; because Jesus revealed everything to them that he heard from his Father; and because he chose them and made them his disciples. Jesus' first proof is self-evident—he died for them. In human terms, no one can offer a greater proof of friendship than to give one's life for one's friend. Here Jesus asserts that he has offered this supreme proof of his sacrificial love for us, his friends. This reason must have been most obvious to his disciples for the rest of their lives. And for all of us Christians, this overwhelming proof of Christ's friendship is central to our love for him. Regarding Jesus' second proof, people throughout history would agree that friendship certainly requires a mutual sharing of experience and knowledge, but in the last century or so, psychologists would add that friendship requires much more, if it is to be distinguished from mere acquaintance or superficial friendship. Real friendship requires some regular external contact as well as sharing of deepest emotions, and revealing all aspects of one's life. But we cannot expect to find such clear-cut definitions two thousand years ago. When we hear Jesus call the disciples "friends" because he revealed everything that he was about, and everything God wanted to reveal, John is speaking in terms of first-century notions of friendship. The same can be said for us, for Jesus implies the same friendship to "those who will believe in me through their word . . . the words you gave to me I have given to them." (John 17:6–8) Jesus indicates the third proof of friendship with him when he adds: "I chose you and appointed you to go and bear fruit." (15:16) That means Jesus gives the disciples the mission to continue his personal work when he sends them out to bring his word to others, to convince them that Jesus is "the way and the truth and the life." Could that work of Jesus be carried out without a close friendship with Jesus? Something similar is true for us. We know that we are "chosen" by God (Rom. 8:33; Col. 3:12). And when Jesus prays "for those who will believe in me through [the disciples'] word" (17:20), he adds an equivalent basis of friendship: "I made known to them your name . . . that the love with which you loved me may be in them and I in them." (John 17:26).

We might add one additional evidence of our friendship with Jesus that follows from our own experience of friendship with others. All friendship demands presence; no human friendship can survive for a long period of time without regular physical presence. We all recall many past friendships that just faded away because we stopped seeing each other over time. Likewise, our friendship with Jesus is a human friendship, and unless we are present to each other, even this friendship will begin to fade. John assures us not only of the occasional presence of Jesus (as in the Eucharist) but also of his constant intimate presence within us by means of his Spirit. Notice how his first promise of the Paraclete is worded: "The Father . . . will give you another Advocate to be with you always, the Spirit of truth . . . [who] will be within you. I will not leave you orphans; I will come to you." (John 14:16–18) We are assured that Jesus our friend will dwell within us always in the person of his Spirit. Our prayer can be inspired by all these proofs of Jesus' friendship for us.

Now let us concentrate on Jesus' second reason mentioned above: "I have called you friends, because I have told you everything I have heard from my Father." Here Jesus establishes his friendship with his disciples on the basis of "making known everything I heard from my Father." However, in the next chapter he adds, "I have much more to tell you, but you cannot bear it now . . . the Spirit of truth will guide you to all truth." (16:12–13) At the actual time when Jesus spoke these words to the disciples, he could not reveal to them some hard truths about God, nor make them understand everything he taught them. But the Spirit of Truth would come to them after his resurrection and "guide [them] to all truth." (16:13) Once they received the gift of the Spirit, they would know more clearly what Jesus' revelation meant. So as the Spirit helped them understand more and more about Jesus and his revelation, they could become more intimate friends of Jesus.

E. Brother (Luke)

"Then [Jesus'] mother and his brothers came to him but were unable to join him because of the crowd. He was told, 'Your mother and your brothers are standing outside and they wish to see you.' He said to them in reply, 'My mother and my brothers are those who hear the word of God and act on it.'" (Luke 8:19–21; note a second parallel passage in Luke 11:27–28) The other synoptics relate the same incident (Matt. 12:46–50; Mark 3:31–34). Fitzmyer has an incisive commentary on this passage:

> Jesus' reply does not imply a denial of family ties . . . ; it does imply that another relationship to himself can transcend even that of family ties. Genuine relation to him consists not so much in descent from common ancestry as a voluntary attachment involving the acceptance of God's word . . . as the norm of one's life.[1]

It is difficult for us to come to the realization of just how radical this teaching of Jesus is. In all three synoptics, Jesus identifies his real relatives with those "who do the will of God." Jesus' words are clear and forceful, affirming that the primary relationship to him is not through blood ties or other earthly connections but through hearing and acting on the word of God. Luke assures us that this relationship is real and spiritual, so much so that we are even more intimately united with Jesus than we would be by blood ties or by being a family relative.

However, Luke makes no direct connection with the Holy Spirit here. We have to turn to our theology to find any connection between this intimate relationship with Jesus and the Holy Spirit. For what our theology does teach us is that this intimate relationship to Jesus is acquired and maintained through Baptism, faith, and sanctifying grace; and all these are free gifts of the Holy Spirit. What a profound source of intimacy these words of Jesus are for us! He tells us that we become his real brothers, sisters, or mother as long as we "hear the word of God and act on it." Especially during our prayer can we learn to appreciate just how amazing this declaration of Christ is for us.

Two other considerations may help us to appreciate Jesus' words. Some of us may not have a brother, sister, or mother to whom we are very close; we may even be at odds with some family members at this time in our lives. Such an experience of an estranged family relationship may easily get in the way of the manner of our relating to Jesus. Perhaps by dwelling on the person of Jesus as our ideal brother or close relative, we may experience a warm and loving relationship with him. We also have another way that we can be assured that on Jesus' part, this relation as our brother is greater than that of any brother, sister, or friend we might have: "No one has greater love than this, to lay down one's life for one's friends." (John 15:13) We cannot doubt that Jesus' love for us as our brother is profound; we can only strive more and more to "hear the word of God and act on it" that this mutual relationship may grow.

Note

1. Joseph Fitzmyer, *The Gospel According to Luke, I–IX*, Anchor Bible, vol. 28 (New York: Doubleday, 1981), 723.

CHAPTER TWELVE

The Spirit of Jesus as the Agent of the Sacraments

❧

Our Catholic faith is a sacramental faith; we have more sacraments and sacred rites than almost any other religion. These sacraments are a great gift to us, for they are an extraordinary source of God's grace and love for us through visible signs—something we can see, touch, experience. Notice too, that we receive each sacrament as individuals, one at a time. Why is this important? Because it is not enough for us to believe that God loves all people; we each need to know that God loves me as an individual. And one clear, sensible evidence for that is God's sacraments, because we receive every sacrament one person at a time. That is the genius of our sacraments: in each one we experience his grace, forgiveness, and love for us as individuals.

The entire liturgical life of the church revolves around the eucharistic sacrifice and the sacraments. And the Holy Spirit is the "source and principle" of all the sacraments, as Pope John Paul II affirms:

> The Holy spirit is . . . the source and principle of the sacramental life through which the church draws the strength of Christ . . . is nourished by his grace and grows and advances on her journey toward eternity. The Holy Spirit . . . is the living source of all the sacraments instituted by Christ and at work in the church.[1]

How do Scripture and the church present the Spirit of Jesus as the "source and principle" of the sacraments? Scripture itself presents three sacraments as coming from Christ. Matthew and Mark represent Jesus as the author of Baptism (Matt. 28:19; Mark 16:16). Mark and Luke describe Christ's institution of the Eucharist (Mark 14, 22–24; Luke 22:19–20). And John reports Christ's giving the disciples the authority to forgive sins, as in Reconciliation (John 20:22–23).

The other four sacraments were determined later by the church and with the inspiration of the Holy Spirit:

> Alexander of Hales and St. Bonaventure attributed the definitive institution of the sacraments of confirmation, ordination, marriage and the anointing of the sick to the Holy Spirit, that is to the active inspiration of the Spirit in the church and its councils. [Later theologians] thought that Christ had determined the communication of sacramental grace, but the form taken by the sacramental signs was determined and even modified by the church, subject to the guidance and inspiration of the Holy Spirit.[2]

After Vatican II and the revision of all the sacramental rites, our sacraments almost always invoke the Holy Spirit. Our revised sacramentary clearly mentions the Spirit of Jesus as the **agent** of each sacrament. For example, in Baptism: "God . . . has given you a new birth by water and the Holy Spirit"; in Holy Orders, before the bishop lays his hands on the ordinand, he prays: "Hear, O Lord, and pour out upon this servant of yours the blessing of the Holy Spirit and the grace of the power of the priesthood." Also, in most of the eucharistic prayers (E.P.), the power of the Spirit is invoked to sanctify the gifts or to transform them into the body of Christ. For example, "Let your Spirit come upon these gifts to make them holy, so that they may become for us the body and blood of Christ" (E.P. II); "We ask you to make [these gifts] holy by the power of your Spirit" (E.P. III); "May this Spirit sanctify these offerings." (E.P. IV)

Also in the new sacramentary, the Holy Spirit is mentioned in the essential **form** of four sacraments. In Baptism the essential form is: "I baptize you in the name of the Father and of the Son and of the Holy Spirit." In Reconciliation the form begins: "God the

Father of mercies . . . sent the Holy Spirit among us for the forgiveness of sins." In the anointing of the sick, the necessary form is: "Through this holy anointing, may the Lord in his love and mercy help you with the grace of the Holy Spirit."

So our modern sacramentary and theology have made us more aware that the Holy Spirit is the "source and principle" of our seven sacraments. For they present the Spirit of Jesus as the inspiration of the sacraments and as the agent who is active in each sacrament. That means that the Spirit of Jesus is the common agent of all sacramental grace and the source of our subjective salvation.

Now let us concentrate on the sacrament of Confirmation, whose proper effect is the gift of the Holy Spirit. A vexing problem for theologians who study this sacrament is just how Confirmation is distinct from Baptism. They know that, in Scripture, both Baptism and Confirmation confer the Holy Spirit, and they also know that, in the practice of the early church, Baptism and Confirmation were generally joined together. In Scripture, the synoptic Gospels begin with the figure of John the Baptizer who baptized his followers and even Jesus himself, even though he admitted, "I have baptized with water; [Jesus] will baptize you with the Holy Spirit." (Mark 1:8–9) The synoptics end their gospels with Jesus' commission to baptize (Matt. 28:19; Mark 16:16). But the Acts of the Apostles begins not with the baptism of believers but with the coming of the Holy Spirit at Pentecost: "they were all filled with the holy Spirit." (Acts 2:4) Then when Peter finished his first sermon and was asked, "What are we to do?" (Acts 2:37), he answered, "Repent and be baptized . . . and you will receive the holy Spirit." (Acts 2:38) Throughout Acts Luke follows this pattern and joins Baptism and the gift of the Holy Spirit (see: 1:5; 10:44–48; 11:15–17). Sometimes the gift of the Spirit follows Baptism (see: 2:38; 19:5–6); other times it precedes Baptism (see: 9:17–19; 10:44–48). For Luke in Acts then, Baptism and the gift of the Spirit are generally united. Rather than proclaiming a separate rite of Confirmation, the Spirit was usually given in connection with Baptism.

In the early church, Baptism and Confirmation along with the Eucharist formed one sacramental rite of initiation into Christ. After being baptized, the Christian was anointed and then received the

Eucharist. As Bernard Cooke notes, "In the writings of the early church fathers and theologians, it is impossible to find a description of Confirmation apart from Baptism."[3] It took almost a millennium for the two rites of Baptism and Confirmation gradually to be separated. As early as Augustine, the practice of infant Baptism (along with the anointing and the gift of the Spirit) became quite common. This led to a practical difficulty, for in the western church only bishops could perform the postbaptismal rites. And since bishops were not always available to perform those anointings of the Spirit, the two rites of Baptism and anointing of the Spirit were often separated and given at different times. Then, from the ninth century on, the special anointing by the bishop became a self-contained "rite of Confirmation." In the twelfth to thirteenth centuries, the scholastic theologians treated Confirmation as a separate sacrament. Peter Lombard and Thomas Aquinas described Confirmation as the gift of the Spirit "for strengthening" (*ad robur*) in contrast to the grace of the Spirit in Baptism, which was "for forgiveness" (*ad regenerationem*).[4] Thomas Aquinas described the proper effect of Confirmation in two ways: strength for professing the faith (as a special calling beyond Baptism), or spiritual maturity and growth toward perfect Christian living in the Spirit.[5] Today these same two effects are regularly presented as the distinguishing characteristics of Confirmation.

Some modern theologians clarify the distinction between these two sacraments by appealing to Scripture in a different way. They point out that in Scripture and the early church, Baptism was strongly associated with Christ's death and resurrection; in Paul's words: "We were . . . buried with him through baptism unto death, so that, just as Christ was raised from the dead . . . we too might live in newness of life" (Rom. 6:4); whereas the gift of the Spirit was conferred at Pentecost: "they were all filled with the holy Spirit." (Acts 2:4) Edward Schillebeeckx then concludes that these two sacraments can be justly separated:

> [B]aptism makes us members of the ecclesial people of God . . . [and] children of the Father . . . in the Spirit of sonship. Then in confirmation . . . we are "established in power"; . . . we receive a share in the bestowal of the Spirit and thus in the Pentecost mystery of

Christ himself. Therefore confirmation makes us adult members of the church. . . . The *robur* or strength of which theological tradition has spoken since the Middle Ages undoubtedly reflects an essential aspect of confirmation.[6]

Notice how Schillebeeckx parallels the **Easter** mystery of Christ's death and resurrection (relating it to Baptism and new life in Christ) and the mystery of Christ's sending of the Spirit at **Pentecost** (relating it to Confirmation and our fullness of life in the Spirit).

Scripture itself offers a subtle corroboration of Schillebeeckx's reasoning above. For Jesus' commission to baptize was given to the apostles in the context of the **Easter** mystery of his death and resurrection (see: Matt. 28:19; Mark 16:16). However Jesus' fuller commissioning of the disciples was connected to his gift of the Holy Spirit (**Pentecost**). That is, in John's Gospel, Jesus confers the spirit on the disciples permanently as he gives them further powers: "Receive the holy Spirit. Whose sins you forgive are forgiven them . . ." (John 20:22–23). And similarly in Luke's Gospel, Jesus promises that the Spirit will come to them at Pentecost and give them special power: "I am sending the promise of my Father upon you [at Pentecost] (cf. Acts 1:4–5)], [when] you will be clothed with power from on high." (Luke 24:49) We might summarize the distinction between Baptism and Confirmation this way: Baptism is the sacrament of our new life in Christ won for us by his death and resurrection (the Paschal mystery); it justifies us before God and makes us children of God our Father. Confirmation is the sacrament of our mature life in Christ, made possible by the sending of the Holy Spirit (the promised Pentecost event); it strengthens us so we can give mature witness to Christ.

Notes

1. Pope John Paul II, *The Spirit, Giver of Life and Love* (Boston: Pauline Books and Media, 1996), 351.

170 ❦ Second Part: The Spirit of Jesus in Prayer

2. Yves Congar, *I Believe in the Holy Spirit,* vol. 2 (New York: Seabury Press, 1983), 9.

3. Bernard Cooke, *Christian Sacraments and Christian Personality* (New York: Holt, Rinehart, and Winston, 1965), 91, 94–96.

4. Thomas Aquinas, *Summa Theologica, III,* q. 65, a. 1, resp; q. 72, a. 1, resp.

5. Aquinas, *Summa Theologial, III,* q. 72, aa. 4–5.

6. Edward Schillebeeckx, *Christ, the Sacrament of Our Encounter with God* (New York: Sheed and Ward, 1963), 161.

THIRD PART

COMPARISONS BETWEEN THE SPIRIT OF JESUS IN THE EARLY CHURCH AND TODAY

∞

CHAPTER THIRTEEN

Every Church Is Divine and Human

∞

The Holy Spirit is the divine element in every Christian community since the time of the apostles. We can see the Spirit's influence in all the apostolic communities; but Scripture also shows us that each community had its own characteristics. The reason for this diversity is that each church was made up of very human members and very different leaders. This is especially evident in the communities of Paul, Luke, and John. These men were all inspired by the Holy Spirit, and what they wrote is recognized as the Word of God precisely because it was inspired by the Spirit.

In this chapter, we want to describe three different approaches to church existence in the New Testament period—those of Paul, of Luke, and of John. We want to keep our focus very narrow—so as not to lose our primary emphasis on the work of the Holy Spirit in each community. These three scriptural views can be a powerful corrective and encouragement when we consider our very human church in this twenty-first century.

A. Paul

Paul's concept of community is based on the members' common faith in Jesus Christ (Rom. 8:9; 2 Cor. 1:21–22) and the shared experience of the Spirit (1 Cor. 12:13; 2 Cor. 13:13–14). For Paul the church is divine, for it consists of the people of God of the new covenant who make up the temple of God (1 Cor. 3:16; 2 Cor. 6:16). In this sanctuary, God's Spirit dwells, filling each member as well as the entire edifice of the church. This concept of church as temple, however, was not original with Paul; but he did give this metaphor new richness and depth.[1]

Another powerful Pauline image of the church is that of the body of Christ. Paul is indeed the originator of this image. He first introduces it in his Letters to the Corinthians and Romans. Later, the deutero-Pauline letters of Colossians and Ephesians bring his theological insight to full splendor. In all the New Testament, this precise metaphor is unique to Paul and his followers.

The life of this body of Christ is due to the Spirit of Jesus, who dwells in the faithful (Rom. 8:9–11) and continues in them the work of redemption. For Paul, the community of Jesus' disciples only **becomes** a church through the Holy Spirit. It is the working of the Holy Spirit that gives the church its origin and existence as well as its form and continuance. Indeed, for Paul, the Spirit comprises and fills, unites and directs all who believe and are begotten of "water and the Holy spirit."

It is in Romans and Corinthians, however, that the ongoing life of the community is often seen as charismatic in character. The functions of the body are precisely the manifestations of the Spirit (Rom. 12:4). The charisms constitute the heart of the living movements of the body (1 Cor. 12:14–26; Rom. 12:4–8). These dynamic gifts of the Spirit were external proofs of justification by God; they led directly to the acceptance of the Gentiles into the one body of Christ.

But Paul also saw the human and flawed element of these manifestations of the Spirit. Much of his writing was directed to the turmoil that was sometimes caused in Corinth by these very charisms. He remonstrated with them: "stop being childish . . . ; everything must be done properly and in order" (1 Cor. 14:20, 40) and not be a cause for disunity. Obviously, he was worried that these very charisms might tear apart the body of Christ; he knew their very strength could also be a grave weakness.

B. Luke

Luke's primary concern in his Acts of the Apostles was to show the continuity of the early church with what went before. The Jesus who ascended into heaven at the end of Luke's Gospel (Luke 24:51) appears again at the beginning of Acts to introduce all that follows. Those who were with Jesus during his public ministry became the critical group to ensure the continuity Jesus wanted. Even Paul had to be commissioned by the risen Jesus. And the Spirit of Jesus is conspicuous in Acts, playing a connective role between the ministry of Jesus and that of his early followers. In fact, the distinguishing feature of Luke's church is the overshadowing presence of the Spirit. For example, he uses *pneuma* (spirit) seventy times in Acts. Throughout Acts the Spirit empowers the church at every turning point; in this sense Luke presents the early church as divine. Thus, the Spirit inspires the apostles at Pentecost (Acts 1:5, 8), effects the spread of the faith along with baptism (Acts 2:38), gives the impetus for Paul and Barnabus (Acts 13:2–4), inspires the church-altering decision to permit Gentiles to join the church (Acts 15:28), empowers Paul's decision to go to Rome (Acts 19:21), and provides overseers in place of Paul (Acts 20:28). Thus, at every essential step the Holy Spirit guided the early church and encouraged the human agents to spread the Word. In addition, Luke gives us an apparently idyllic church in Acts; for example, in chapter 4, he presents an amazingly peaceful and united church: "The community of believers was of one heart and mind, and no one claimed that any of his possessions was his own, but they had everything in common." (4:32) Besides that, Luke paints a somewhat triumphal picture of the church in Acts, as the Christian movement grows continually, so that even setbacks are only temporary. All of this could easily lead us to believe that the Holy Spirit so governed the early church in all her decisions and crises that we might expect the Spirit to come to the rescue of the church in every crisis, to lead it unfailingly through every problem and division. Not so.

The human side of the church, its many weaknesses and disputes, is also evident in Acts; and it's important for us to recognize this human side of the early church. Thus, in chapter 5, he describes the deceit and chicanery of Ananias and Sapphira; in chapter 6, he notes that "the Hellenists complained against the Hebrews" (6:1) that they were being neglected by the apostles; in chapter 8, he describes the first case of simony in the church, when the eponymous Simon tried to buy the power of the Spirit; in the beginning of chapter 15, Luke first shows a church very divided over the question of the Gentiles: "Unless you are circumcised . . . you cannot be saved" (15:1); at the end of chapter 15, he describes the bitter dispute of Paul and Barnabas ("So sharp was their disagreement that they separated," v. 39). In Luke's church, even the Holy Spirit was not a Deus ex machina (a divine solution for every problem).

These observations about the Lukan church can be very encouraging for our church in this century, whenever we become distressed by the human side of our church today. When we see scandals among our clergy, abuse of authority by Rome, injustice for minorities or women in the church, we rightly feel betrayed by our human church. No excuse can be given for these failures. History teaches us that our church will always be terribly human, just because it has leaders and members who are human and flawed. Despite all the turmoil this causes in our church, we can take some comfort in trusting the Holy Spirit to continually heal the body of Christ.

C. John

John's ecclesiology emphasizes the relation of the individual Christian to Jesus Christ and to the indwelling Spirit. He teaches that we are all begotten by God; we are God's children through water and the Holy Spirit (John 1:12–13; 3:3–6). John also uses life-giving and relational images to describe life in Christ. Jesus is the vine and Christians are the branches receiving life from the vine (John 15:2–6); he is the shepherd who tends the sheep that belong to him (John. 10:27–28). In Jesus, John sees the reign of God as being perfectly realized. But after Jesus has returned to the Father, the Spirit emerges as the ongoing presence of Jesus, "another Advocate," who

Chapter Thirteen: Every Church Is Divine and Human 177

is clearly a personal presence in each Christian. He is the replacement for Jesus, so much so that almost everything said about the Spirit has already been said about Jesus. The Spirit is the individual advocate dwelling within all Christians to give them confidence before the world and to help them interpret the significance of Jesus (John 16:8–11); in Jesus' words, this teacher "will teach you everything and remind you of all that I told you." (John 14:26) In John's church, the Spirit/Paraclete was the divine presence in each member of the community.

Paradoxically, this very strength in the Johannine church also led to its greatest human weakness. The assurance that there is a living, divine teacher in the heart of each believer was a profound contribution to the church; but this same appeal to the Spirit, possessed individually, led to uncontrollable divisions. What could the community do when believers, who possessed the Spirit, disagreed with each other? To whom would they listen? There seemed to be no way to control such a division in a community guided totally by the Paraclete. All three Johannine epistles tried mightily to correct this problem. Yet it seems that the majority of Johannine Christians seceded from the Johannine faithful and went out of existence. Only those who accepted even a limited amount of authority in the person of Peter remained faithful. As Raymond Brown concludes, "The epilogue to the fourth gospel [chapter 21, added later], which may represent the final stage of the Johannine writings preserved for us, acknowledges the authority of a human shepherd."[2] Without that corrective in the form of some kind of church direction, people supposedly "led by the Spirit" believed what they felt inspired to believe and could claim their own Spirit-inspired way of following Jesus.

The fundamental difficulty here is that John's original Gospel (including only the first twenty chapters) taught Jesus' disciples that they can depend on the individual enlightenment and guidance of the Spirit for their faith and life in Christ. Many of them wrongly understood that such inner guidance by the Spirit was all they needed to be true Christians; they didn't realize the havoc that would result in rejecting the influence of the Spirit in those who proclaimed, taught, and led the community. Chapter 21 of John's Gospel and

John's First Letter insisted on the need for the authority of Peter and the teaching of the church as also inspired by the Spirit of Jesus. Very quickly the Johannine community learned that tensions and conflicts were inevitable in the church of Christ and could not be solved without leaders intended by Christ and inspired by his Spirit.

So while Johannine ecclesiology may be the most attractive and exciting in the New Testament, it can also lead to division and instability. At the time of the Reformation, this instability became most obvious. The churches of the Reformation insisted that all believers possess the Spirit who bears witness in them individually. Without the guidance of the Spirit in the leadership of the church as a whole, they broke away from the rest of the church. In the last couple of centuries, similar ecclesiologies have led to all sorts of Pentecostal groups and Spirit-led sects that continually divide into smaller groups.

In our Catholic Church, the problem occurs at the opposite extreme. Sometimes the leaders of the church appeal to the inspiration of the Holy Spirit as an excuse to decide everything from the top down without the consultation and consent of the rest of the church. Vatican Council II insisted that the gifts of the Spirit are possessed by all Christians, so that consultation and collegiality are necessary in the church of Christ. Sadly, this teaching of Vatican II is not fully implemented yet.

D. The Pastoral Epistles

Even though the Pastoral Epistles (1 and 2 Timothy and Titus) most likely were not written by Paul himself, they are written in his name and by his disciples. These three epistles constitute the deliberate effort to show continuance between the church of the apostles and the later (subapostolic) church. They show a significantly different concept of church and community; they evidence a definite change from a missionary church to a pastoral church—hence the term "pastoral." The advice given to Timothy and Titus and to the Christian communities is in terms of structure. Now that Paul has "competed well [and] . . . finished the race" (2 Tim. 4:6–7), several Pauline churches are without local authority and leadership. That deficiency is to be remedied by appointing presbyters and overseers (which would develop into bishops and priests in the church of the succeeding centuries). These leaders had the responsibility to keep the faith pure by teaching sound doctrine and holding firmly to the sure word as it was taught (1 Tim. 3:1–4; Titus 1:9), to be a model for the church (1 Tim. 3:1–10), to order the life and relationships of the community (1 Tim. 5:1–16; Titus 2:1–10). Also, they were to exercise discipline and mete out justice (1 Tim. 5:19–22); they were directed to lay on hands and appoint elders (Titus 1:5). In a word, in the Pastoral Epistles, we see the beginnings of a hierarchical structure. This is the way Paul (or his immediate disciples) envisioned the stability and unity of the later church. Such an approach served the church well as it slowly changed from a movement to an institution (as all movements eventually do).

But we also see a definite weakness hidden in such an ecclesiology. For the primary effort in these letters is to find good pastoral leaders who would be responsible people, of sound doctrine, and easy to get along with; they should be safe and considerate, resident pastors. That implied that they were not likely to be dynamic missionaries or charismatic movers who would convert and change the world. For the qualities of a missionary—like Paul!—are quite different from the qualities of a peace-loving pastor.

Another very human quality also showed up in time. Just because these pastoral leaders were so strongly urged to teach sound doctrine, to order the life of the community, to exercise discipline and mete out justice, they were not inclined to let ordinary Christians corrupt doctrine, disturb unity, or follow their own way of living. Some of them felt it was their duty to restrain others, to correct them severely, and to establish certain laws without much consultation or advice.

Notes

1. Rudolph Schnackenburg, *The Church in the New Testament* (New York: Herder and Herder, 1965), 83.

2. Raymond Brown, *The Churches the Apostles Left Behind* (New York: Paulist Press, 1985), 123.

CHAPTER FOURTEEN

Experienced Presence versus Presence by Faith

A. In the Early Church

For the early church, Jesus was an **experienced** presence for many people; he was humanly experienced by some followers face to face. This experience was so dominant in their faith, they wondered what would happen when Jesus was no longer with them, when Jesus had left them. This was a great problem for all the disciples. The hopeful answer in John's church was that they would have another Advocate, the Spirit of Jesus "to be with [them] always" and "to teach [them] everything." This continuing presence of Jesus' Spirit was real and apparently experienced by them.

Similarly in the Acts of the Apostles and in the Pauline church the Holy Spirit was an **experienced** presence. In Acts the Spirit was dramatically experienced at three Pentecost occurrences (Acts 2:1–13; 10:44–48; 19:1–7); these were considered as proof from God that both Jew and Gentile were equally accepted. In Corinth and other churches, the Spirit was often experienced through charisms (1 Cor. 12), by miracles, and by prophetic preaching. In the early church, then, the shock of no longer experiencing Jesus firsthand was somewhat alleviated by the profound experience of Pentecost as well as the power and presence of the Paraclete.

B. In the Modern Church

For Christians after the first century and into our own time, the absence of Jesus is not offset by the experienced power of the Holy Spirit. Instead, we do have Christ's promise and our own faith that the Spirit of Jesus is present in **every Christian individually**. He dwells in each one of us as the Spirit of the Son, by whom we call out "*Abba*." (Gal. 4:6) Now we know his presence only by **faith**. Generally we are without external evidence of his presence. Nevertheless, we do have many helps that the early church did not have.

For example, we have the Paraclete dwelling within us from the beginning of our life in Christ; this Spirit of Jesus is present in each of us individually as our "other Advocate" who is "with [us] always." (John 14:16)

We have the complete Scriptures inspired by the Spirit. The New Testament contains the only adequate proclamation of Jesus, the Word of God, and Jesus himself is the entire truth, the whole revelation about God. Jesus was very clear when he told his disciples that they did not have the entire truth: "I have much more to tell you, but you cannot bear it now. But when he comes, the Spirit of truth, he will guide you to all truth." (John 16:12–13) Only with the help of the Spirit could they come "to all truth." It took centuries for the church to formally declare many truths about God, Christ, and universal salvation. And we individual Christians only grow "to all truth" throughout our lives with the help of the Spirit of Truth.

We occasionally have a real, though internal, experience of Christ in prayer by the grace of the Spirit. At times, when we meditate on the life of Christ or on his passion, we experience a genuine personal bond of love or commitment.

We have all seven of the sacraments, while the early church may have had only three. These sacraments, empowered by the Holy Spirit, continue to be our individual personal experience of Christ. As St. Ambrose expressed this forcefully in the fourth century: "You have shown yourself to me, Christ, face to face; it is in your sacraments that I meet you."

We have the constant intercession of his Spirit in prayer. As Romans 8:26–27 encourages us: "The Spirit too comes to the aid of our weakness, for we do not know how to pray as we ought, but the Spirit . . . intercedes for the holy ones according to God's will." That is, we each possess our personal intercessor with God; with the help of this Spirit, we can be confident of praying according to God's will.

CHAPTER FIFTEEN

How Is It "Better for You That I Go"?

The disciples must have been stunned when Jesus asserted, "It is better for you that I go." No way could they believe that they could be better off without his presence. Let us consider this and other challenging words of Jesus regarding the Paraclete and try to understand the full import of Jesus' promises to his disciples then, and to us in the modern church.

A. "It Is Better for You That I Go."

"I tell you the sober truth: it is better for you that I go. If I fail to go, the Paraclete will never come to you; whereas if I go, I will send him to you." (John 16:7) Here Jesus boldly claims that it is better for each of his disciples to possess the Paraclete as their individual Advocate, and he adds that this can happen **only** after Jesus has finished his work on earth. It appears that Jesus wants to instill a very high degree of appreciation of the Paraclete in the community of disciples. To accomplish this, Jesus implies that he himself is not the ultimate gift, and that his words alone are not sufficient. Rather, the Spirit will be that gift, present in the community, and will continually reveal the lasting understanding of those words and their significance for all future disciples.

From our vantage point, we might agree with Jesus regarding the early Christians; for though they no longer had the real experience of Jesus' presence, we know from the Acts and elsewhere that they soon **experienced** the Holy Spirit externally and powerfully. His Spirit was the driving force for the dramatic spread of the early church. It was only after Jesus' departure that they could have the assistance of the Spirit to understand Jesus fully. Jesus himself explained this to them very pointedly: "you cannot bear it now. But when he comes, the Spirit of truth, he will guide you to all truth." (John 16:12–13)

But would we agree with Jesus that it is better for us today, who have the multiple graces of the Holy Spirit only through **faith**? In response, notice how John's Gospel describes the mission of the Holy Spirit. Especially in John's Gospel Jesus clearly identifies that mission of the Paraclete. Just as the mission of Jesus was to be "the way and the truth and the life" and the universal source of redemption, so also the mission of the Spirit of Jesus is to be the Spirit of Truth to carry on the work of Jesus and be the universal agent of our individual sanctification. In God's plan, the Spirit's mission only begins after Jesus' departure; Jesus himself tells us here: "If I fail to go, the Paraclete will never come to you." And John earlier explained: "There was as yet no Spirit, since Jesus had not been glorified." (John 7:39) Both these quotes teach that the role of the Spirit of Jesus is to take the place on earth of the glorified Jesus.

From John's Gospel alone, we can learn the elements of the mission of the Spirit of Jesus. There are five that stand out. The Paraclete is to be the permanent presence of God in the individual disciples of Jesus (14:16). The Paraclete is to be the Spirit of Truth for them to understand Jesus fully (14:26). The Spirit is the unique principle of divine life (3:5). Only by means of the Spirit of the Son of God can they become actually children of God (1:12–13; cf. Gal. 4:6). The Spirit is the agent for the forgiveness of sins; Jesus' redemption from sin comes to us personally by the power of the Holy Spirit (John 20:22–23). The Paraclete will bear witness within the disciples (15:26) and through them, there will be a permanent witness of Jesus to the world for all time (16:8–11). Now, when we consider these five elements, we realize they do not require external experiences but only **faith**. That is why Jesus could truthfully say, "It is better for you that I go." For only then could the mission of the Paraclete begin in the hearts of all who believe.

One last point. Even though we appreciate that, by God's plan, the mission of the Paraclete generally works internally through faith, we still may feel personally inadequate; we know only too well how we obstruct the work of the Spirit to "lead [us] into all truth." So we look for more, for some external sign from God, some powerful experience. John of the Cross has a wonderful answer for us at such times; he speaks to us as if his words come from God himself:

> If I have already told you all things in my Word, my Son, and I have no other word, what answer or revelation can I now make that would surpass this? . . . Since that day when I descended upon Him, with my Spirit on Mount Tabor proclaiming: 'This is my beloved Son, in whom I am well pleased, hear him' [Matt. 17:5], I have relinquished these methods of answering and teaching [that is, by visions or revelations]. Hear him because I have no more faith to reveal nor truths to manifest.[1]

And when Jesus himself assures us that the Paraclete "will teach you everything and remind you of all that I said to you" (14:26), that promise refers above all to understanding Jesus and his word, for "I have told you all things in my Word, my Son, and I have no other word."

Finally, we can observe the actual inspiration of the Holy Spirit throughout history: the testimony of many martyrs who gave witness with their lives in the strength provided by the Spirit; the example of so many saints who led heroic lives inspired by the Spirit; the prayerful model of authentic contemplative saints; the inspired creativity of so many founders of religious orders; and the reliable development of dogma by numerous ecumenical councils of the church guided by the Spirit. This same Spirit continues to surprise our modern world in countless ways.

B. "You Cannot Bear It Now."

"I have much more to tell you, but you cannot bear it now." (16:12) Jesus' disciples could not understand his way of redemption; he knew they would be utterly confused by his suffering and death. Only after the resurrection could they begin to reflect on the scandal of his passion and death. They needed the powerful help of the Spirit of Truth in order to understand this great mystery of salvation by means of the cross. The mission of the Paraclete was precisely "to remind [them] of all [he] had told [them] . . . and guide [them] to all truth."

We also need help to fully fathom Christ's way of redemption by suffering, which is almost unintelligible to most: "we proclaim Christ crucified, a stumbling block to Jews and foolishness to Gentiles." (1 Cor. 1:23) We yearn to understand how our own spirituality can be more Christ-centered; we try to respond more to Jesus' invitation: "If anyone wishes to come after me, he must deny himself, take up his cross daily and follow me." (Luke 9:23) We hope to come to terms with Jesus as our model for living the Christian life: "to this you have been called, because Christ also suffered for you leaving you an example that you should follow in his footsteps." (1 Pet. 2:21) We want to face the great tragedies of our time—dire poverty, ethnic cleansing, AIDS and other epidemics, countless wars, recent terrorist attacks—and see them as the result of misused human freedom, though still a part of the mystery of Christ's redemption. There is no doubt that Christians of our generation need more than ever the Spirit of Jesus to come to terms with human evil of our day.

C. "He will Remind You of All That I Told You."

"The holy Spirit will instruct you in everything and remind you of all that I told you." (14:26) Earlier in John's Gospel, Jesus often promised to come back, by means of the Paraclete, and teach them everything. Notice how often he mentioned that they would understand him only later:

> 12:16: His disciples did not understand this at first, but when Jesus had been glorified they remembered that these things were written about him.
>
> 13:19: "From now on I am telling you before it happens, so that when it happens you may believe that I AM."

14:20: "On that day you will realize that I am in the Father and you are in me and I in you."

14:29: "And now I have told you this before it happens, so that when it happens you may believe."

15:26: "When the Advocate comes whom I will send you from the Father . . . he will testify to me."

16:4: "I have told you this so that when their hour comes you may remember that I told you."

16:12: "I have much more to tell you, but you cannot bear it now."

20:9 (after the resurrection): For they did not yet understand the scripture that he had to rise from the dead.

What Jesus meant at that time was that the Paraclete would help them understand the symbolic actions he performed and the great mystery of God's plan of redemption. He would give a new depth and conviction to their faith.

In our day, how much we still have to learn about the way of Jesus! We still find a suffering Savior to be a stumbling block for us at times. The Spirit of Jesus is necessary to give us a new depth and conviction to our faith, and to remind us that Jesus is forever a suffering Savior who did not come to remove all suffering in this life. When tragedies strike, we too need the Spirit of Jesus to reflect on what Jesus said to us, and "to remind you of all that I told you."

D. "I Will Come Back to You."

"[The Father] will give you another advocate, the Spirit of truth. . . . I will not leave you orphaned; I will come back to you." (14:16–18) In the early church, Christ's disciples felt bereft after Jesus died. He had been "the way, the truth and the life" (14:6) for them. But Jesus "would not leave [them] orphaned"; he sent them "another Advocate to be with them always." With the Paraclete as the new presence of Jesus, they had the courage to face all the turbulent times of the early church. Many mistakes would be made; many challenges to their faith would confront the disciples; but the church could depend on the presence of the Holy Spirit. They were never without the power of Jesus' Spirit.

Our church today has a similar need for the constant presence and help of Jesus' Spirit, so that we can give witness to Jesus. We can face our own turbulent times with the assurance that we are never without the power of Jesus' Spirit. Each one of us is not without Jesus' presence, for we each have the Spirit of Jesus within us. With the courage of the Spirit we can strive to bring change to our church and world.

E. "You Also Will Testify [to Me]."

"When the Advocate comes . . . the Spirit of truth . . . he will testify to me. And you also testify." (15:26–27) In the early church, there was ample evidence of the disciples' giving witness to Jesus throughout the Acts of the Apostles: Acts 2:4–11; 4:8–12; 4:18–31; 5:27–32; 7:2–60. In all these situations, they gave witness to Jesus with the expressed help of the Holy Spirit.

In our day, it is also difficult to give witness to Jesus for other reasons. For instance, some countries today are positively inimical to Christianity; often the church is ridiculed because of its sexual morality; our American society is no longer simply Judeo-Christian but much more diverse in religious background. And within the church itself, many point to grave defects that are real or imagined: troublesome scandals, such as pedophilia; inequality for women and gays in the church; and disciplining of leading theologians. All of these make our witness to Jesus more complex or problematic. Without denying such conditions, we can still give witness to Jesus—with the promised help of the Spirit of Jesus. That kind of witness is also part of Jesus' promise: "the Spirit . . . will testify to me. And you also testify."

Note

1. St. John of the Cross, *The Ascent of Mount Carmel*, II, 22, #5, 180.

CHAPTER SIXTEEN

Problems Regarding the Spirit of Jesus in the Modern Church

∞

A. External vs. Internal Working of the Holy Spirit

As we look at the first-century church, much of the activity of the Holy Spirit was **external** and visible. The Spirit at the three Pentecosts of the Acts of the Apostles made his presence known by speaking in tongues and by "signs and wonders" (Acts 5:12); the charisms of the Corinthian church were varied and convinced multitudes of the Spirit's presence; the testimony of the apostles was strengthened by the felt power of the Holy Spirit. Of course the Spirit was also an **internal** force; as the Letter to the Ephesians put it: may God "grant you . . . to be strengthened with power through his Spirit in the inner person, and that Christ may dwell in your hearts through faith." (Eph. 3:16–17)

But in our modern church, the work of the Holy Spirit is mostly **internal**. The internal presence of the Spirit is the essential and universal power for us to experience Christ on the individual level. In the above quote, the Spirit strengthens us "in the inner person," so that we may live our faith in Christ more effectively. The verses immediately following this contain the beautiful summary of our Christian life: "that you, rooted and grounded in love, may have strength to comprehend with all the holy ones what is the breadth and length and height and depth, to know the love of Christ which surpasses all knowledge, so that you may be filled with all the fullness of God." (Eph. 3:17–21) The strengthening by the Holy Spirit in the "inner person" means that we will know the love of Christ and be "rooted and grounded in love." In the Pauline corpus, that love of God is "poured into our hearts through the holy Spirit." (Rom. 5:5) So this empowering by the Spirit leads to Christ dwelling in us by faith and love, which is the essence of our spiritual life.

Let me mention one aspect of the internal working of the Spirit of Jesus that is often overlooked. That is, not only is our faith essential to our following of Christ, it is also critical for the universal church. Vatican II reminds us of the importance of the *sensus fidelium*, that is, the common faith of the universal church. The idea, here, is that all the faithful, responsive to the Spirit, have an instinct for the truth. Without this universal consensus in matters of faith, the universal church could no longer give strong and united witness to Christ our Savior:

> The holy people of God shares also in Christ's prophetic office; it spreads abroad a living witness to him, especially by a life of faith and love and by offering to God a sacrifice of praise. . . . The whole body of faithful, who have received an anointing which comes from the holy one (I Jn. 2:20, 27, referring to the Holy Spirit), cannot be mistaken in belief. It shows this characteristic through the entire people's supernatural sense of the faith, when . . . it manifests a universal consensus in matters of faith.[1]

B. We Are Not Usually Attentive to the Spirit

Once we understand that the Holy Spirit is the permanent Spirit of Jesus dwelling in us, to whom we can relate personally and individually, we desire to be attentive to the Spirit in our daily living. However, we are often inattentive to the indwelling Spirit and squander this source of grace and powerful prayer.

Perhaps we can take comfort from the famous words of Jesus in Matthew 25:40: "Whatever you did for one of these least brothers/sisters of mine, you did for me." Jesus assures us that even when we are inattentive to Christ's presence in others, **he** accepts what we do for others as done to him. Similarly, Paul assures us (Rom. 8:26–27) that even when we are inattentive to the presence of the Holy Spirit in us, "the Spirit too comes to the aid of our weakness, for we do not know how to pray as we ought but the Spirit itself intercedes with inexpressible groanings." That is, the Holy Spirit continues to identify with us in prayer even when we are not aware of him. Even though the parallel is not perfect, it is comforting to believe that the Spirit works for us despite our conscious inattention and inadequacy.

C. Why Is the Paraclete Not Called the Spirit of Love?

John consistently presents the Paraclete as the Spirit of **truth**, not the Spirit of **love**. The emphasis on truth is not so attractive for our Christian faith today, for we are very aware of Jesus' command in John's Gospel: "This is my commandment: love one another as I have loved you." (John 15:12; cf. 13:34) And yet there is no Johannine statement about the Spirit as the source of love. Personally, I was shocked when I first realized this fact—until I understood that John writes from a unique paradigm centered on truth and faith. However, recently I have found two indirect ways of connecting the Holy Spirit with this all-important commandment of Jesus. Consider, first, the fifth Paraclete saying: Jesus tells the disciples, "the Spirit of truth . . . will guide you to all truth." (John 16:13) This seems to include more than a deeper intellectual understanding of "the way of truth"; that is, it involves teaching a way of life in conformity with Jesus' teaching. The reason for saying this is bound up with the whole Johannine understanding of "the way of truth." For John's Gospel thinks of truth not as an abstract system of faith but as a sphere of action, similar to the Old Testament notion of "the way" so prominent in the Acts of the Apostles (Acts 9:2; 19:9, 23; 22:4; 24:14, 22).[2] Second, when Jesus affirms that he is "**the way**" (John 14:6), according to scripture scholars that has a double reference: he is the **channel** of salvation, he is the **model** for our living. Now Jesus is our model principally in terms of love: "Love one another as I have loved you." (John 13:34–35) If the Paraclete is to "teach us everything" about Jesus, that includes both knowing Jesus as the way and learning how to follow him. All of that includes loving as he loved.

Also, the First Letter of John connects keeping Jesus' commandment of Christian love with the Spirit:

> [God's] commandment is this: we should believe in the name of his Son, Jesus Christ, and love one another just as he commanded us. Those who keep his commandments remain in him, and he in them, and the way that we know that he remains in us is from the Spirit which he has given us. (1 John 3:23–24)

That is, 1 John asserts that if Christians keep God's commandments, God remains in them and "the way we know that he remains in us is from the Spirit that he has given us." Thus, faith in Jesus includes keeping God's commandment of love so that he may dwell with us; and the criterion for that is the person of the Holy Spirit given to us. Alternately, we can only possess God's Spirit if we keep his commandment of love; so—in John's peculiar logic—if we have God's Spirit, we have the essential element of salvation.

This teaching of the Johannine community leads us to rely on the Spirit of Jesus to teach us how to follow Jesus our model, and to be our assurance that we are keeping his commandment of love. Perhaps that conclusion does not move us to identify the Spirit as the Spirit of love, but it does help us to discover important qualities of the Paraclete without doing violence to John's teaching.

D. Why Doesn't Scripture Say More about the Spirit of Jesus?

Why doesn't Scripture say more about the Spirit of Jesus? In the first few years after Christ's death, the early Christians did not have the written word of God in the New Testament, but they did have the powerful, external presence of the Spirit of Jesus, which emboldened them and filled so many with the powerful charisms of the Spirit, as we see in the Acts of the Apostles.

For the later church and for us today, when we look to Scripture to inspire our church and our lives, we find precious few verses that deal directly with the Holy Spirit. We get some sense from Luke in Acts, from Paul in his major epistles, and from John's wonderful Paraclete sayings. But these make up only a very small percentage of the New Testament. How can we, at this time in our history, really understand the age of the church and of the Spirit of Jesus, when Scripture does not give an adequate description of the functions of the Spirit for the later church?

We need to start with the perspective of the Gospel writers. It was necessary for them to be primarily concerned with the life, death, and resurrection of Christ—with the real history of our salvation. That is, the heart of our faith is simply the good news of what God did in Jesus Christ. Our faith is an historical religion; the description of that foundational faith must be **objective** and external. The apostles wrote what they experienced firsthand or what came to them from the early followers of Jesus. There would be no Christianity without this careful proclamation about Christ, without this historical foundation. With their testimony, they established our objective salvation on solid grounds.

Christ did, however, indicate, especially at the end of his public life, that his Spirit would come to continue his work on earth. This Spirit of Jesus was to carry on his work and Jesus gave us the general outline of how the Spirit would inspire, teach, guide, support and encourage the church throughout history. And Luke witnessed to Pentecost and to all the charisms and work of the Spirit of Jesus in Acts. This was enough for us to understand that the **subjective** work of our salvation is to be guided and empowered by the Spirit of Jesus.

Still we can press our point: why don't we have a better, clearer description of the function of the Spirit in the church and a realistic picture of how the Spirit of Jesus works in our world? To try to find an answer, let us see what Scripture tells us about God's salvation—a salvation based on Jesus becoming incarnate and human beings remaining free. We look, first, at what Scripture tells us about God's objective salvation in Christ. All we know about Jesus comes from Scripture, especially the four Gospels. And the image of Jesus our Savior in the Gospels is not crystal clear, nor absolutely historical, nor always compelling. In fact, it is two thousand years old; it originated in a culture that is thoroughly different from ours. It would be more compelling if that image were perfectly clear, without divergences among the authors, without cultural differences, and with utterly convincing proofs. Our faith, we imagine, would be so much more compelling if we ourselves could experience Jesus, or if he personally taught us the mysteries of faith and the wonders of God's plan for us. How much easier we think it would be if we could have our own personal experience of Jesus, with clear proofs and inspiring message.

God's answer for us is implied in Scripture. But there is a favorite passage of mine in John of the Cross that states God's response to our question imaginatively yet forcefully:

> If you desire me to declare some secret truths or events to you, fix your eyes on [Christ], and you will discern hidden in him the most secret mysteries, and wisdom and the wonders of God, as my apostle proclaims: "In [the Son of God] are hidden all the treasures of the wisdom and knowledge of God." (Col. 2:3) These treasures of wisdom and knowledge will be far more sublime . . . and advantageous than what you want to know.[3]

This revelation about our **objective** salvation in Jesus is God's whole revelation; it is quite adequate for our faith. It may not be all the evidence and personal experience we might prefer, but it lets us free to believe in Jesus in a reasonable and human way.

Now, let us take a similar look at what Scripture tells us about our **subjective** salvation in the Spirit. God could have sent the Spirit in a very forceful, charismatic way not only at Pentecost but for all times and places. God could have given external gifts and charisms of the Spirit to every Christian, as was done for some people in the apostolic church. These gifts could have been so evident and powerful that no one could doubt God and his power in our world; they would be almost compelled to believe. Their faith, however, would be almost forced upon them, not a free human choice.

Instead, Scripture reveals enough about the Spirit of Jesus for us to freely believe in the Spirit of Jesus. For Scripture assures us that the Spirit is our personal teacher dwelling within us, encouraging us to cry out, "*Abba*, Father," as children of God, and leads us to become intimate friends of Jesus. All of this is not so forceful to people without faith, but it is real and sufficient for people of faith.

In a word, Scripture gives us all the evidence we need to believe in Jesus our Savior. That evidence, however, does not compel us to believe in him; we can freely choose to reject him, as many did even during his public life. And Scripture gives us all the evidence we need to be convinced that the Holy Spirit makes us true sons and daughters of God and will lead us in the way of all truth. Yet the work of God's Spirit is internal and depends on a living faith. That is what Scripture tells us about the work of the Spirit. It may not be what we would wish to find there, but we can only believe that it is sufficient for us in the plan of God.

Notes

1. Walter Abbott, S.J., gen. ed., *The Documents of Vatican II* (New York: Guild Press, 1966), *Lumen Gentium*, #12, 29.

2. See Raymond Brown, *The Gospel According to John, 12–21*, Anchor Bible, vol. 29A (New York: Doubleday, 1966), 628–29.

3. St. John of the Cross, *The Ascent of Mount Carmel*, II, 22, #6; 181.

CHAPTER SEVENTEEN

The Spirit of Jesus and Christology

∞

From all that has been said in this book, we see that there are different christologies and pneumatologies in the New Testament. These differences cannot be reduced to one overarching paradigm without negating the distinctiveness of each one. Modern scripture scholars all affirm such a pluralism, though they would also admit a fundamental unity. In this chapter, we want to look at two basic christologies: a Spirit christology and a Word or Logos christology, for most present-day christologies can be so divided. First we will describe them as found in Scripture and the early church. In the process, we will be careful to point out the function of the Holy Spirit in each christology. Then we will describe how these christologies lead to different pneumatologies and how these can help our spirituality today. Hopefully, this approach will also offer a kind of summary to this entire study on the Spirit of Jesus.

By way of introduction, recall how the Old Testament used many mental or conceptual symbols to express the experience of God. Those symbols—such as God's "Wisdom" or "Word" as well as God's "Spirit" or "Presence"—all relate to particular experiences of God in the world. And the experience reflected in each symbol is somewhat distinctive; for example, Word and Spirit are not identical ideas. However, each of these symbols refers in some way to

God; it is God's presence, power, wisdom, or word that is being experienced. And when these same symbols are used with reference to Jesus, they signify that God is encountered in Jesus.

So when Jesus is identified as the Word or Wisdom of God, that means the transcendent God has been manifested or revealed in the person of Jesus. To speak of Jesus as Word means that he portrayed God's truth and revelation.[1]

Similarly, when the New Testament writers speak of the Spirit of God at work in Jesus' life, they mean that God was encountered in Jesus' person and ministry. So that just as the prophets and leaders in the Old Testament were filled with God's spirit, so Jesus was permanently empowered by God's Spirit. To speak of the Spirit of God in Jesus means that Jesus portrayed God's power and grace.

A. Spirit Christology

Let us consider Spirit christology. The synoptic Gospels all depict God as Spirit at work in Jesus' ministry. Luke especially represents a consistent Spirit christology in narrative form. It begins with Jesus' conception by the overshadowing presence of God as Spirit, so that Jesus is conceived by Mary, yet is born "Son of the most high."

At the beginning of his public life, the Spirit empowers Jesus at his baptism, so that Jesus is able to heal by the power of the Spirit. After Jesus' resurrection, he sends his Spirit to animate the community of his followers. This is what we mean by **Spirit** christology; the focus is on Jesus, in whom God's Spirit is present and active. It was the common way that early Christians expressed their recognition of the presence and power of God in Jesus' life and person; that is, God as Spirit was the principle of life and dynamic energy present and active in Jesus in a wondrous way. The central idea of this christology is empowerment. Such a christology emphasizes Jesus' humanity, for the metaphor of empowering implies an integral human being in whom the Spirit dwells and acts. As a result, it offers our faith a way of life empowered by God as Spirit toward realizing God's values and purposes in all of human history.

Once Christ has returned to the Father, Luke continues to show the Spirit as present and empowering the church. At Pentecost, the Spirit becomes the presence and power of God within the Christian community. That is how Luke continues his Spirit christology in the later church.

B. Word Christology

Word or Logos christology is quite different. The prologue of John's Gospel (John 1:1–14) is the purest form of Word or Logos christology: the Word was; the Word was with God; the Word was God; the Word became flesh. In the incarnation the Word did not just take on flesh or have the appearance of flesh; he became flesh. The word and wisdom that came to the prophets has now become personal in Jesus. And John's entire Gospel continues to present Jesus as the definitive Wisdom and revelation of God. That is, the Wisdom of God, prominent in the wisdom books of the Old Testament, is represented and even personified in Jesus and his teaching. The central idea of **Word** christology is incarnation: God as Word "comes down" and is embodied in the person and ministry of Jesus; the Logos is the manifestation or revelation of God in history; in him we have seen God's glory (John 1:14, 18). Such a christology emphasizes Jesus' **divinity**, because the personification of the Word of God implies a personalized form of being with God from the beginning. As a result, it finds in Jesus the total revelation of God in terms of human life and salvation.

C. Pneumatology Flowing from Spirit Christology

In sections A and B above, we described two **christologies**, two ways of understanding Jesus Christ. Spirit christology describes the person of Christ as empowered by God's Spirit; that is, God is present and active through his Spirit in Jesus, so that Jesus can teach, heal and save us. Word christology describes the person of Jesus as

God's word; that is, God is incarnate in Christ, so that he is the total revelation of God for our salvation. In sections C and D now, we want to describe two **pneumatologies**, two ways of understanding the Holy Spirit. Both of these pneumatologies flow from the two christologies; they each tell us how God is present and active in his Spirit, so that his faithful may know God, love God, and follow in the way of Jesus.

Luke gives us a clear picture of Spirit christology; he describes the Spirit's presence and power at work in Jesus; that is, God as Spirit was the principle of life and dynamic energy present and active in Jesus. Then in Acts, beginning with Pentecost, Luke continues to show the Spirit as present and empowering the early church; and he does this in a way that is quite parallel to his Spirit christology. This is Luke's theology of the Spirit or "pneumatology flowing from Spirit christology."

This kind of pneumatology can be powerful for us today in terms of our own spirituality, because it shows the continuity between the Spirit that empowered Jesus and the Spirit empowering each of us. We can easily see the parallel in our Christian lives; that is, God's Spirit is the presence of God in us by grace in such a way as to empower us to live after the model of Jesus.

D. Pneumatology Flowing from Word Christology

John offers a clear example of Word christology. The prologue of John's Gospel majestically presents Jesus as the Word, the Logos. Then, chapters 1–13 present Jesus as the Truth, the Revelation of God; these chapters are the best example of Word christology. Then in chapters 14 through 16, John's Jesus promises his disciples a "new Advocate," who would take his place and "be with [them] always." John implies that just as Jesus himself is the Word of God and the complete truth of revelation, so the Spirit of Truth will be Jesus' mirror image present in all Christians to the end of time. We see how Jesus himself describes the functions of his Paraclete: "he will teach you everything"; "he will remind you of all that I told you"; "he will guide you to all truth"; "he will take from what is mine and declare it to you"; "he will declare to you the things that are coming." All of these works of the Spirit of Jesus are precisely the same functions of Jesus, the Word, in John's Gospel. This is how John continues his Word christology in the early church.

What this implies is that the Word christology takes on a new persona; the Spirit of Truth now takes the place of Jesus after he has ascended. That's what is meant by "pneumatology flowing from Word christology"; that is, the theology of the Spirit or pneumatology describes the Spirit at work in our lives similar to the way that Word christology describes Christ, the Word, revealing the whole truth about God and our salvation.

Notice how Jesus describes the work of the Paraclete as totally parallel to his own work as the Word of God, the revelation of God. For example, the Spirit of Jesus will "not speak on his own, but he will speak what he hears . . . ; he will take from what is mine and declare it to you." In the very next verse, Jesus adds that just as he himself spoke the very words of God, because "everything that the Father has is mine," so now the Spirit of Truth will precisely "take from what is mine and declare it to you." (John 16:15) These five Paraclete sayings of Jesus constitute what is meant by "pneumatology flowing from Word christology."

Such a pneumatology can be a powerful source of spirituality for us today. It reminds us that we live in the age of the Spirit; we are to be guided by the Spirit of Jesus; we can put great trust in the Spirit of Jesus who "will guide [us] to all truth." It teaches us that Jesus himself intends that the Paraclete be his new persona dwelling within us; it encourages us to believe that what Jesus was to his disciples, the Paraclete is meant to be for us. This is why this recent development of pneumatology in the church is so promising, and why the new appreciation of the Spirit of Jesus in our spirituality and prayer life can be so fruitful.

E. Holy Spirit Spirituality

These two pneumatologies suggest a spirituality based on the Spirit of Jesus. Such a spirituality based on the Holy Spirit might include two principal themes: first, the heart of such a spirituality springs from the four sources of **intimacy** with God found in the New Testament (see above, chapter 11); second, Jesus himself **promises** that the Holy Spirit will be the power, the guide, and the new presence for Christians after he returns to the Father.

1. Intimacy with God

John presents the foundational source of intimacy for us: "Whoever loves me will keep my word, and my Father will love him, and we will come to him and make our dwelling with him." (John 14:23) This presence of the Father and Jesus is established by means of the Paraclete: "the Father . . . will give you another Advocate to be with you always, the Spirit of truth . . . [who] remains with you and will be in you." (John 14:16–17) In this instance, Jesus tells us that the Spirit is the one who dwells in us permanently, and by means of this Spirit both the Father and the Son come to us and love us.

Paul bases our intimacy with God on our real relationship to God as our Father: "those who are led by the Spirit of God are children of God . . . the Spirit itself bears witness with our spirit that we are children of God." (Rom. 8:14–16) He tells us that we are children of our Father because we possess the Spirit of God's Son (Gal. 4:6), so we can cry out familiarly, "*Abba*, Father."

John, on the other hand, presents our intimacy with Jesus as one of friendship: "I have called you friends, because I have told you everything I heard from my Father." (John 15:13–15) For John, our personal friendship with Jesus is permanently based on the new Advocate whom he sends: "I will not leave you orphans; I will come to you"; Jesus means he will come back to us by means of his Spirit "who will remain with [us] always."

Luke and the synoptics describe our intimacy with Jesus as stronger than a blood or family relationship to him: "My mother and my brothers are those who hear the word of God and act on it." (Luke 8:19–21) He means that our primary relationship to Jesus is as his brother or sister, which is based on our "hearing the word of God and acting upon it." True, Luke makes no connection to the Holy Spirit here, but our theology teaches that our spiritual relationship is acquired and maintained through Baptism, faith, and sanctifying grace, and all these are appropriated to the Holy Spirit.

These are the ways that Scripture describes our intimacy with God and with Christ. Simple faithfulness to the way that Scripture describes these sources of intimacy will assure us that our spirituality is Spirit-based. When we reflect on God's presence in us, we remember Jesus' words: "[the Father] will give you another Advocate to be with you always." When we cry out to God in prayer, we can pray "*Abba*, Father," because the Spirit makes us "children of God." When we ask Jesus, our friend, to know him more intimately, we recall his promise that the Paraclete "will teach [us] everything . . . and remind [us] of all" he taught us. When we need assurance that Jesus considers us his brother or sister, we ask his Spirit to help us "hear the word of God and keep it."

2. The Promises of Jesus

Christ himself in Scripture encourages us to base our spirituality on the Holy Spirit. When Jesus is about to die, he promises his apostles the spiritual power and knowledge they will need in order to know him, give witness to him, and follow his way. Luke and John present these promises prominently at the end of their Gospels.

In Luke, Jesus attested, "I am sending the promise of my Father upon you" (Luke 24:49), and repeated his pledge: "You will receive power when the holy Spirit comes upon you, and you will be my witnesses . . . to the ends of the earth" (Acts 1:8); then he fulfilled that promise to them: "they were all filled with the Holy Spirit." (Acts 2:4) For at Pentecost the early church was given the power of the Holy Spirit to witness to Jesus and to live out that witness. Jesus' promise is also meant for all his followers throughout time.

In John, Jesus' five Paraclete sayings are an all-inclusive promise to the disciples: "The Advocate . . . will teach you everything and remind you of all that I told you." (John 14:26) Here Jesus means that the Paraclete will remind us of all that he told us and lead us in the way of all truth; the Paraclete is to take the place of Jesus within us. Because we believe in Jesus' promise, then, our spirituality is rightly centered on the Spirit of Jesus.

Note

1. For a clear presentation of these two main categories of christology today, see Roger Haight, S.J., "Two Types of Christology," in *Chicago Studies* 38, no. 2 (Summer/Fall, 1999): 117–27.

CHAPTER EIGHTEEN

A Simple Pneumatology Based on Luke, Paul, and John

∞

In this last chapter, it might be helpful to offer one theological synthesis of the pneumatology presented in this book. It will be a deliberate oversimplification in terms of emphasizing one primary mission of the Spirit of Jesus in Luke, in Paul, and in John.

A. The Spirit as Gift

Christian theology teaches that all three divine persons are specially present in everyone who has been transformed in grace through the sacrament of Baptism. But when theologians describe this union with God, they do not traditionally speak in terms of the Trinity but of the "indwelling of the Holy Spirit." What is behind this tradition of theology? Apparently theologians are following the lead of Scripture, which implies that God and Christ dwell within us by means of the Holy Spirit: [the Father and I] "will come to [them] and make our dwelling with [them]" (John 14:23), and the immediate context explains: "I will ask the Father, and he will give you another Advocate to be with you always, the Spirit of truth." (John 14:16–17) That is, just as Scripture **appropriates** the divine indwelling to the Holy Spirit, so do theologians.

Theologians would also add a profound historical reason that is generated by their description of the internal life of the Trinity; that is, just as the Father and Son express their love for each other in the Spirit, so the Father and the Son make themselves present to us in love precisely by sending us their Spirit. The Spirit is their gift of love and the sign of their presence: as the expression of the Father's love, the Spirit forms us into sons/daughters of God and draws us to the Father; as the expression of the Son's love, the Spirit molds us after the image of Christ and unites us in his body. By this gift of the Spirit in baptism, we are anointed to live this new divine life as children of God the Father; by this gift we are incorporated into Christ, we belong to him, we live in him.

What constitutes the **manner** of the Spirit's presence; what are the effects of the Spirit within us? This whole study is meant to be an answer to that question. But by deliberate oversimplification, we can point to **three** main works of the Spirit of Jesus, as found in Luke, in Paul, and in John.[1]

B. The Spirit in Luke: The Source of Power and Inspiration

In Luke, the Spirit was the source of Christ's power. Throughout Luke's Gospel Jesus is filled with "the power of the Spirit" (Luke 4:14) and his word and work are accomplished with the help of the Spirit. Then in Acts, Luke presents the coming of the Holy Spirit at Pentecost as the moving power and inspiration for the early Christians and for the community of the church. Peter, Paul, and Stephen are inspired to give witness to Christ and effect the conversion of thousands by means of the Spirit. The Christian community is aided in its particular decisions and actions by the Spirit. Acts is dominated by the power and the inspiration of the Spirit. And that same power and inspiration of the Spirit of Jesus is ready to direct us in our day, to the degree that we are willing to depend on the Spirit.

C. The Spirit in Paul:
An Indwelling Presence and Sanctifier

In 1 Corinthians Paul tells the Corinthians: "you are the temple of of God and . . . the Spirit of God dwells in you." (1 Cor. 3:16–17) And later, he applies this same metaphor to individual Christians (6:19). He means that just as God made his dwelling with Israel as a holy sanctuary among them (Ezek. 36:26–27 and 37:26–28), now the Corinthians form a new sanctuary or temple of God because of the Holy Spirit dwelling among them and within each one. Later in Corinthians, Paul describes them as members of the body of Christ: "in one Spirit we were all baptized into one body." (1 Cor. 12:12–13) This is Paul's inspired way of describing their profound union with Christ by means of baptism and the Spirit; he wants them to realize that their bodies are holy, they belong to Christ, each one must be respected.

The third effect of the indwelling of the Spirit of Jesus is that we each become a son or daughter of God: "God sent the Spirit of his Son into our hearts, crying out, '*Abba*, Father.'" (Gal. 4:6) Because we possess "the Spirit of his Son" in our hearts, we can address God familiarly as "Father." Again, this sanctification is activated by the Holy Spirit.

Three Pauline metaphors teach that we are dedicated to God because of our anointing with the Spirit in baptism; we are made holy by means of the presence and action of the Spirit of God dwelling within us. All of Paul's spirituality flows from these realities; in more than a dozen different ways, he teaches that because we live in Christ by his Spirit, we should grow into the likeness of Jesus.

D. The Spirit in John:
Our Personal Teacher and Advocate

In John's Gospel, chapters 14 through 16, the Advocate takes the place of Jesus once he has finished his earthly work: "the Father will give you another Advocate to be with you always." (John 14:16)

From then on, the Spirit of Jesus will dwell within each of us as our personal teacher: to remind us of all Jesus taught, to teach us everything that Jesus revealed, to lead us in the way of Jesus, to announce the things to come; he will be our personal counselor: to testify to the truth of Jesus, to take up the defense of Jesus before the unbelieving world.

The very purpose of the Paraclete within us individually is to help us understand the deeper meaning of his words, to remember what Jesus taught by his words and example, to clarify the way of Jesus in our present world, to know how to apply the teaching of Jesus in the "things that are coming," to encourage us in the face of our unbelieving world. This inspiration of the Spirit of Truth acts from within us to form our personal life of faith and understanding, to teach us how to mold our life after the model of Jesus.

One of the most effective ways that the Spirit of Jesus teaches us internally is in mental prayer, for that is the primary method we have for studying the words, actions, example, and way of Jesus. Our entire prayer life is rightly centered on Jesus. In John, that is exactly the purpose of the Spirit of Truth within us.

* * * * *

Let me conclude this book with the insights of two outstanding scholars regarding the work of the Holy Spirit. Karl Rahner summarizes what Pentecost means for Christ's church:

> Pentecost is not a mere transitory visitation by the Spirit. . . . Rather Pentecost . . . is at basis only the outward manifestation of the much more vital fact that henceforward the Spirit will never more be wholly withdrawn from the world until the end of time. For this permanent dwelling of the Spirit in the world is only the outcome of that overshadowing of the Spirit which took place in the incarnation of the Son of the Father. And because the church is nothing else than the visible manifestation of the Spirit in the world, therefore the church . . . only becomes visible and manifest for the first time at Pentecost.[2]

That is, Pentecost is the beginning of the **era of the Spirit**; from that day on, the Spirit of Jesus dwells permanently in our world and is manifested in the church until the end of time.

Raymond Brown summarizes the work of the Spirit of Jesus in God's whole plan of salvation this way:

> God was diffusive of his being in creating a good world that mirrored him and especially in creating intelligent human beings that mirrored his intelligence. But God could not be satisfied until he became embroiled in human history with all its successes and failures by identifying himself with one people (Israel). . . . Still God was not satisfied, and so he further embroiled himself in one human life, that of Jesus Christ. But God's ultimate act of presence to the world that he created and redeemed involves his entrance into individual human lives as the Holy Spirit. The Holy Spirit is the ultimate revelation of God . . . the Spirit is the supreme presence of God . . . : "The Father will give you another Paraclete, the Spirit of truth, to be with you forever. . . . He remains with you and is within you." (John 15–17)[3]

That is, God's plan of salvation included a progressive means of revealing himself to us and of being embroiled in our world. God's ultimate involvement in our lives is accomplished **by the Spirit of Truth,** who is intimately present in each one of us as our personal teacher of the way of Jesus.

Notes

1. For a similar development of these three functions of the Holy Spirit, see Bernard Cooke, *Christian Sacraments and Christian Personality* (New York: Holt, Rinehart and Winston, 1965), 45–50.

2. Karl Rahner, *Theological Investigations,* vol. 7 (New York: Herder and Herder, 1971), 187.

3. Raymond Brown, *Biblical Exegesis and Church Doctrine* (New York: Paulist Press, 1985), 112.

Select Bibliography

Abbott, Walter, S.J., gen. ed. *The Documents of Vatican II*. New York: Guild Press, 1966.

Anderson, James B. *A Vatican II Pneumatology of the Paschal Mystery*. Roma: Editrice Pontificia Universita Gregoriana, 1988.

Arintero, J. G., OP. *Stages in Prayer*. St. Louis, MO: B. Herder Book Co., 1957.

Barrett, C. K. *The Holy Spirit and the Gospel Tradition*. London: SPCK, 1975.

Bermejo, Luis, S.J. *The Spirit of Life*. Chicago: Loyola U. Press, 1989.

Bloesch, Donald. *The Holy Spirit, Works and Gifts*. Downers Grove, IL: InterVarsity Press, 1996.

Brown, Raymond, S.S. *The Gospel According to John*. New York: Doubleday, 1966. Vols. 29 and 29A, Anchor Bible Series.

———. *The Epistles of John*. New York: Doubleday, 1982. Vol. 30, Anchor Bible Series.

———. *The Churches the Apostles Left Behind*. New York: Paulist Press, 1984.

———. *The Community of the Beloved Disciple*. New York: Paulist Press, 1979.

———. *Biblical Exegesis and Church Doctrine*. New York: Paulist Press, 1985.

———. "Diverse Views of the Spirit in the New Testament," *Worship* 57 (May 1983): 225–36.

Burgess, Stanley. *The Spirit and the Church: Antiquity.* Peabody, MA: Hendrickson, 1984.
———. *The Holy Spirit: Eastern Church Traditions.* Peabody, MA: Hendrickson, 1989.
Carillo Alday, Salvador, MSpS. *Power from on High: The Holy Spirit in the Gospel and Acts.* Ann Arbor, MI: Servant Books, 1978.
Collins, Gerald, S.J. *Christology.* Oxford, NY: Oxford U. Press, 1995.
———. *First Corinthians.* Collegeville, MN: The Liturgical Press, 1999. Vol. 7, Sacra Pagina Series.
Congar, Yves, M.J. *I Believe in the Holy Spirit.* 3 vols. New York: Seabury Press, 1983.
Cooke, Bernard, S.J. *Christian Sacraments and Christian Personality.* New York: Holt, Rinehart and Winston, 1965.
De la Croix, Paul-Marie, OCD. *The Biblical Spirituality of St. John.* Staten Is., NY: Alba House (St. Paul Publications), 1966.
De la Potterie, Ignace, S.J., and Stanislaus Lyonnet, S.J. *The Christian Lives by the Spirit*, Staten Is., NY: Alba House, 1971.
Dunn, James D. G. *Jesus and the Spirit.* Philadelphia: Westminster Press, 1975.
———. *The Christ and the Spirit.* 2 vols. Grand Rapids, MI: Wm. B. Eerdmans, 1998.
———. *The Theology of Paul the Apostle*, Grand Rapids, MI: Wm. B. Eerdmans, 1998.
Durrwell, Francois-Xavier. *Holy Spirit of God (An Essay in Biblical Theology)*, trans. Sr. Benedict Davies, OSU. London: Geoffrey Chapman, 1986.
Ellis, Peter. *Seven Pauline Letters.* Collegeville, MN: The Liturgical Press, 1982.
Fatula, Mary Ann, OP. *The Holy Spirit: Unbounded Gift of Joy.* Collegeville, MN: Liturgical Press, 1998.
Fee, Gordon D. *God's Empowering Presence: The Holy Spirit in the Letters of Paul.* Peabody, MA: Hendrickson, 1994.
———. *The First Epistle to the Corinthians.* Grand Rapids, MI: Wm. B. Eerdmans, 1987.
———. *Paul, the Spirit and the People of God.* Peabody, MA: Hendrickson, 1996.
Ferguson, Sinclair. *The Holy Spirit.* Downers Grove, IL: InterVarsity Press, 1996. Part of *Contours of Christian Theology*, ed. G. Bray.
Fitzmyer, Joseph, S.J. *The Gospel According to Luke.* New York: Doubleday, 1981. Vols. 28 and 28A, Anchor Bible Series.

―――. *The Acts of the Apostles*. New York: Doubleday, 1998. Vol. 31, Anchor Bible Series.

―――. *Romans*. New York: Doubleday, 1993. Vol. 33, Anchor Bible Series.

―――. *According to Paul*. New York: Paulist Press, 1993.

Furnish, Victor Paul, *II Corinthians*. New York: Doubleday, 1984. Vol. 32A, Anchor Bible Series.

Garrigou-Lagrange, R., OP. *The Three Ages of the Interior Life*. Vol. 2. St. Louis, MO: Herder, 1948.

Gaybba, Brian. *The Spirit of Love: Theology of the Holy Spirit*. London: Cassell, 1987. Vol. 6, Geoffrey Chapman Theology Library.

Haight, Roger, S.J. *Jesus, Symbol of God*. Maryknoll, NY: Orbis Books, 1999.

―――. "Two Types of Christology," *Chicago Studies* 38, 2 (Summer/Fall 1999): 117–27.

Hays, Richard B., *First Corinthians*. Louisville, KY: John Knox Press, 1997. Part of the series Interpretation: A Bible Commentary for Teaching and Preaching.

Hull, J. H. E. *The Holy Spirit in the Acts of the Apostles*. Cleveland: World Publishing, 1967.

John Paul II. *The Spirit, Giver of Life and Love*. Boston: Pauline Books and Media, 1996.

Johnson, George. *The Spirit-Paraclete in the Gospel of John*. Cambridge: London University Press, 1970.

Johnson, Luke Timothy. *The First and Second Letters to Timothy*. New York: Doubleday, 2001. Vol. 35A, Anchor Bible Series.

Johnson, William. *Mystical Theology*. London: HarperCollins Publishers, 1995.

Karris, Robert. *Prayer and the New Testament*. New York: Crossroad, 2000.

Kasper, Walter. *The God of Jesus Christ*. New York: Crossroad, 1986.

Kavenaugh, Kieran, OCD, and Otilio Rodriguez, OCD, eds. *The Collected Works of St. John of the Cross*. Washington, DC: ICS Publications, 1979.

―――. *The Collected Works of St. Teresa of Avila*. 3 vols. Washington, DC: ICS Publications, 1976.

Kinn, James. *Contemplation 2000; St. John of the Cross for Today*. Petersham, MA: St. Bede Publications, 1997.

Kung, Hans. *The Church*. New York: Sheed and Ward, 1967.

MacDonald. Margaret Y. *Colossians, Ephesians.* Collegeville, MN: The Liturgical Press, 2000. Vol. 17, Sacra Pagina Series.

Marie-Eugene, P., OCD. *I Want to See God; A Practical Synthesis of Carmelite Spirituality.* Chicago: Fides Publishers, 1953.

Marmion, Dom Columba, OSB. *The Trinity in Our Spiritual Life.* Westminster, MD: Newman Press, 1953. An anthology of the writings of Dom Columba Marmion, by Dom Raymond Thibaut, OSB.

———. *Fire of Love.* London: Sandsand Co., 1964. An anthology of the writings of Dom Columba Marmion by Charles Dollen.

Marshall, I. H., and D. Petersen, eds. *Witness to the Gospel: The Theology of Acts.* Grand Rapids, MI: Wm. B. Eerdmans, 1998.

Martin, Ralph. *The Catholic Church at the End of an Age.* San Francisco: Ignatius Press, 1994.

Martyn, J. Louis. *Galatians.* New York: Doubleday, 1998. Volume 33A, Anchor Bible Series.

McBrien, Richard. *Catholicism.* San Francisco: Harper and Row, 1981.

McDonnell, Kilian, OSB, and George Montague, SM. *Christian Initiation and Baptism in the Holy Spirit.* Collegeville, MN: Liturgical Press, 1991.

Menzies, Robert P. *The Development of Early Christian Pneumatology.* Sheffield, England: Sheffield Academic Press, 1991.

Moloney, Francis J., SDB *The Gospel of John.* Collegeville, MN: The Liturgical Press, 1998. Vol. 4, *Sacra Pagina Series.*

Moltmann, Jurgen, *The Spirit of Life.* Minneapolis, MN: Fortress Press, 1992.

Morwood, Michael, S.J. *Tomorrow's Catholic.* Mystic, CT: Twenty-third Publications, 1997.

O'Carroll, Michael, CSSP. *Veni Creator Spiritus: A Theological Encyclopedia of the Holy Spirit.* Collegeville, MN: Liturgical Press, 1990.

O'Connor, Edward. *Pope Paul and the Spirit; Charisms and Church Renewal in the Teaching of Paul VI.* Notre Dame, IN: Ave Maria Press, 1978.

Rahner Karl, S.J. *The Spirit in the Church.* New York: Crossroad Seabury, 1979.

———. *The Content of Faith.* New York: Crossroad, 1993.

———. *On Prayer.* Collegeville, MN: Liturgical Press, 1993.

———. *Theological Investigations.* Vol. 7. New York: Herder and Herder, 1971.

Richard, Earl J. *First and Second Thessalonians.* Collegeville, MN: Liturgical Press, 1995. Vol. 11, Sacra Pagina Series.

Schillebeeckx, Edward, OP. *Christ, the Sacrament of the Encounter with God.* New York: Sheed and Ward, 1963.

Schnackenburg, Rudolph. *The Gospel According to St. John*. 3 vols. Kent: Burns and Oates, 1992. This is part of Herder's Theological Commentary on the New Testament.

———. *The Church in the New Testament*. New York: Herder and Herder, 1965.

Schweizer, Eduard. *The Holy Spirit*. Philadelphia: Fortress Press, 1980.

Sheets, John, S.J. *The Spirit Speaks in Us*. Wilkes-Barre, PA: Dimension Books, 1968.

Squires, John T. "The Plan of God." In *Witness to the Gospel*. Grand Rapids, MI: Eerdmans, 1998, 24–32.

Stanley, David M., S.J. *Boasting in the Lord*. New York: Paulist Press, 1973.

Swete, H. B. *The Holy Spirit in the Ancient Church*. London: Macmillan, 1912.

Turner, Max. "The 'Spirit of Prophecy' as the Power of Israel's Restoration and Witness." In *Witness to the Gospel*. Grand Rapids, MI: Eerdmans, 1998, 328–47.

Van Roo, William, S.J. *Telling about God*. Vol. 2, *Experience*. Roma: Editrice Pontificia Universita Gregoriana, 1987.

Von Balthasar, Hans Uhr. *Prayer*. New York: Sheed & Ward, 1961.

Index

Abraham, 124
Acts, 53, 57, 77, 93, 103, 190, 193, 194; church, baptism and gift of Spirit and, 39–40, 99, 167; counsel and, 38; courage and, 38; faith, baptism and gift of Spirit and, 38–39; Luke's symbolism for Spirit of Jesus and, 40–41; number of times Holy Spirit in, 31, 93, 175; Ordo Salutis in, 38–39; Pentecost, gifts of Holy Spirit and, 37–38, 102, 169, 191, 195, 201, 202; Pentecost and, 33–34, 41; Pentecost as foundation for witness throughout, 34–36, 78–79, 190; Pentecost transforming Jesus' following into missionary movement and, 36–37, 96, 106, 109–10, 208; soul of church and, 105–6; understanding and, 37; wisdom and, 37; (overview of) work of Spirit in, 32
Advocate, 129–30. *See also* Paraclete
Agabus, 35, 36
Alexander of Hales, 166
Ambrose, St., 182
Ananias, 108, 176
Anchor Bible Series, xi
apostles: courage of, 38; healing by, 19, 34
Aquinas, Thomas, 37, 145, 168
arrabon (first installment), 111
Augustine, Saint, 103

baptism, 6, 13, 17, 25, 31; church, gift of Spirit and, 39–40, 43–44, 73, 108, 126, 137, 166–67; confirmation v., 167–69; faith, gift of Spirit and, 38–39, 43–44, 72; fire and, 40–41; forgiveness in, 168; of Gentiles, 99; of Jesus, 30, 40, 43–44, 65–66,

117–18; with public purpose, 69; as rebirth, 87; resurrection and, 168; as sacrament, 166–69, 207; salvation from, 43–44; sealing and, 69; of 3000, 36; water of, 44, 99–100, 167
Barnabas, 32, 102, 106, 108, 175, 176
Barth, Markus, 69
Bermejo, Luis, 76
body, 99; of Christ, 12–14, 67, 68, 72, 74, 76–77, 99, 137, 174, 176; of church, 12–13, 21, 72, 74, 76–77, 104, 105, 174, 176; leading sin and death, 16, 23; against Spirit, 23; as temple, 11–12
Bonaventure, St., 166
brother, Jesus Christ as, 161–63
Brown, Ray, viii, 57, 59–61, 93–94, 108, 132, 177, 211

Calvin, John, viii
Catholic church: Holy Spirit for, viii; leaders, gifts of Spirit and, 168; love and, 82; mental prayer of, 138; reforms in, 88–89; sacramental faith of, 165
charisms, 18, 20, 67, 73–74, 75–76, 85, 101, 105, 137, 174, 191, 193
Children of God, 6–9, 63–64, 71–72, 101, 124–25, 158–59, 176, 197, 204, 205
Christ: body of, 12–14, 67, 68, 72, 74, 76–77, 99, 137, 174, 176; mind of, 15; Mystical Body of, 77; putting on (armor) of, 70; witness to, 32

Christians: bearing witness of Jesus, 54–55, 190; guide to truth for, 57–58, 102–3, 131–32, 141; in image of Christ, 23; Spirit of Jesus in, 92, 103–8, 182; as temples of God, 5, 11–12
christology: Holy Spirit spirituality and, 203–6; Spirit, 199, 200–202; Word, 199, 201, 202–3
church, 32; auguration of, 33; baptism and gift of Spirit and, 39–40, 43–44, 73, 108, 126, 166–67; believers lost in, 80; body of Christ and, 12–13, 68, 72, 74, 76–77, 104, 105, 174, 176; building of, 21; christology, Holy Spirit and, 199–206; Christ's goal in, 67; continuity of early, 175–76; disputes in, 79; as divine, 174, 175, 176–79; experienced presence in early, 181, 191; external v. internal working of Holy Spirit in modern, 191–92; gifts of Spirit and, viii, 17, 104–5, 178, 207–8; human/flaws of, 174, 175–76, 177–78, 179; Jesus, suffering, redemption and, 187–88; Jesus, Holy Spirit, scripture's lacking and, 194–97; Jesus, Spirit, reminding and, 188–89; Jesus' departing better for, 185–87; Jesus' returning and, 185–87, 189–90; leaders of, 86, 87–89, 177–79; not attentive to Spirit, prayer and, 192–93; Paraclete, Spirit of Truth not Love and,

193–94; Pentecost and, 33–34, 201, 202, 210; Pentecost transforming Jesus' following into missionary movement, Luke and, 36–37, 93, 96, 106, 109–10; pneumatology of Luke, Paul and John for, 207–11; presence by faith in modern, 182–83, 190, 191–92; salvation history of, 29, 32, 77, 102; scandal's of modern, 57, 176; as temple of God, 5, 11–12, 70, 103–4, 174; witnessing in modern, 190. *See also* Johannine church; Lukan church; Pastoral Epistles church; Pauline church
circumcision, 176
Colossians, 12–13, 140, 160
commandment: double, 60–61; of God, 60–61
condemnation, 56
confession, 18
confirmation, 167–69
Cooke, Bernard, 168
1 Corinthians, xiii, 6, 11–12, 14, 17, 18–21, 68, 69, 95, 101, 104, 137, 139, 148, 174, 188, 209
2 Corinthians, 17, 25, 155
Cornelius, 87
cosmology, 75
Council of Jerusalem, 106
Council of Trent, 44
counsel, 38
courage, 38

David, 3
De La Potterie, Ignace, 55
de Sales, St. Francis, 141
deacons, 32, 86

Dei Verbum (On Revelation), xi, xiv
Deuteronomy, 22
disciple(s): bearing witness to Jesus, 53–55, 61, 81, 96, 129–30, 190; beloved, never dying, 81; as choosen community and faith, 62–63, 106; disciples teaching and making of, 157, 160; in early church, 86, 173, 181; forgiveness of sin done by, 107, 166; Holy Spirit reminding, 47, 50–51, 94, 129, 169, 189–90; Jesus friendship with, 160; Jesus' departure as better and, 185–86; Jesus' final commission in terms of Spirit and, 30–31; Jesus' privileges/promises to, after resurrection, 132–33, 185–87, 189–90, 204, 205–6; leader passing of spirit on to, 47; prayers of, 48, 132–34; recalling Jesus, 50–52; Spirit testifying to, 53–54, 190
discipleship *(mathetes)*, 31
dove, 40
down payment *(arrabon)*, 16–17

Easter mystery, 169
Elizabeth, 101
Ephesians, xii, 12–13, 24, 67–70, 191–92; baptism, sealing and, 69; Christ's goal in church and, 67; church as temple of God in, 103–4; wisdom and, 68, 70
eschatological spirit, 111–13
eternal life: from faith, 45; Spirit as pledge of, 9, 111, 131, 186

Eucharist, 10, 137, 161, 166, 167–68
evil: God, sin and, 9, 84, 119–20; from imperfection of humans, 9
evolution, 75
Exegetes, 44, 69
Exodus, 15, 119
Ezekiel, 4, 10–11, 209

faith, 6, 13, 15, 73: baptism, gift of Spirit and, 38–39, 72; Confirmation of, 168; effects of Spirit with, 19, 23, 191; eternal life from, 45; in hostile world, 81; in Jesus Christ, love, and chosen by God, 62–64; keeping, pure, 179; objective, 195; with Paraclete, 186–87; prayer of, 143–44; presence by, in modern church, 182–83, 190, 191–92; sacramental, 165; salvation from, in Jesus Christ, 45–46, 113; weak, 130
family, Jesus Christ as, 161–63, 204–5
Father: *Abba* (my), 6, 7–8, 9, 72, 120, 124–25, 141, 158–59, 182, 197, 204, 205; God as, 158–59; identities between God, Jesus and, x, xi, 58–59, 60; incomprehensible, xi; knowledge of, 133; Old Testament and, 7; operations of Jesus Christ and, x, xi; our, 8, 75, 118–20; Spirit sent by, ix, 53; spiritual origin from, ix
Fee, Gordon, xii, 76
filioque, viii
fire, 40–41

first fruits *(aparche)*, 16–17
Fitzmyer, Joseph, 7, 112, 162
flesh. *See* body
forgiveness, 8–9; in baptism, 168; from sacraments, 165; of sin, 31, 32, 77–78, 107, 119, 131, 166, 186
free will, 80, 84, 195
freedom, Spirit of, 15–16, 23
friend, Jesus Christ as, 159–61

Galatians, 6–7, 15–16, 22–23, 25–26, 63, 72, 92, 101, 125, 150–51
generosity, 23
Gentiles, 106; conversions of, 32, 36, 108–9; Jews and, 69, 73, 104
glossolalia. *See* tongues, speaking in
God: children of, 6–9, 61, 63–64, 71–72, 101, 124–25, 158–59, 176, 197, 204, 205; commandment of, 60–61; depths of, 14; dwelling place of, in Spirit, 68; as Father, 158–59; as forgiving and loving, 8–9, 119; good and evil and, 9, 84, 119–20; grace (gift) of, 25–26; as holy, 119; humble reliance on, 119; as judge, 8; love and, 61, 62, 72, 126, 131, 145, 150–52, 157, 165, 204; mighty deeds of, 19; personal presence of, 156–58; personified wisdom of, 47, 68, 70; providence of, 83; salvation of, 195; the soul and, 151; symbols of, 199–200; temple of, 5, 11–12, 70, 103–4, 139, 174; transcendent, 74–75;

union with, 150–51; will of, 123, 134, 137, 146, 162, 183; WORD of God, Jesus Christ and, 45, 70, 140, 173, 199, 201, 202–3. *See also* Father; intimacy with God
God's Empowering Presence (Fee), 76
grace (*charis*): as gift, 26; as greeting, 25; from Holy Spirit, ix, 25–26, 97, 148, 186; from sacraments, 165, 167
Green, Michael, 76

healing, 73; by apostles, 19, 34; by Jesus, 67
Holy Spirit: definition of, vii; disciples reminded by, 50–51, 94, 129, 169, 189–90; East v. West approach to, viii; external v. internal working of, 191–92; functions of, x; impersonal aspects of, vii–viii, 3–4, 37; leaders of church guided by, 86, 87–88, 178; personal aspect of, x; power of, 32; Scripture inspired by, xiv–xv; sealing of, 69; Word and, 70, 173. *See also* Spirit
hope, 9; as fruits of Spirit, 24–25
Huios (son), 63; adoptive son v., 6–7
Huiosthesia (adoptive son), 6–7

I Believe in the Holy Spirit (Green), 76
immanence, indwelling, 49–50
intimacy of God: Jesus as brother/family with, 161–63, 205–6; Jesus as friend with, 159–61; our Father, 158–59; personal presence with, 156–58; spirituality and, 204–5
Isaiah, 66–67, 117
Israel: period of, 29–30; spirit of leaders of, 3–4

Jeremiah, 10
Jeremias, Joachim, 7, 8
Jerome Biblical Commentary, xi
Jesus Christ: *Abba* (my) Father unique to, 6, 7–8, 72, 120, 125, 158–59, 182.197, 204, 205; baptism of, 30, 40, 43–44, 65–66, 117–18; birth of, 30, 200; as brother/family, 161–63, 205–6; confidence/persistence in prayer by, 120–22; crucifixion/suffering of, 126, 188–89; death of, 160, 168, 194; departure of, better, 185–87; difficult virtues of, 55; disciples bearing witness to, 53–57, 61, 96, 129–30, 190; disciples given Spirit by, 47, 169; disciple's prayers to, 48, 132–34; disciples recalling, 50–52; divine indwelling of Spirit of, 49–50, 80, 87, 92–93, 96, 98–99, 101, 120, 123, 134, 176–78, 182, 201, 207, 209; Father and, as one, 49; final commission in terms of Spirit, 30–31, 77; as friend, 159–61; guiding along way of truth and, 57–58, 102–3, 131–32, 157, 186, 193; Holy Spirit, scripture's lacking and, 194–97;

Holy Spirit after, returned to Father, 37, 44, 49, 56, 60, 80, 93–94, 113, 127, 155, 185–87; Holy Spirit and, x, 60–64, 65–66, 69, 74, 76, 98–110, 118; identities between God, the Father and, x, xi, 58–59, 60; justice, innocence of, 56; as Lord, x, 21; love of, 82, 97–98, 141, 155, 192, 204; Messiahship of, 27, 69; as model of prayer, 122; new life in, 98–100, 150; opposition between world and, 55–56; Paraclete and resemblance/continuance of, 59–60, 81, 127–28, 132–33, 185–87; Pentecost transforming Jesus' following into missionary movement, Luke and, 36–37, 96, 106, 109–10, 208; personal presence of Spirit of, 48, 156–58; personal relationship with, 97–98, 135–36, 155; praying of our Father by, 118–20; promises of, 108–10, 132–33, 185–87, 189–90, 204, 205–6; resurrection of, 37, 92, 107, 129, 131–33, 168; salvation and, xii, 29, 40, 77, 193–94; as truth and salvation, 45–46, 57, 95–98, 102; two natures of, viii; uniting Jews and Gentiles, 69; as WORD of God, 45. *See also* Christ

Jews, 69, 73, 104

Joel, 33, 35, 87, 111

Johannine church: authority issues in, 85; divine/human side of, 176–78; egalitarianism of, 82; experienced presence in, 181; free will and, 84; general description of, 80–81; God's providence with, 83; love and, 82; Paraclete, Jesus returned to the Father and, 80; soul of, 106–8; Spirit, prayer and, 81–82; strengths of, 81–84; weaknesses of, 84–85

John (apostle), 8, 155, 207; baptism, faith and gift of Spirit and, 38–39, 43–44, 108; children of God in, 61, 63–64, 176, 205; discernment of Spirit and, 22; disciples, forgiveness of sins and, 107, 166; disciples bearing witness to Jesus in, 53–57, 61, 81, 96, 129–30, 190; disciples recalling Jesus and, 50–52; divine indwelling of, 49–50, 80, 96, 134, 152, 157–58, 176–78, 182, 207; eschatological spirit of, 112–13; five Paraclete text by, 47–58, 81–82, 186, 195; guiding along way of truth and, 57–58, 102–3, 131–32, 157, 186, 193; identities between God, the Father and Jesus in, 58–59, 60; individual Christians influenced by, 106–7; Jesus as friend in, 159–61; Jesus, God's personal presence and, 156–58; Jesus' promises and, 110, 204, 205–6; Jesus' teaching everything and, 50, 52, 94, 128–29, 133, 136, 139, 149–50, 152, 181, 188–89, 205, 209–11; John 14:16–17 of, 48–50,

127–28, 189; John 14:25–26 of, 50–52, 128–29; John 15:26–27 of, 53–55, 129–30; John 16:8–11 of, 55–57, 130–31; John 16:12–13 of, 57–58, 131–32, 189; John 16:23–26 of, 132–34; love of one another in, 160–61, 193–94; new life (born again) from Jesus in, 99–100; opposition between Jesus and world and, 55–56; Paraclete after Jesus returned to the Father in, 44, 49, 56, 80, 93–94, 113, 127, 185–87, 189–90; Paraclete and resemblance/continuance of Jesus, 59–60, 81, 127–28, 132–33, 185–87; Paraclete's meaning and, 46–47; personal teacher, advocate and, 209–11; prayers and, 48, 127–34, 146–47, 149, 152; sacrificial love of, 159–60, 162; Spirit as successor to Christ and, 93–95; Spirit of Jesus in first letter of, 60–64; Spirit of truth and, 44–46, 54, 57, 83, 84–85, 94, 96–97, 100, 102–3, 107, 110, 128, 130, 140, 146–47, 156, 157, 161, 182, 188–90, 193–94, 202–3, 204, 208, 210–11; Spirit testifying in, 53–54, 129–30, 190; Word christology of, 201, 202–3
John of the Cross, St., 140, 144–46, 147, 149, 150, 151, 196
John Paul II (pope), viii, 52, 165
John the Baptizer, 40–41, 101, 167

John XXIII (pope), 79, 88, 105
joy, 132; as fruits of Spirit, 24

knowledge, 18–19, 132–33; acquired v. infused, 145, 149; natural v. supernatural, 147

Last Supper, 118
law: love as fulfillment of, 23–24, 72; love's rule v., 82–83; Mosaic, 15–16, 23, 24, 25, 57, 102; not under, 15–16
leader(s): of church, 86, 87–88, 177–79; exaggerated authority by, 88; passing of spirit on to disciple, 47; reforms of, 89; Spirit relativing work of, 79
Lehodey, Dom Vitalis, 138
Leo XIII (pope), viii
Lombard, Peter, 168
love: as fruits of Spirit, 23–24, 72, 74; of Jesus, 82, 97–98, 141, 155, 159–60, 192, 204; Lord/God and, 61, 62, 72, 126, 131, 145, 150–52, 157, 165, 204; one another/neighbor, 52, 61, 62, 63, 82–83, 101, 108, 160–61, 193–94; of outcasts, 55; Paraclete not, 193–94; rule of, v. law, 82–83; from sacraments, 165; sacrificial, 159–60, 162; of Trinity, sending Spirit, 208; truth v., 45, 193–94
Lukan church: charismatic, 78; continuity of early church and, 175–76; divine/human side of, 175–76; general description of, 77–78; salvation history and,

77–78; soul of, 105–6; strengths of, 78–80; weaknesses of, 80
Luke (apostle), 34, 48, 155, 166, 188; church, Acts and, 31–41, 105–6; early missionary preaching and, 93, 96; eschatological spirit of, 111–12; fire, baptism and, 40–41; gospel of, 29–31, 40; Jesus as brother/family in, 161–63, 205–6; Jesus' final commission in terms of Spirit and, 30–31, 77; Jesus' fulfillment of promises and, 109–10, 205; new life from Jesus in, 99; number of times Holy Spirit in, 29, 93, 101, 105; power, inspiration, Spirit and, 208; prayer, confidence/persistence and, 120–22; prayer of our Father in, 118–20, 136; repentance of sins and, 31; salvation history by, 29–30, 33–34, 40, 77–78, 93, 101–2, 112; Spirit as successor to Christ and, 93; Spirit christology of, 200–201, 202; truth, witness, redemption and, 95–96; vocal prayer and, 136–37; witness and, 31, 32, 78–79, 96, 112, 190. *See also* Acts
Lumen Gentium (On the Church), xi
Luther, Martin, viii

Mark (apostle), 60–61, 102, 120, 159, 166; Jesus' final commission in terms of Spirit and, 30–31; number of times Holy Spirit in, 29; prayer and, 120, 122; Spirit of Jesus and, 65–66
martyrs, 187
materialism, scientific, 54, 56
Matthew (apostle), 54, 102, 120, 159, 166; Jesus always with us in, 156–57; Jesus Christ as Lord, Spirit and, 21, 66–67; number of times Holy Spirit in, 29; teaching, disciple making and, 157
Merton, Thomas, 83
Messiah, 27, 69
missionary movement, 36–37, 93, 96
Moses, 4, 41
Mystici Corporis (Pius XII), 76

new convenant, 10–12
Nicodemus, 43–44, 99–100
Noah, and flood, 40

Old Testament: Father and, 7; fire and, 41; God's temple and, 11–12; Noah, flood and, 40; Paraclete and, 47; prophets, spirit and, 47, 124; prophets tested by, 22; Spirit of, 3–4, 29, 37, 101; symbols of God in, 199–200; way of truth and, 57

Paraclete: condemnation of Jesus, world judged and, 56, 130–31; disciples bearing witness to Jesus in, 53–57, 61, 81, 96, 129–30, 190; divine indwelling of Jesus' Spirit and, 49–50, 80, 96, 134, 152, 157–58, 182, 207;

faith with, 186–87; guiding along way of truth with, 57–58, 102–3, 131–32, 157, 186–87, 193; guilty of sin in, 56, 130–31; identities between God, the Father and Jesus in, 58–59, 60; Jesus and resemblance/continuance with, 59–60, 81, 127–28, 132–33, 185–87; after Jesus returned to the Father, 44, 49, 56, 60, 80, 93–94, 113, 127, 185–87, 189–90; Jesus' departure as better and, 185–87; Jesus' justice, innocence in, 56; Jesus' teaching everything and, 50, 52, 94, 128–29, 133, 136, 139, 149–50, 152, 181, 188–89, 205, 209–11; meaning of, 46–47; not Love, 193–94; Old Testament and, 47; opposition between Jesus and world and, 55–56, 130–31; as Spirit of Jesus, 60; as Spirit of Truth, 44–46, 54, 57, 83, 84–85, 94, 96–97, 100, 102–3, 107, 110, 128, 130, 145–46, 156, 157, 161, 182, 186, 188–90, 193–94, 202–3, 204, 208, 210–11

Pastoral Epistles church: on church after disciplines, 86; divine/human side of, 178–79; general description of, 85–87; leaders and, 87–89, 178–79; Spirit-directed calling of, 86; strengths of, 87–88; weaknesses of, 88–89

Paul (apostle), 36, 37, 79, 106, 178, 208; Barnabas and, 32, 102, 106, 108, 175, 176; body of Christ and, 12–14, 67, 68, 72, 74, 76–77, 99, 104, 174; children of God and, 6–9, 63, 71–72, 101, 124–25, 158–59, 204; before conversion, 21; as converter, 32; death near for, 85–86; discernment of Spirit and, 19–20, 22, 73; downpayment, first fruits and, 16–17; eschatological spirit of, 111; faith and, 6, 13, 15, 72; forgiving/loving God and, 8–9; fruits of Spirit and, 22–25; gifts of Spirit and, 17–22, 104–5; God as Father and, 158–59; grace and, 25–26, 97; healing and, 19; hope and, 9, 24; indwelling Spirit of, 10–12, 13, 72, 87, 92–93, 97–98, 101, 120, 123, 158, 209; interpretation of tongues and, 20–22; Jesus, relationship with and, 155–56; Jesus Christ as Lord, Spirit and, 21, 175; Jesus' fulfillment of promises and, 108–9; joy and, 24; knowledge and, 18–19; love and, 61, 62, 72; meditation and, 139; mental prayer and, 139–40, 144; mystical prayer and, 145, 148, 150; new life from Jesus in, 98–99; number of times Holy Spirit in, 98; Pastorals not authored by, 85; peace and, 21–22, 24; prayer as Holy Spirit interceding and, 73, 123, 124, 134, 137, 144; prayer, children of God and, 124–25; prayer, God's love and, 126; prayer internal teacher, and, 125–26; prayer, power in weakness and, 124; prophecy and, 21–22; revealer of Truth and, 14–15, 95; revelation, Spirit and, 5, 14, 68; salvation, Holy Spirit and, xii, 5, 25–26; Spirit as first installment (*arrabon*) in, 111; Spirit as successor to Christ and, 92–93; Spirit of freedom and, 15–16, 23; Spirit's activities and, 5–6; vocal prayer and, 137; wisdom and, 18, 68, 70. *See also* 1 Corinthians; 2 Corinthians; Galatians; Pastoral Epistles church; Pauline church; Romans

Paul VI (pope), viii

Pauline church, 191; body of Christ, Holy Spirit and, 12–13, 72, 74, 76–77, 104, 105, 174; building of, 21; charismatic, 73–74, 105; community, faith in Jesus and, 173–74; divine/human side of, 174; experienced presence in, 181; general description of, 71–74; intimate relationship, children of God, and, 71–72; love with, 72, 74; multifaceted functions of Holy Spirit in, 74; personal intercessor of, 72–73; soul of, 103–5; strengths of, 74–75; transcendent God of, 74–75; weaknesses of, 75–77

peace, 21–22, 24

Pentecost, xiii, 41, 76, 84, 87, 110, 169, 181; church and, 33–34, 201, 202, 210; early missionary preaching of, 93, 96, 175; feast of, 142; as foundation for witness throughout Acts, 34–36, 78–79, 190; gifts of Holy Spirit and, 37–38, 102, 169, 191, 195, 201, 202; transforming Jesus' following into missionary movement and, 36–37, 96, 106, 109–10, 208

Pentecostals, viii, 178

persecution, 109

Peter, xiii, 19, 35, 79, 188, 208; baptism, Holy Spirit and, 36, 38–40, 87; Gentile converts by, 32, 36, 99, 106; Holy Spirit's inspiration of, 34, 102; Last Supper and, 118; Messiahship of Jesus and, 27; as role of shepherd/authority, 107, 177, 178

Phillip, 36, 102

Pius XII (pope), 76

pledge. *See* downpayment

prayer, 135; of *Abba* Father, 158–59; Advocate always with you and, 127–28; Advocate convicting world and, 130–31; Advocate teach everything and, 128–29, 133, 136, 139, 149–50, 152, 210; affective, 140–42; asking Father in my name and, 132–34; confidence/persistence in, 120–22; contemplative, 144–47; of disciples, 48, 132–34; of faith, 143–44; God's love of us and, 126; infused, 145–47, 149; as intercessor, 73, 123, 124, 134, 137, 144; as internal teacher, 125–26, 210;

Jesus Christ as model of, 122; meditation, 139–40; mental, 138–44, 210; mystical/passive, 144; of our Father, 118–20; power in weakness and, 124, 137, 148, 183, 193; of quiet, 147–48; romantic, 143; Spirit empowering, 70, 73, 81–82, 193; Spirit guiding way of all truth and, 131–32, 136; Spirit testifying to me and, 129–30; transforming union and, 151–52; (full) union, 150–51; of (simple) union, 148–50; vocal, 136–37. *See also* intimacy of God; sacraments

prophecy, 18, 19, 73; Acts, Luke and, 34–36, 78, 111; enlightenment from multiple, 21–22

prophets, 4; intercession of, 124; spirit of God with, 47; Spirit-directed calling of, 86; testing, 22

Protestants, viii

quiet, 147–48

Rahner, Karl, xi, 2310
rebirth, 87, 100
Reconciliation, 107, 166–67
redemption, 186
through crucified/suffering Christ, 126, 188–89; mystery of, 95; not understanding, 187–88; objective and subjective, 100, 101; through remembering Jesus, 51; through revelation, 68–69

Reformation, 178
responsibility, 23
resurrection, 37, 92, 107, 129, 131–33, 168–69, 175, 188
revelation, 57, 68; now, 112–13; plan of God for, xiii–xiv, 112, 201; through Spirit, 5, 14; through Trinity, xiii–xiv; wisdom and, 68–69, 70
righteousness, 24
Rohr, Richard, 137
Romans, xii, 5, 6, 7, 9, 11, 13, 16, 17, 24, 25–26, 63, 70, 72, 92, 98, 100–101, 111, 123, 125, 134, 137, 144, 145, 148, 158, 159, 160, 174, 181, 192
Ruah, 3

sacraments, 182; of Baptism, 166–69; of Catholic church, 165; of Confirmation, 167–69; Eucharist and, 166, 167–68; Holy Spirit source of, 165–67; from Jesus, 166; of Reconciliation, 166–67
salvation, 182; from baptism, 43–44; economy of, xi–xii; God's, 195; through Holy Spirit, xii, 5, 25–26, 112; from Jesus Christ, 45–46, 113, 193, 211; Luke history of, 29–30, 33–34, 40, 77–78, 93, 101–2, 112; through resurrection, 37, 92; subjective, 195, 196; through Trinity, ix, xi–xii; witness of, 31, 78
Sanhedrin, 34, 36, 54, 55
Satan, 56
Saul, 3, 102, 108

scandal, 56; modern, 57, 176; of secessionists, 54
Schillebeeckx, Edward, 168–69
Schnackenburg, Rudolph, 62
science, 54, 56, 75, 130
Scripture, God inspiring, xiv–xv
secessionists, 54, 63
Second Vatican. *See* Vatican II
self-control, 23
sexual misconduct, 12, 13
sickness, 83–84
Simon, 176
sin: evil, God and, 9, 84, 119–20; forgiveness of, 31, 32, 77–78, 107, 119, 131, 166, 186; free from, 15, 16; guilty of, 56, 130–31; human tragedies/sickness not as, 83–84; law and, 15; repentance of, 31
Son, 63; of God, 149; Spirit of, 8, 120, 158, 182. *See also* Huios (son)
soteriology, ix
the soul, 151
speaking in tongues, 20, 73, 96, 109, 191
Spirit: activities of, 5–6; Acts' overview of work of, 32; baptism and gift of, 38–39, 43–44, 126, 137, 166–67; against body/flesh, 23; children of God from, 6–9, 63–64, 71–72, 101, 124–25, 158–59, 176, 204, 205; church, baptism and gift of, 39–40, 108, 178; in Confirmation, 37; discernment of, 19–20, 22, 73; downpayment, first fruits and, 16–17; faith, baptism and gift of, 38–39; free choice and, 80, 85; of freedom, 15–16, 23; fruits of, 18–17, 22–25; gifts of, 17–22, 37–38, 104–5, 207–8; of grace and salvation, 25–26, 97, 148; human/flaws of, 174, 178; indwelling, 10–12, 13, 49–50, 72, 80, 87, 92–93, 96, 98–99, 101, 120, 123, 152, 157–58, 176–78, 182, 207, 209; Jesus' final commission in terms of, 30–31; leader's work relativized through, 79; new convenant of, 10–12; of Old Testament, 3–4, 29, 37; of peace, not confusion, 21–22, 24; as personal intercessor, 72–73, 137, 144, 178; as pledge of eternal life, 9, 111, 131, 186; prophets and directed calling of, 86; as revealer of Truth, 14–15, 95, 97; sighs of, 124; of Son, 8, 120, 158, 182; as successor to Christ, 92–95; testifying, 53–54, 129–30, 190; of Truth (Paraclete), 44–46, 54, 57, 83, 84–85, 94, 96–97, 100, 102–3, 107, 110, 128, 130, 140, 146–47, 156, 157, 161, 182, 188–90, 193–94, 202–3, 204, 208, 210–11. *See also* Paraclete
spiritual marriage, 151
spirituality: Holy Spirit, 203–6; intimacy with God and, 204–5; Jesus' promises and, 204, 205–6; Stephen, 37, 102, 208
synoptics, 53–54, 55, 60–61, 159, 162; double commandment of, 60–61

temptation, 119–20
Teresa, St. (of Avila), 139, 141, 150
Theresa, Mother, 105
Thessalonians, 20, 25
Timothy: indwelling Spirit in, 87; Spirit-directed calling of (prophet), 86. *See also* Pastoral Epistles church
Titus, 87. *See also* Pastoral Epistles church
tongues: of fire, 40–41; interpretation of, 20–22; speaking in, 20, 73, 96, 109, 191
tribunals, 54, 55
Trinity: internal v. external workings of, ix; love of, 208; as one and three, x–xi; personal presence of, 156; revelation through, xiii–xiv; salvation through, ix, xi–xii
truth: guiding along way of, of Jesus/Spirit, 57–58, 94, 102–3, 131–32, 136, 157, 186, 193; Jesus as whole, 45–46, 140; love v., 45, 193–94; revealer of, 14–15, 95, 97; Spirit of (Paraclete), 44–46, 54, 57, 83, 84–85, 94, 96–98, 100, 102–3, 107, 110, 128, 130, 140, 146–47, 156, 157, 161, 182, 188–90, 193–94, 202–3, 204, 208, 210–11; witness, redemption and, 95–96

understanding, 37
union: full, 150–51; prayer of simple, 148–50; transforming, 151–52

Vatican II, xiv–xv, 79–80, 88–89, 105, 166, 178, 192

wisdom, 18, 34, 37, 69, 199–200; personifed, 47, 68, 70, 201
witness, 78, 108–9, 112, 178; disciples bearing, to Jesus, 53–57, 61, 81, 96, 129–30, 190; of forgiveness of sins, 31, 32, 77–78; modern bearing of, 190; Pentecost as foundation for, 34–36, 78–79, 109–10
Word (*Logos*) christology, 199, 201, 202–3

Yahweh, 3–4

Zechariah, 101

About the Author

James W. Kinn received a doctorate in theology from the University of St. Mary of the Lake, Mundelein, Illinois in 1961. He taught theology at Quigley Seminary for ten years, during the exciting times of Vatican Council II and its aftermath. Most of his life he was a parish priest in the Archdiocese of Chicago. He was pastor of Santa Maria del Popolo for nineteen years. His special interest in the last thirty years has been scripture study, especially all the Anchor Bible commentaries of the New Testament. He is the author of *Contemplation 2000: St. John of the Cross for Today*, which was also published in Chinese. This book on the Spirit of Jesus is the result of several years of research, teaching, and pastoral experience.